Giant Book of
CARD
TRICKS
By BOB LONGE

Main Street
A division of Sterling Publishing Co., Inc.
New York

Material in this collection was adapted from

Great Card Tricks,
World's Best Card Tricks,
World's Greatest Card Tricks, and
Clever Card Tricks for the Hopelessly Clumsy
© Bob Longe

10 9 8 7 6 5 4 3 2

Published by Sterling Publishing Co., Inc.
387 Park Avenue South, New York, NY 10016
© 2003 by Sterling Publishing Co., Inc.

Distributed in Canada by Sterling Publishing
℅ Canadian Manda Group, One Atlantic Avenue, Suite 105
Toronto, Ontario, Canada M6K 3E7
Distributed in Great Britain by Chrysalis Books
64 Brewery Road, London N7 9NT, England
Distributed in Australia by Capricorn Link (Australia) Pty. Ltd.
P.O. Box 704, Windsor, NSW 2756, Australia

Sterling ISBN 1-4027-1052-6

CONTENTS

INTRODUCTION 8

Getting Started:
THE MOVES

TIPS 12

THE PEEK 14

THE GLIDE 15

CONTROLLING A CARD
Double-Cut 17
Delayed Shuffle 18
Simple Overhand Shuffle 18
Don't Pass It Up 19
Easy Way 21
Easy Control 21
Even Easier Control 22
Key-Card Control 23

FALSE CUTS
Casual Cut 25
Multiple-Pile Cut 26
Gall Cut 26
The One-Finger Cut 26

SHUFFLES
Hindu Shuffle 29
Overhand Shuffle 30
  Normal Shuffle 30
  Bringing the Top Card to the Bottom 31
  Bringing the Bottom Card to theTop 31
  Controlling a Group of Cards 32

FORCES
Standard Force 34
Two Tricks With the Force 36
  Quick Trick 36
  Blackstone's Stunt 36
Riffle Force 36
Simon Says 37
One-Cut Force 38
The Face-Up Force 39
Double-Turnover Force 39
Crisscross Force 40

DROP SLEIGHT 41

DOUBLE LIFT
Snap Double-Lift 42
Efficient Double-Lift 44
Original Double-Lift 47

The Great
CARD TRICKS

PREDICTION
Presto Prediction 50
Colorful Prediction 54
Three-Card Surprise 57

TRANSPOSITION
Tick Tock Trick 60
Easy Aces 62
Tricky Transpo 64
One in Four 66
Travelling Hearts 69
Joker Helps 71
Join the Knavery 73
Quite Quaint Queens 77

ESTIMATION
Easy Estimation 80
Digital Estimation 82
The Perfect Pile 84

FACE-UP, FACE-DOWN
Do-It-Yourself Discovery 87
Behind My Back 89
The Rare Reverse 90
My Favorite Card 92
Ups and Downs 94

SPELLING
Impromptu Speller 96
Quick Speller 98
A Hot Spell 103

GAMBLING
Impossible Poker Deal 105
Freedom of Choice 108
From the Land Down Under 112
Two-Handed Poker 115

GAMBLER'S BONUS
Mind Control Poker 118
Flush of Success 120

Gambling Aces 123
Ace Surprise 125

GRAB BAG
Countdown 127
The Four Aces Again 128
Get Out of This World 130
The Process of Elimination 136
The Double-Match Trick 138
Astounding Appearance 140
Murder 143
Quaint Coincidence 146

MIND READING
A Word About Mind Reading 148
In the Palm of Your Hand 149
Crisscross 152
The Big Deal 154
The Three Piles 156
The Three Location 158
Either/Or Force 161

PREPARATION
Two-Faced Card Trick—1 162
Two-Faced Card Trick—2 164
Lucky 7 168
Color Confusion 170

DISCOVERY
No Touch, No Feel 173
Sheer Luck 176
Double Discovery 178
Four Times Four 181
Sixes and Nines 185

SETUP
Blind Choice 190
The Ideal Card Trick 193
Seven for Luck 194
What Do You Think? 195
A Face-Up Miracle 197

FOUR ACES
It's Out of My Hands 199
An Ace Collection 201
Double or Nothing 204
Wally's Wily Ace Trick 206
Sneaky Aces 212
Grand Illusion 213

MISCELLANEOUS

I Guess So 215
Oily Water 218
More Oily Water 220
Most Oily Water 222
Big Turnover 223
Easy Match 226
List to One Side 229
Pop-Up Card 231
Those Mysterious Ladies 232
Good Choice 236
Spin-Out! 238

GOTCHA!

Second Deal 240
No Wonder 242
Dunbury Delusion 243

RECOVERY

An Out 246

Clever Card Tricks for the
HOPELESSLY CLUMSY

MOVES AND MANEUVERS

Preposterous Patter 250
Control 252
   Simplicity Itself 252
False Cuts 255
   Just a Casual Cut 255
   And Another 256
   Roll-Up Cut 257
Milking the Cards 261
The Up-and-Down Shuffle 262
What If Things Go Wrong? 265

TRICKS

Mental Tricks 266
   The Way Back 266
   Out of My Hands 269
   My Variation 270
   Five-and-Ten 272
   Let's Prognosticate 272
   Two for One 274
   Something Old, Something New 277
Coincidence Tricks 279
   Very Little Turnover 279
   Who Has a Match? 281

It's All Up to You 283
Another Way 284
Just a Little More 288
Dynamic Duo 289
Location Tricks 291
Don't Take that Tone with Me 291
Double Discovery 293
The Long Count 298
Impromptu Liar's Trick 301
What Else? 307
Piles of Magic 308
Meet Madam Flaboda 310
These Are Gold 314
You Need All 52 317
Take Your Q 321
Let's Lose Your Card 326
Easy Speller 328
General Tricks 329
Point with Pride 329
Crime Does Not Pay 331
B'Gosh 334
The Ten Trick 337
Four of a Kind 341
Piles of Aces 341
Aces by the Number 344
Kings in a Blanket 350
Better Than Four of a Kind 354
I Win, You Lose 356
Suits Me 357
Big Odds 357
Very Close 358
Lower Is Higher 359
Solitaire 359
Can't Lose 1 360
Can't Lose 2 361
The Time is Now 362
Mistakes Are Fun 362
It's That Time 365
Number Tricks 366
Twenty-Card Trick 367
A Prime Trick 368
A Fun Trick 371
Nothing Up My Sleeve 371

PARTING THOUGHTS 374

AFTERWORD 376

INDEX 379

INTRODUCTION

The purpose of this book is to teach you great card tricks and tell you exactly how to perform them. This includes step-by-step instruction and tips on presentation.

The ability to perform good card tricks is not unlike the gift of playing a musical instrument well. As with a musical instrument, you can enjoy the solitary practice, and you can share your skill with others.

Are there other rewards? Certainly. The admiration of spectators, for instance. Who doesn't enjoy being the center of attention? But even better is the sharing. You, the card expert, enliven every occasion and contribute to everyone's enjoyment.

When performing card tricks, however, some magicians miss the main point. The object is not merely to fool spectators, nor to impress with a variety of flourishes. The object is to *entertain*. And magic is the central theme. The tools are many: good tricks, practiced skill, interesting patter, humor, and—above all—a sharing of the fun.

The idea is to entertain an audience, as well as yourself.

You'll feel enormously pleased with yourself as you develop greater skill with your tricks, and well you should. Just don't forget to share the joy.

Getting Started
THE MOVES

Every trick, whether it calls for prestidigitation or not, requires considerable skill. What skill? The skill of *presenting a trick properly.* I have seen performers with amazing technical ability who never amaze, nor do they entertain or amuse. Worst of all, they never perform *magic.* They do astonish with their flourishes, in the same way a juggler astonishes. We want to astonish, all right, but we also want to do magic, to create an atmosphere of mystery and romance. It takes skill.

It is not enough merely to "know" a trick. Even the simplest trick requires the four Ps: *preparation*, thorough *practice*, convincing *patter*, and smooth *presentation.*

Preparation: Read over the trick, going through every aspect with a deck of cards. Run through it a few times to make sure you understand the basic principle. Now *think* about it. No two persons are going to do a trick exactly the same way. See if you can develop a unique angle or a simplification that will particularly suit you.

There is nothing absolutely binding about anyone's instructions, including mine. Understand, however, that in this book the method given is tried and true; the trick has been done hundreds of times to good effect using the exact method described.

Practice: Work out every move precisely. You must be *smooth.*

Patter: Here is where mystery, romance, and magic come in. Spectators *want* to be amazed; give them an excuse, a reason. Make strength of weakness. Why must they count the cards? You want to be scrupulously fair. Why are you removing a card from the top? It's your lucky card, and the spectator must tap the deck with it. It doesn't matter how preposterous the story is. Often as not, the more ridiculous the story, the more entertaining the trick.

Do *not* narrate, "Now I deal three cards, and now I place them over here." No spectator likes being treated like an idiot. Obviously, you must sometimes explain what you are doing and why you are doing it, but do not make this your standard procedure.

Develop the kind of patter appropriate to your personality. If you are bombastic, develop lively, high-tension patter. If you are reserved, present reasoned experiments. Don't try to be something you aren't. In other words, don't don the magician's cape, becoming the all-knowing, the all-powerful. Just be yourself. Knowing a few cards tricks does not make you superior. And if you are, in fact, superior, try to keep this fact concealed. In other words, try not to be obnoxious. Many magicians neglect this step.

Presentation: Take care of the first three Ps, and you won't have to worry about the fourth P, *presentation.* There are two rules: Never do a trick twice, and quit while you're ahead.

Some tricks are designed to be repeated—the mystery is enhanced with repetition—but most should be done only once. A repetition could lead to discovery.

Occasionally spectators will insist that you do a trick again. Perhaps they will say, "You're afraid we'll catch on." This is quite true, of course. But you respond, "Not at all. A repetition would bore you. It would certainly bore me. I have many other wonders to show you."

When asked to perform, you will be tempted to do at least a dozen tricks. Three or four are plenty. If your audience begs for more, you can always accommodate them.

I explain the tricks in considerable detail, perhaps more than you need or want. One reason is that I have always resented it when a card-book author left out important details. Another reason is that it is not enough for you to know just the basic trick; it's important that you learn *exactly* what I do. Often enough, the real secret of a successful trick is something which may, to the casual reader, seem insignificant: a word, a gesture, pacing, whatever.

I recommend, then, that you try each trick in much the same way as it is presented here. Inevitably, you will come to perform it your own way.

You have heard of "self-working" tricks. There is no such thing. *All* tricks—from those requiring several sleights to those requiring none—must be worked skillfully by the performer.

TIPS

You are about to learn lessons I paid for with failure, chagrin, and self-recrimination.

1. When a card is selected, have it shown to other spectators. Yes, it's true—sometimes a spectator will lie.

2. No matter how ardently you are importuned, do not reveal how a trick is done. This applies to even the simplest trick. When you give a trick away, you spoil it for the spectators, and you ruin your reputation as "Mr. Magic." The spectators can no longer enjoy the mystery and the romance, and instead of a magician, you have become someone who bought a book the spectators did not buy. You will be delighted to follow this advice once you have explained a trick and have heard a spectator say, "Oh, is that all?"

Spectators *want* to believe in magic. Years ago, I violated this principle. A lady I knew fairly well told me that she had seen a marvellous trick the night before. A friend of the family had placed an empty beer bottle on the kitchen table, had wrapped it in paper, and had then squashed the paper. The bottle had disappeared!

I reluctantly gave in to her entreaties to explain the trick. "He was sitting at the table, right? The paper he wrapped the bottle in had to be stiff enough to hold the shape. As he talked, he brought the wrapped bottle over the edge of the table and let the bottle drop in his lap."

"But that isn't what he did," my friend insisted.

"No problem," I said. "Then it was magic."

Since then, I have *never* explained a trick.

3. *Never* let a spectator do a trick. If pressed, tell the spectator he can perform when you are done. If he insists, you *are* done. Give him the deck and walk away.

Sometimes I explain, "I don't think I could survive seeing for the five-hundredth time someone dealing out three rows of cards with seven cards in each row."

Quite often, disappointment marks the face of the aspiring performer. "Oh, do you know that one?" he asks ruefully.

4. A card is selected, and you find it. No matter how many different ways you find the card, you are still doing only one trick. You can do this several times, and it might be entertaining. But throw in some variety. Very few of the tricks in this book begin with "Take a card," so you have a nice variety to choose from. Mix up your tricks. The more diversity you display, the more entertained the spectators will be, and the more impressed they will be with your ability.

5. If you are fascinated with performing card tricks, you will undoubtedly consult many other books of legerdemain. Just remember this: It's not enough that a trick may be easy to do; it must also be *worth* doing.

THE PEEK

Magicians use *The Peek* to sneak a look at a card without being observed. There are many methods, most of them requiring some sleight of hand.

The Peek is often called *The Glimpse.* I prefer the former term—it sounds sneakier.

The methods I present here are actually *Peek* substitutes, but that does not matter. You need to know the name of a particular card in the deck—the top, the bottom, or the second from the bottom—but you do not wish to unduly arouse the suspicions of your audience.

Suppose you wish to learn the name of the top card. Choose from these four methods.

1. Peek at the bottom card while toying with the deck and chatting with the spectators. Give the cards an overhand shuffle, (pages 28 & 29) drawing off the last few cards individually so that the bottom card ends up on top.

2. Look at it ahead of time.

3. Fan through the deck, saying, "I want to get a mental picture of all the cards," or (even more preposterously), "I want to make sure all the cards are here." Note the top card.

4. Fan through the cards, saying, "I want to remove my bad luck card. Otherwise this might not work." Fan through once, noting the top card. Then find the queen of spades, or some other "bad luck card," and toss it aside. This method is particularly effective.

There are many other methods of sighting a card. If you investigate card-trick literature, you will come across at least a half-dozen.

THE GLIDE

Used properly—which is to say, sparingly—this is one of the most useful moves in card magic. You show the bottom card of the deck and, presumably, place it on the table. Only it is not the same card. You actually deal out the second card from the bottom.

The maneuver, of course, should never be used as a trick by itself. Even the dullest spectator will have an inkling as to what actually happened.

ILLUSTRATION 1:
Hold the deck in your left hand,
at the sides, and from above.

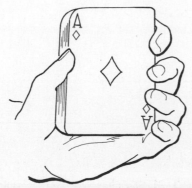

ILLUSTRATION 2:
Lift the cards and show the
bottom card to the spectators.

The deck is held in the left hand at the sides from above (Illustration 1). The cards are lifted, showing the bottom card to the spectators (Illustration 2). Note that the hand is gripping nearer the back of the deck than the front, and that the second and third fingers extend over the side of the deck past the first joint. The reason will become apparent.

The deck is tilted down again, and the second and third fingers bend under and draw the bottom card back one-half inch or so. Illustration 3 shows the view from underneath. The second card from the bottom is now drawn out with the second and third fingers of the right hand. When the card is drawn out about an inch, the right thumb takes it at the top so that the card is gripped beneath by the second and third fingers and at the top by the thumb. The card is placed face down on the table.

ILLUSTRATION 3:
Draw the bottom card back one-half inch.
This view is from underneath.

CONTROLLING A CARD

It's vital that you be able to control a selected card, usually bringing it to the top. Here are eight different ways to accomplish this.

Double-Cut

This is a complete cut of the deck. Suppose you wish to bring a card to the top. Spread the deck for the return of a selected card. The spectator sticks the card into the deck. As you close up the deck, slightly lift the cards above the chosen card with the fingers of your right hand. This will enable you to secure a break with your little finger above the chosen card (Illustration 4). (If the card is to be brought to the bottom, secure a break *below* the selected card.)

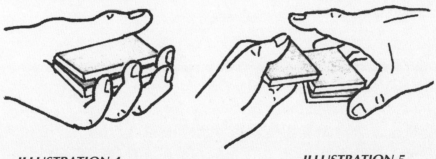

ILLUSTRATION 4   **ILLUSTRATION 5**

Holding the deck from above in your right hand, transfer the break to your right thumb. With your left hand, take some of the cards from the bottom and place them on top (Illustration 5). Take the remainder of the cards below the break and place them on top. (It is perhaps more deceptive if you move three small packets from below the break instead of two).

This is, by far, the most common way in which magicians control a card to the top or bottom.

As you will see, this is also a sleight which has many other uses in certain tricks.

Delayed Shuffle

You do *not* get a little-finger break when the selected card is returned. Instead, in the process of closing up the deck, you move the cards above the selected card *forward* about half an inch. With your left thumb, push the chosen card to the right. Continuing the process of closing up the deck, move forward the remaining cards in your left hand (Illustration 6). You now have an in-jogged card above the chosen card.

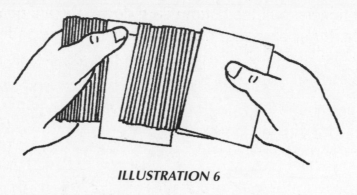

ILLUSTRATION 6

Immediately drop your left hand with the deck to your side and chat for a moment with the spectators. When you're ready, bring your left hand up in the overhand shuffle position. Your right hand takes the deck, and your right thumb *pushes up* on the protruding card, obtaining a break. Small packets are shuffled into your left hand until the break is reached. All the cards below the break are dropped on top. The chosen card is now on top. (See *Controlling a Group of Cards*, page 32, for a complete explanation of the overhand shuffle using an injogged card. Note particularly Illustrations 17 and 18).

Simple Overhand Shuffle

Have the spectator place his card on top. False-shuffle the cards and give them a false cut. This works as well as anything else. (See *False Cuts*, page 25, and *Shuffles*, page 29).

Don't Pass It Up

I thought I'd invented this method of bringing a card to the top, but I discovered that Martin Gardner had beaten me to it by a considerable number of years.

A card is selected. As you ask the spectator to show it around, hold the deck in the dealing position in your left hand. Your right hand also holds the cards, gripping them from above with your fingers at the outer end and your thumb at the inner end. With your left fingers, pull the bottom card down about a quarter inch. Your right thumb secures a break between this card and the rest of the deck (Illustration 7). The maneuver is completely covered by your right hand.

ILLUSTRATION 7:
For clarity,
the left hand isn't shown.

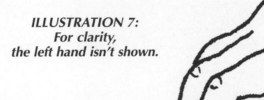

You're about to perform the first part of a legitimate one-finger cut in preparation for a very tricky move indeed. Bring your left hand behind the deck and, from below with your left forefinger, revolve about half the cards so that they fall into your hand at the front of the deck (Illustration 8). At this point you're holding half the deck in your left hand, which is in front of your right hand. Extend the cards in your left hand, indicating that the chosen card should be replaced on top. In your right hand is the original lower portion of the deck, at the bottom of which you are holding one card separated with your right thumb.

After the spectator places his card on top of the pile in your left hand, bring the cards in your right hand, ever so briefly, over

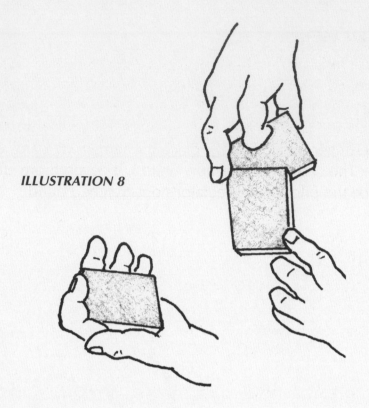

ILLUSTRATION 8

those in your left hand. Let the bottom card of the packet in your right hand drop on top of the packet in your left hand. As you begin the forward motion of your right hand, say something like, "You had complete freedom of choice, right?" At the beginning of the question, drop the card on top of the packet in your left hand. As you complete the question, continue moving your right hand forward with its packet. Raise your right first finger from the packet and point your finger at the spectator. The whole procedure should appear to be one movement, as you apparently are merely emphasizing your statement by moving the packet forward and pointing a finger at the spectator.

Thumb off the top card of those in your left hand onto the top of those in your right. Place the rest of the cards in your left hand on top of all.

Apparently, you very fairly placed the spectator's card in the middle; actually, it's on top.

Easy Way

Get a little-finger break above the selected card. With your right hand, cut a small pile from the top of the deck. Place the pile face down on the table. Cut off another small pile and place it on top of the pile on the table. Repeat, taking off all the cards above your little-finger break. Finally, place the remaining cards on top of the pile. The chosen card is now on top. It's even more effective if you place the piles on a spectator's outstretched hand.

Easy Control

Ian Land and I independently arrived at a similar card control. Let's call mine *Easy Control* and his *Even Easier Control.* My method is not a complete cut of the deck, so it is useful only for bringing a chosen card to the top or within a few cards from the top.

You are holding a break above the chosen card with your left little finger. Fan through about half of the cards *that are above the break,* saying, "We know your card is in here somewhere." With your right fingers on the right side, flip this group face up onto the deck. Rapidly fan through these face-up cards, saying, "Could be here." Stop fanning when you get to the first face-down card.

Close up the fanned cards so that they slide into your right hand. Hold this group separate as you continue fanning down to the break held by your left little finger. With the tips of the right fingers flip over the cards you just fanned out so that they are now face up on the balance of the deck.

Here's the situation: In your right hand is a group of face-up cards. On top of the balance of the deck is another group of face-up cards, which you have just flipped over.

As soon as these cards land face-up, rapidly fan through them, adding them below the cards in your right hand. Say, "Could be here." Stop fanning when you get to the first face-down card (the chosen card).

Again, loosely close up the fanned cards. Hold them slightly to one side as you flip the remaining cards face up with your left thumb. Add these to the bottom (or rear) of those in your right hand as you fan through them, saying, "Could be here." Stop about two-thirds of the way through, saying "Who knows?" Close up the entire bunch and turn the deck face down. The chosen card is now on top.

During this last fanning, make sure you do not reveal the lowermost card, which is the one chosen.

Even Easier Control

Ian Land's method is similar to mine, but his is a complete cut of the deck. Since the bottom card is revealed during the move, you can't use it to bring a card to the bottom. You *can* use it, however, to bring a card within a small number of cards from the bottom. And it can be used to bring a card to the top or within a small number of cards from the top. I think you'll like the simplicity of this method.

Again, you're holding a break above the chosen card with your left little finger. Turn over the top card of the deck, saying, "Your card is not on top." Replace the card face down.

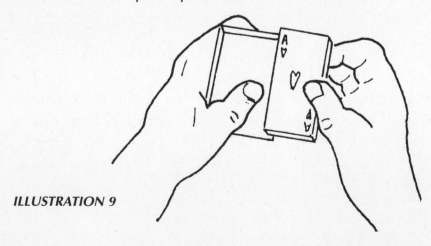

ILLUSTRATION 9

22

With the palm-down right hand, grasp all the cards above the break at the left side. Pivot them in an arc to the right, as though opening a book from the back (Illustration 9). "It's not here in the middle."

Move your right hand with its cards a bit to the right. With your left thumb, flip over the cards that are in your left hand, saying, "And not on the bottom."

Place the face-up cards that are in your right hand on top of the face-up cards that are in your left hand. Turn the deck over. The chosen card is now on top.

Key-Card Control

In some instances, using a key card for control works best. For example, you might want to bring the chosen card to within a fairly high number of cards from the top. This control would do perfectly, as I'll explain.

Before the spectator chooses a card, sneak a peek at the bottom card of the deck. This is your key card. You can do this as you separate the deck in two, preparing to do a riffle shuffle. Easier yet, look at the bottom card as you tap the side of the deck on the table, apparently evening up the cards. Then, when you shuffle, keep the card on the bottom.

So you know the bottom card of the deck. Fan out the deck, and a spectator selects a card. Close up the deck. From the top of the deck, lift off a small packet of cards and drop it onto the table. Lift off another small packet and drop it on top of the first one. After dropping several packets like this, say to the spectator, "Put your card here whenever you want." After you drop one of your packets, he places his card on top. You put the rest of the deck on top of it. Even up the cards and pick them up. The key card which you peeked at is now above the chosen card.

Start fanning through the cards, faces towards yourself. Mutter something such as, "This is going to be really hard." Fan off several cards. Cut them to the rear of the deck. Fan off several more. Again, cut them to the rear. You're establishing a pattern so that it won't seem so odd when you finally cut the chosen card into position.

Let's say you simply want the card available on top of the deck. Continue fanning groups of cards and placing them at the rear until you see that you'll soon arrive at the key card. Cut the cards so that the key card becomes the top card of the deck. Just below it, of course, is the chosen card. Turn the deck face down.

"I can't seem to find your card." Turn over the top card of the deck (the key card). "This isn't it, is it?" No. Turn the card over and stick it into the middle of the deck. Turn the deck face up. "How about this one?" No. Take the bottom card and stick it into the middle of the deck. Turn the deck face down. The chosen card is at your disposal on top of the deck.

Suppose, for purposes of a specific trick, you want the chosen card to be tenth from the top. Again you start by fanning off small groups and cutting them to the rear of the deck. When you get to the chosen card, you start counting to yourself. You count the chosen card as "One." Count the next card as "Two." Cut the cards so that the card at "Ten" becomes the top card. The chosen card is now tenth from the top.

Clearly you can use the same method to arrange to spell the chosen card from the top, dealing off one card for each letter in the spelling.

FALSE CUTS

After a card is returned and brought to the top, it's not a bad idea to further convince spectators that the card is lost by giving the pack a false cut or false shuffle.

False cuts are also very useful when you have a set-up deck and you want to convince the spectators that the cards are mixed.

Casual Cut

Most versions of this false cut involve a sweeping movement which reveals that *something* peculiar has taken place. Hold the cards in the basic dealing position in your left hand, but with the cards tilted clockwise at about a 45° angle. Approach from the rear with your palm-down right hand. With your right thumb and fingers, grasp approximately the *bottom* half of the deck at the sides. Pull this portion towards you. As soon as the packet clears, lower your left hand a few inches. This creates a compelling illusion that the packet came from the top of the deck. Bring the packet *over* the cards in your left hand and slap it onto the table.

Your right hand, from above, now takes the packet from your left hand. Slap this packet on top of the packet on the table. As you do this, grasp the combined packets and pick them up. Return the complete deck to your left hand.

Multiple-Pile Cut

Set the deck on the table at position "A." Cut off a small portion ("B") and set it somewhat away and to the right of "A." Cut another small pile off "A" and set it to the right of "B;" this is pile "C." Continue with piles "D," "E," "F." Place "B" on "C," place "BC" on "D," and so on to "F." Pick up the combined pile. As an afterthought, notice "A." Place the cards in your hand on "A" and pick all up. The cards are back as they were at the beginning.

Gall Cut

This cut, attributed to Jay Ose, takes a bit of nerve.

With your left thumb riffle down about a third of the deck. Lift off this pile and place it on the table. As you place this pile down, with your left thumb riffle down about half of the remaining cards. Lift these off and place them to the right of the first pile.

Your right hand takes the remaining pile and slaps it down to the right of the other two piles. With your right hand, place the first pile on the second. Pick up the combined pile and place it on the third. The deck is back in its original order.

The One-Finger Cut

This is unique among false cuts, in that the phony one looks more genuine than the real one.

First, the *real* cut. The deck is held from above in the right hand near the right edge, second finger at the front, thumb at the back, and first finger either curled or slightly bent. The left hand, fingers up, approaches the deck from the rear (Illustration 10).

The first finger of the left hand does the work. With the tip, it pivots the top half of the deck, revolving the cards around the second finger of the right hand (Illustration 11). The left hand moves directly in front of the of the right hand so that the top half of the deck drops into the left hand (Illustration 12).

To complete the legitimate cut, the right hand places its half on top of the cards in the left hand.

Here is the *false* cut. After you pivot the top half into the left hand, bring the cards in the right hand directly over the top of the portion in the left hand and set them on the table. The right hand returns, takes the pile from the left hand, which has remained stationary, and places the pile on top of the cards on the table.

There are two keys: bringing the pile in your right hand *directly over* the cards in your left hand as you set the pile on the table, and keeping your left hand stationary when you return with your right hand to get the other half. The cut takes just a few seconds and is totally deceptive.

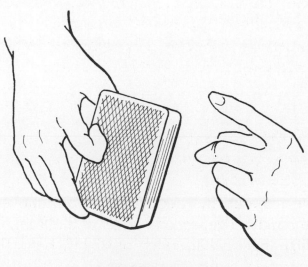

ILLUSTRATION 10:
The first step of a "true" cut.

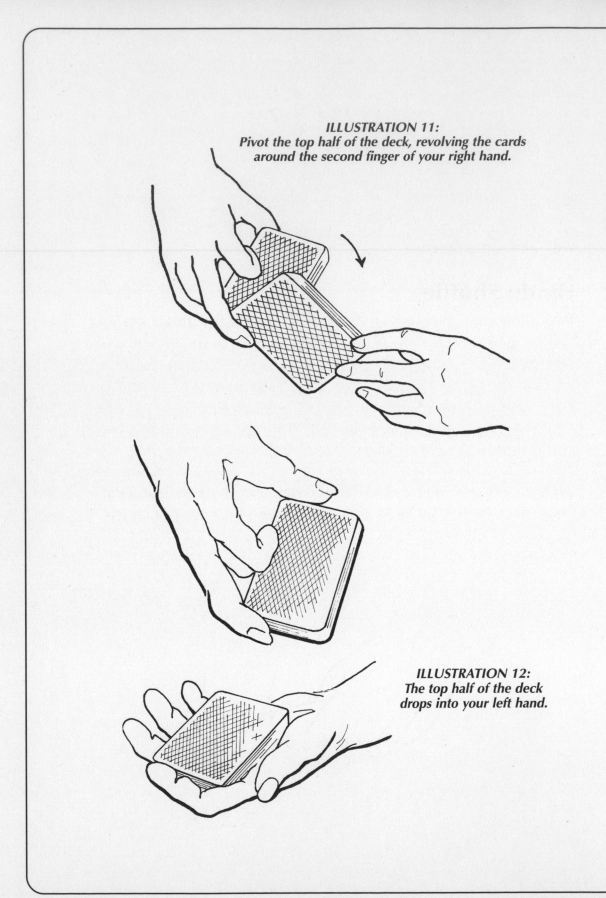

ILLUSTRATION 11:
Pivot the top half of the deck, revolving the cards around the second finger of your right hand.

ILLUSTRATION 12:
The top half of the deck drops into your left hand.

SHUFFLES

To perform some of the tricks in this book, you must know how to do two kinds of shuffle, the Hindu shuffle and the overhand shuffle. Neither is difficult, but mastering the *false* overhand shuffle will take some practice.

Hindu Shuffle

With the Hindu shuffle, you can do a variety of sleights. Here we are just concerned with the mechanics of the shuffle, as well as a very easy force.

Start with the deck in the dealing position in your left hand. With your palm-down right hand, grasp the cards at the near narrow end. Bring the deck towards you with your right hand, allowing your left fingers to draw off a small packet from the top (Illustration 13). This packet falls into your left hand. Draw off another packet, letting it fall onto the one in your left hand. Continue until only a small packet remains in your right hand. Drop this on top of the others.

Now the force: You have your force card on the bottom of the deck. With your first move, you not only withdraw a packet from the top, but you also cling to a small packet on the bottom with

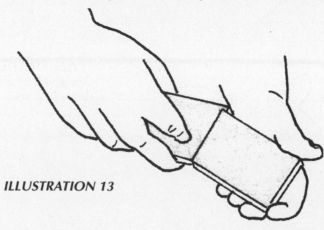

ILLUSTRATION 13

29

your left thumb and left fingers. The packet from the top falls on top of this packet. Complete the shuffle in the usual way. Apparently you've performed a regular Hindu shuffle; actually, the bottom several cards remain exactly as they were. This means, of course, that the force card is still on the bottom. Perform this maneuver a few times.

Ask a spectator to tell you when to stop as you shuffle the cards. Perform the regular Hindu shuffle, taking quite small packets with each move. When the spectator tells you to stop, avert your head and tilt up the packet in your right hand, showing the spectator the bottom card. Then place this packet on top of the cards in your left hand.

Overhand Shuffle

Normal Shuffle

Hold the deck in your left hand as shown in Illustration 14. With your right hand, pick up from the bottom of the deck all but a small packet (Illustration 15). Bring your right hand down (Illustration 16) and let a small packet drop from the top of these cards onto the top of the cards in your left hand.

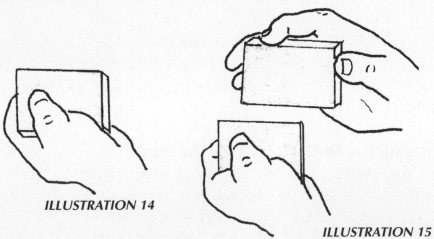

ILLUSTRATION 14

ILLUSTRATION 15

Your left thumb lifts a little, allowing passage. The release of these cards from the top of those in your right hand is effected by very slightly relaxing the pressure of your thumb and fingers at the ends.

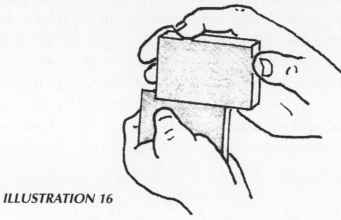

ILLUSTRATION 16

As the packet is lifted again by your right hand, your left thumb, which was drawn back, returns to the back of the cards being accepted by your left hand. (This is particularly important in the various false shuffles, as you will see.)

Continue dropping packets in the same manner until all the cards are in your left hand.

Bringing the Top Card to the Bottom

In the first move of an overhand shuffle, draw off a single card with your left thumb. Shuffle the rest on top of it. The top card is now on the bottom.

Bringing the Bottom Card to the Top

Start the overhand shuffle. When all that remains in your right hand is a very small packet, draw off cards singly with your left thumb until all have been shuffled off. The bottom card is now on top. (In the same way, you can bring several cards to the top, simply making sure that you draw off the last several cards one at a time.)

Controlling a Group of Cards

The key to all false shuffling is performing casually. Don't stare at your hands. Chat as you do your dirty work.

The idea is to keep a packet on top in order. Again start by picking up from the bottom of the deck all but a small packet. (This small packet will eventually be returned to the top.) As your right hand returns, it's slightly closer to your body. A packet is not released; instead, your left thumb draws off one card. Because your right hand is slightly closer to your body, the card is automatically jogged inward approximately half an inch (Illustration 17). (This move is known as the *injog*.)

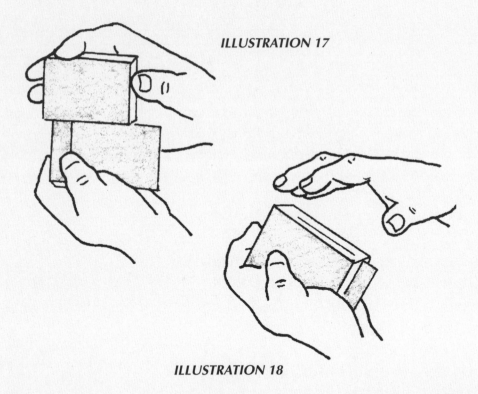

ILLUSTRATION 17

ILLUSTRATION 18

Your right hand moves slightly forward; now the cards released into the left hand in small packets will be even with the rest of the deck. At the conclusion of this phase, the deck should look like Illustration 18.

In phase two, as your right hand takes the deck, your thumb pushes up on the protruding card, obtaining a break (Illustration 19). In the overhand shuffle, small packets are dropped into your left hand until the break is reached. All the cards below the break are dropped on top. Thus, the original top packet is back on top.

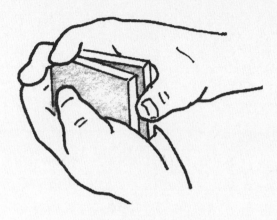

ILLUSTRATION 19:
For clarity, the break is exaggerated.

FORCES

Usually, the magician forces a card as an essential part of a trick. Every force, however, can be presented as mind reading. The judicious choice of some of these can enhance a mental routine. When using a force as mind reading, explain that you don't want to influence a spectator psychologically, so the card to be thought of should be chosen completely by chance; then proceed with the force.

Standard Force

The standard force isn't perfect for even the most advanced card expert, but it's well worth learning. No method appears more natural. What's more, if you fail to force a particular card, you simply proceed with a trick where a force isn't required. Any time you do a trick where a card is chosen, try to force a card. The more you practice, the better you'll get. Eventually, you'll be able to force nine times out of ten.

My method is standard, except perhaps for setting up the force card. Clearly, whenever you force a card, you must peek at a card and then get it in position for the force.

To use my method of preparing for the force, you must know how to do the Hindu shuffle (page 29). Take the deck in the Hindu shuffle position, both hands slightly tilted clockwise. Draw off a small packet in the first move of the Hindu shuffle. As you do so, you are holding most of the deck in your right hand. Turn your right hand even more clockwise until you can see the bottom card (Illustration 20). This is your force card. Now tilt your right hand back to the normal position. Continue drawing off small packets to about half the deck, and then toss the rest of the deck on top, letting the cards fall on top of your inserted little finger, which holds a small break (See Illustration 4, page 17).

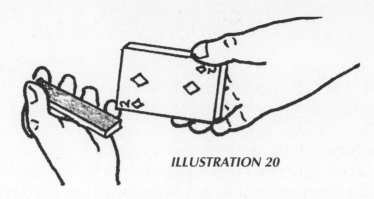

ILLUSTRATION 20

The little finger is now holding a break at the middle of the deck below the card you sighted. Immediately begin to fan the cards into your right hand, pushing with your left thumb on top and pulling with your right fingers underneath. Approach a spectator, saying, "I'd like you to select a card." As he reaches, arrange to have your sighted card fall under his fingertips. How? Coordinate the speed of your fanning and the extension of the deck towards the spectator. Also, you expose the surface of the sighted card a little more as the spectator's hand nears the deck (Illustration 21).

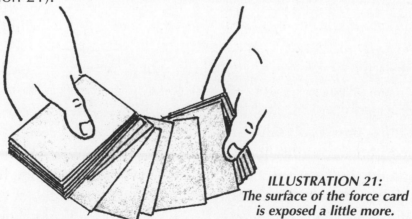

ILLUSTRATION 21:
The surface of the force card
is exposed a little more.

If all this seems a bit vague, it is because forcing is more of an art than it is an exact science. There's only one way you'll really get the knack: practising on spectators.

Two Tricks with the Force
Quick Trick
When you successfully force a card, say to the spectator, "Now show the ten of clubs around, but don't let me see it." You'll be quite gratified by the delayed reaction.

Blackstone's Stunt
Harry Blackstone (the elder) used to force a card and, just as the spectator was withdrawing it from the deck, he'd say, "Take any card but the five of spades." When the spectator showed that he indeed had taken the five of spades, Blackstone would express chagrin, and proceed to force it on him again.

Riffle Force

Sneak a peek at the bottom card. Shuffle it to the top in an overhand shuffle. Perform another overhand shuffle, lifting about half the deck with the first move. Draw off one card with your left thumb, injogging the card. Shuffle off the rest. (See *Controlling a Group of Cards*, page 32.) Place the deck in the dealing position in your left hand. Retaining the deck in your left hand, grip the cards from above with your right hand, fingers at the outer end, thumb at the inner end. As you do so, with the right thumb lift the injogged card. Now you're holding a break above the force card with your right thumb.

Riffle down the left side of the deck a few times with your left thumb. Say to a spectator, "I'd like you to tell me when to stop as I riffle the deck." Slowly riffle down the side of the deck with your left thumb. The spectator will probalby tell you to stop somewhere around the middle. If the spectator waits until you're well past the middle, quickly riffle down the remainder of the deck. Start the riffle again, saying, "Tell me to stop anytime." When you're told to stop, tilt the deck slightly forward as you lift off all the cards above the break. Move these cards forward and then to one side. Offer the pile in your left hand, saying, "Take a look at your card, please." Or, if the trick calls for it, say "Take your card, please, and show it around."

Simon Says

The first person I saw using this force was Simon Lovell; hence the title.

The top card of the deck is your force card. Hold the deck in the dealing position in your left hand. Fold your left first finger under the deck; this will facilitate the following move. Riffle down the left side of the deck with your left thumb, saying to a spectator, "Tell me when to stop." Stop immediately at the exact point he indicates. Your left thumb now is bending down all the cards below the break. (Illustration 22).

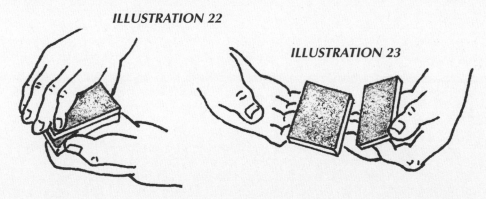

ILLUSTRATION 22

ILLUSTRATION 23

Hold your right hand palm up next to your left hand. Tilt your left hand clockwise, until the cards above your left thumb fall face up on the extended fingers of your right hand. The right edge of the pile in your right hand should rest along the first joint of your right fingers (Illustration 23). The second and third fingers of your left hand flip the pile over so that it falls face down in your right hand. Immediately extend your right hand towards the spectator. Say, "Please look at your card." He looks at the original top card of the deck.

One-Cut Force

You must know the top card. See *The Peek* (page 14). As you hold the deck, have a spectator cut off a portion of cards and turn them face up on the rest of the deck.

Immediately turn the deck over and spread the cards out on the table (Illustration 24).

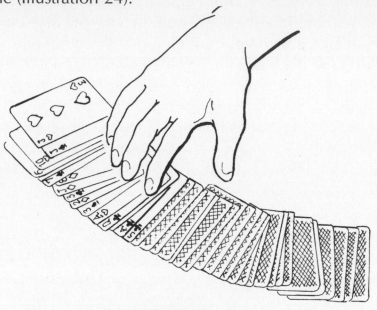

ILLUSTRATION 24:
One means of forcing the top card in a deck.
As you hold the deck, have a spectator cut off a portion of the cards, and then have him place them face up on the rest of the deck. Turn the deck over and spread the cards out on the table.

Push through the face-up cards to the first face-down card. Point to it, saying, "Please take a look at the card." It is, of course, the original top card which you sighted.

There is a temptation to say, "Look at the card you cut to." I think it's a mistake to be that specific. I don't want the spectator to be thinking, "Hmm. *Is* that the card I cut to?"

The Face-Up Force

This is a quick, deceptive force, which I occasionally use to discover a chosen card. You must know the top card. Have a spectator take a card from the deck, turn it face up, and place it on top. He then cuts a pile from the top and sets it on the table. You turn the remaining cards in your hand face up and place them beside the cutoff portion. Take the cutoff portion (with the face-up card on top), turn it face up, and place it on top of the other pile.

Pick up the deck and turn it face down. Hand it to the spectator and ask him to look through to the face-up card and look at the randomly selected card below it.

You may prefer to fan through yourself, chatting about freedom of choice in cutting the cards. Separate the cards below the face-up card and offer the next card (originally the top card, of course) for him to look at.

Actually, all that has happened is that a face-up card was placed upon the force card and the cards were cut. The handling, however, obscures this and convinces the spectator that he has freely chosen the card. Practice this one a bit before trying it in public; smoothness is the key.

Double-Turnover Force

Again you must know the top card. See *The Peek* (page 14). As you hold the deck, ask a spectator to cut off a small packet and turn it face up on the deck. Then have him cut off a larger packet and turn it face up on the deck. Fan through the face up cards to the first face-down card. Extend the face down pile to the spectator, asking him to look at his card. It is the original top card.

Crisscross Force

You must know the top card of the deck. Set the deck on the table. Ask a spectator to cut off a pile and place it on the table. Pick up the bottom portion and place it crosswise on the cut-off portion.

Chat with the spectator for a moment so that he has a chance to forget about the true position of the two piles. (This is known as "time misdirection.") Point to the top card of the lower pile, saying, "Take a look at your card, please." As before, it's the original top card of the deck.

DROP SLEIGHT

This is a wonderful utility move in which one card is secretly exchanged for another. Separate a card at the bottom of the deck, holding a break above it with your right thumb, and then perform the first part of a legitimate one-finger cut: From behind the deck, with your upraised left first finger, revolve about half of the cards from the top of the deck so that they fall into your left hand.

Now for the sleight itself. With your left thumb, push off the top card of those in your left hand. With the left edge of the packet in your right hand, flip this card over so that it turns face up on the lower portion of the deck (Illustration 25). At the conclusion of the move, your right hand, with its packet, swings naturally over the cards in your left hand. Display the card, saying, for instance, "Here we have the six of hearts."

Continue with patter suited to the trick you're doing as you flip the card face down in the same way as you flipped it face up. This time, as your right hand comes over the deck, drop the card separated by your thumb. It falls on top of the lower packet as your right hand continues its sweeping move to the left for an inch or so. This small movement to the left covers the sleight, making it completely invisible.

The original top card of the deck has now been exchanged for the original bottom card of the deck. This maneuver is useful in a number of tricks, as you will see.

Usually, after the sleight is performed, your hands are separated, and the top card of the packet in your left hand is thumbed face down onto the table.

ILLUSTRATION 25

DOUBLE-LIFT

The double-lift is used in many tricks. A proficient card handler should definitely know how to do one. There are at least a dozen different ways of performing a good double-lift. The three below work extremely well.

Snap Double-Lift

I was told that this was one of John Scarne's favorite methods. I don't know whether he invented it.

Apparently a card is casually snapped face up and flipped back on top of the deck. Actually, it's two cards.

First, you should practice the display of a *single* card by snapping it face up. Incidentally, if you want to make the double-lift believable, always display a card in the same way as you do when performing the sleight.

Hold the deck high in your left hand (Illustration 26). Your right hand lifts off the top card, holding it as shown in Illustration 27. Squeeze the card so that it bevels downwards, as shown in Illustration 28.

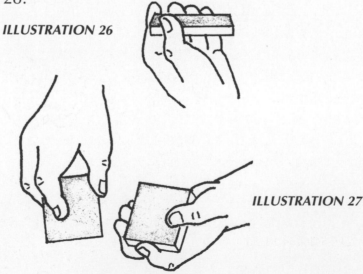

ILLUSTRATION 26

ILLUSTRATION 27

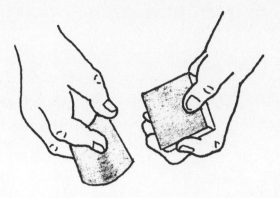

ILLUSTRATION 28

The idea now is to press down slightly with the first finger and continue bending the card, until by straightening the second finger slightly you snap the card loose from that digit and hold the card between your thumb and first finger (Illustration 29). At the same time as you snap the card, turn your hand clockwise so that the card is clearly displayed. The entire move is done in an instant.

The card is returned to the deck by laying its side on the tips of your left hand fingers, and flipping it over with your right hand first finger (Illustration 30).

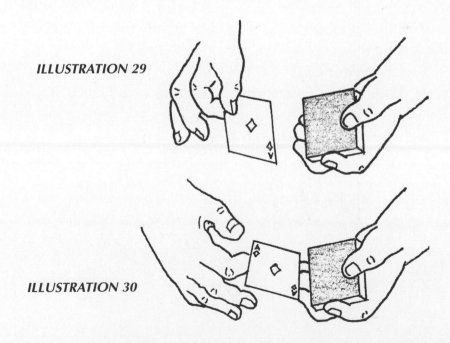

ILLUSTRATION 29

ILLUSTRATION 30

Practice the entire maneuver until you can do it smoothly and naturally.

For the double-lift, you duplicate precisely the actions in the single lift. Holding the deck high in your hand, casually riffle the left side of the deck near the rear with your right thumb (Illustration 31). In doing this, separate the top two cards from the rest of the deck and hold the break with your *left* thumb (Illustration 32).

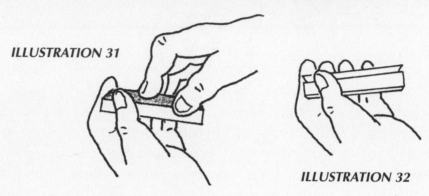

ILLUSTRATION 31

ILLUSTRATION 32

Take the two cards with your right hand *exactly as you took the single card.* Snap the two cards face up. Name the card. Roll the two back on top. Do all this in precisely the same way as you did the single card.

There's a knack. At first, the cards may separate slightly, but if you treat the two *precisely* as you would a single card, they won't. Alternate snapping over a single card and a double card. Within half an hour, you should have the move mastered.

Efficient Double-Lift

I developed this double-lift some time ago. Since then, I've seen other magicians use double-lifts that are similar, if not identical. I believe that the details make this one of the best: It looks natural, it requires no preparatory move, and the return to the deck is extremely simple.

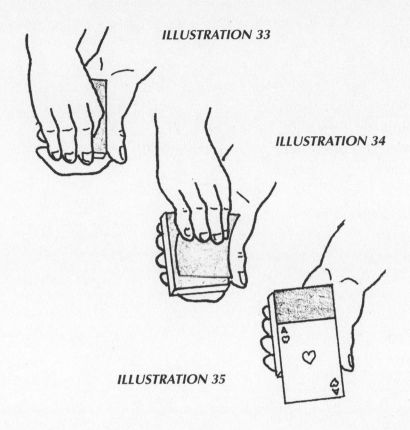

ILLUSTRATION 33

ILLUSTRATION 34

ILLUSTRATION 35

Hold the deck in your left hand, thumb along the left side. With your right hand, grip the deck from above, thumb at the rear, first finger folded on top, and the remaining fingers at the outer end (Illustration 33).

Bevel the cards back slightly. With your right thumb, lift two cards about a quarter inch. The backward bevel helps with this. Slide your fingers back along the surface of the double card so that you're gripping it at the back end between fingers and thumb (Illustration 34). Immediately snap the double card over end for end, moving your right hand forward as you do so. Set the card down so that it projects about an inch-and-a-half beyond the front of the deck (Illustration 35).

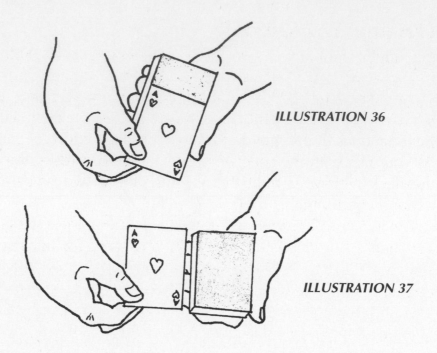

ILLUSTRATION 36

ILLUSTRATION 37

After pausing a few moments, with your palm-up right hand grasp the double card at the right outer side, fingers below and thumb on top (Illustration 36). Lift it off the deck and bring it to the right side of the deck (Illustration 37). With your right fingers beneath, flip the double card face down on top of the deck.

Note: It may be difficult at first to separate two cards from the deck with your right thumb. A good way to practice is to perform the double-lift, then deal the top card down. Perform another double-lift; deal the top card down. Continue on through the deck. Eventually, you'll have no trouble at all.

Original Double-Lift

The double-lift I learned as a kid is quite easy and will still do the job for a great many tricks.

As with *Efficient Double-Lift* (page 44), hold the deck in your left hand with your thumb along the side. Grip the deck with your right hand, as in the previous double-lift (Illustration 33, page 45). As you chat with the spectators, separate two cards at the rear of the deck with your right thumb. Push these two cards forward about a quarter-inch.

With your right hand, grasp the two cards at the outer end, fingers beneath and thumb on top. This is precisely the same grip shown in Illustration 36 (page 46), except that, in this instance, the card taken with your right hand is face down. Turn the two cards over end-for-end, and set them down so that they project about an inch beyond the front of the deck.

When ready, grasp the cards at the outer end again, turn them end-for-end, and return them, face down, to the top of the deck.

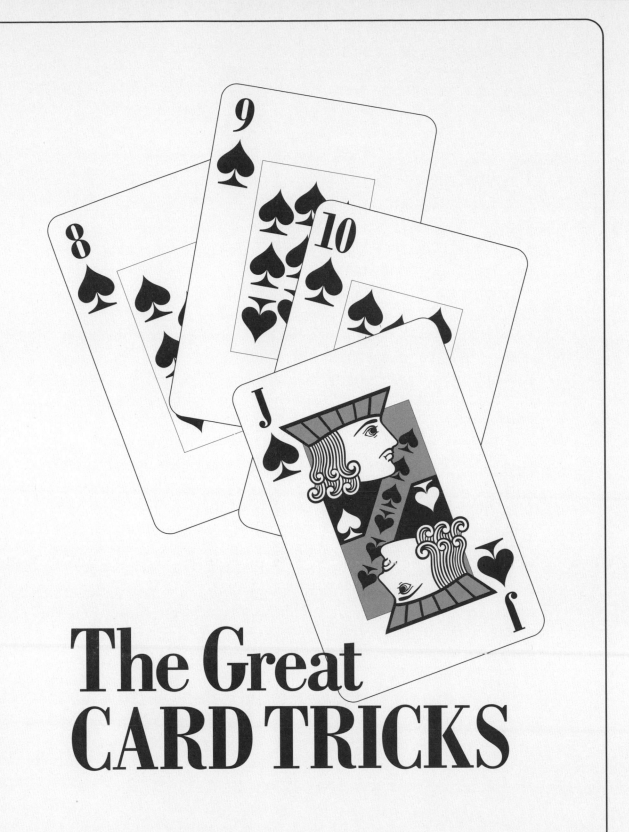

The Great
CARD TRICKS

PREDICTION

Presto Prediction

This trick appeared almost forty years ago in a booklet I published. The trick was recently credited to someone else. I don't invent so many good tricks that I can afford to let that pass: I invented it, and besides, my version is better.

Few tricks have a climax as startling as this one. The principle is just about impossible to detect, but what really makes the trick work is the patter, the romance. I have always felt that a weakness can be turned into a strength if you only give the problem enough thought. In this instance, the spectators are dealing cards, selecting, counting down. In other words, this has all the earmarks of a "mathematical" trick, a no-brainer, a trick anyone could do. Indeed it is. But the patter makes it all seem logical, if not absolutely necessary. So at the climax of the trick, be sure to try the suggested patter.

Hand the deck to a spectator for shuffling, saying, "Now I am going to attempt to predict the future. The odds are fifty-two to one against my doing this, but I think it's going to work this time. You see, I've missed the last sixty-three times, so I'm way overdue."

Take the deck back, holding it with your fingertips, so that all can see that you are doing nothing tricky. "Watch carefully. I want you to see that I do not change the position of a single card. I'm going to fan through the deck and remove a prediction card."

Demonstrate by fanning through the cards, faces towards you, noting the value of the top card. Close up the cards. Let us suppose that the top card is an eight.

"Watch carefully now!" With the cards facing you, again fan through them, starting at the bottom. Since you noted an eight on top, count to eight from the bottom and note the card at that position. Let us say it is the five of diamonds. Continue fanning until you come to the corresponding card in color and value—in this instance, the five of hearts. Meticulously lift the five of hearts from the deck and place it face down on the table, stating, "This is my prediction card." While doing all this, handle the cards openly to emphasize that you are doing *nothing tricky* with the deck.

Hand the deck to a second spectator. "Please turn the deck face up and deal the cards one at a time into a pile." Once he deals past the card you noted, casually say, "You can stop whenever you want." When he does stop, tell him he may deal a few more, take a few back, whatever he wishes.

Take the undealt cards from the spectator and place them face down. Turn the dealt cards face down. The position now is as follows: The top card of the undealt pile indicates the number down in the dealt pile at which the match for your prediction card lies. In our example, the top card of one pile is an eight, and the eighth card down in the other pile is the five of diamonds, which corresponds to your prediction card, the five of hearts.

Point out the two face-down piles to a third spectator. "Perhaps you have seen demonstrations where the performer asks you to choose a pile and then he takes whatever pile he wants. In this case, I want you to pick up a pile. That will be the pile that you will actually use."

Sound convincing? Of course. But, as you will see, it doesn't matter which pile he picks up. Suppose he takes the pile with the eight on top. You say, "What we are going to do is turn over the top card of your pile—not yet—and count down that number in this pile." Pick up the other pile and continue, "An ace has a value of one, a jack eleven, a queen twelve, and a king thirteen."

This statement is particularly effective when the card is *not* one of these, for it creates the impression that you have no idea what the card is.

The third spectator turns over the top card of his pile; you slowly count off the cards from your pile, setting aside the card arrived at. In your example, the spectator turned over an eight, so you count off eight cards, setting aside the eighth one, the five of diamonds.

Suppose that when you offer the choice of piles the third spectator picks up the pile containing the card that matches your prediction card. Simply say, "Now I will turn over the top card of my pile, and we will count down that number in the pile you have chosen." Be sure to mention the business about the value of ace, jack, queen, and king. Let the spectator count off the cards, and you take the final card of the count and place it face down on the table.

You now have two face-down cards on the table: your prediction card and the card "chosen" by the spectators. Gather up the rest of the deck, leaving the two face-down cards.

What you say now triples the trick's effectiveness. "Let's review. First the deck was thoroughly shuffled. Without changing the position of a single card, I removed the prediction card. Then you (the second spectator) dealt off as many cards as you wanted, stopped whenever you wanted. Finally, you (the third spectator) chose a pile, and we actually used the pile you chose. In other words, we tried to arrive at the choice of a card completely by chance. Why did we go through all this? Because if I offered you the choice of a card, you might think I had some way of forcing my selection on you. Instead, we have guaranteed that a card was chosen at random."

Set aside the deck. Take the two cards at the outer edge. "If I have correctly predicted the future, these two cards should match each other in color—and in value." Face the two cards simultaneously. When you gather the cards up after enjoying their astonishment, it's fun to add, "I feel sorry for the next fifty-one people I do this for."

Note: Occasionally, when fanning through the cards for your prediction card, you will see that it is among those that will be counted off. Obviously, the trick will not work. Shake your head, close up the cards and hand them to a spectator, saying, "Please shuffle them again. I can't seem to picture a card; the vibrations just aren't right. Perhaps another shuffle will help."

Colorful Prediction

With this trick, by using an unprepared deck, you apparently correctly estimate the number of red and black cards in two piles.

For this one, you need a complete deck of fifty-two cards. Let a spectator shuffle the deck. Take it back and begin dealing into a face-down pile. After you have dealt fifteen or more, invite the spectator to tell you to stop whenever he wishes.

As you deal, count the cards. Try to keep your lips from moving. When he says stop, give him the dealt pile. Ask him his favorite color, red or black. Suppose he says red, and further suppose that his pile contains twenty-three cards. You say, "Bad luck. I have three more red cards than you have black."

Repeat the assertion. Now deal your cards face up, counting the red cards aloud as you go. The spectator deals his cards face up, counting the blacks. Sure enough, you have three more reds than he has blacks.

Why?

To understand, take a deck of cards, shuffle it, and deal it into two piles of twenty-six cards each. Suppose you have nineteen black cards in one pile. You must also have seven red cards in that pile. This means that the other pile must contain nineteen red cards and seven black cards. So, no matter how you shuffle, when you have two piles of twenty-six cards, you will always have the same number of black cards in one pile as you have red cards in the other.

This will be clearer if we take an extreme example or two. If you have twenty-six black cards in one pile, you will have twenty-six red cards in the other. You could say, "I have the same number of reds in my pile as you have blacks in yours."

It would work the same if you had twenty-five red cards and one black in your pile. The spectator would have twenty-five blacks and one red. And you, naturally would have the same number of red cards as he has blacks.

If you tried to pass that off as a trick, however, very few spectators would be deceived, particularly if you do repeats. Therefore, you disguise the principle by working with unequal piles and perfoming a simple calculation.

When you performed the trick as above, the spectator had twenty-three cards. That's three less than twenty-six. You, therefore, have three more than twenty-six. This means that you have three more red cards than he has black. For that matter, you have three more black cards than he has red.

Back to the trick. The spectator is astonished at your clairvoyance, but you have only just begun. Have the spectator shuffle his packet of twenty-three, and you shuffle your packet. You may even exchange packets and shuffle. Then you take your original packet and begin dealing onto his, asking him again to tell you when to stop. Once more you keep track of the number.

He had twenty-three, so you begin counting with twenty-four. When he tells you to stop, you again know the number of cards he has in his pile.

"Which do you want this time, red or black?" Suppose he chooses black, and that he now has thirty cards in his pile.

"Good selection. You now hold four more blacks than I have reds."

In other words, he has four more cards than twenty-six.

You may repeat the trick a number of times, remembering to deal from the larger packet to the smaller. In our example, the piles would be shuffled again, and you would make sure to deal from the pile of thirty onto the other, which, of course, contains twenty-two.

The trick, like many good ones, is a combination of a hidden principle and verbal chicanery. You can throw spectators off further by stating your prediction in different ways.

There are four ways you could state the preceding prediction:

1. You now hold four more blacks than I have reds.
2. You now have four more reds than I have blacks.
3. I now have four fewer blacks than you have reds.
4. I now have four fewer reds than you have blacks.

Three-Card Surprise

When I invented this trick, I discovered that it is doubly astonishing. It is absolutely baffling and entertaining to spectators. And it is astonishing to me that it should be so well received. I consider it among the best tricks I perform.

The original version of this trick must be as old as card tricks. Long ago I came across a good version. Unfortunately, two decks were required (an automatic turn-off for me), and the move required at the end seemed contrived, unnecessary, and unsatisfactory. Recently I solved the problem of the ending, and in the process came up with what amounts to a new trick—with one deck.

Because the effect is similar to that of *Presto Prediction*, you should probably not do these two in the same set. The effect is that you correctly predict three cards chosen by a spectator or spectators.

Have the deck shuffled. Take the cards back and fan through them, faces towards you, saying, "We are going to take turns selecting cards. First I'll select one, and then you'll select one."

As you spread the cards, note the top card. Remove a card from the deck of the same value and color. If the top card is the six of diamonds, for instance, you remove the six of hearts. Without showing it to the spectators, place it face down on the table. Spread the rest of the cards face down on the table, inviting a spectator to choose one and place it face up on your card. It is important that you make no mention of telling the future or matching cards; you two are simply taking turns selecting cards.

Tell the spectator, "A very good choice. Now I'll select another one." Fan through the cards as before, and remove the card that is the same color and value as the one which he just placed face up. As you do so, mutter about now this must be the world's most tedious card experiment. Place the card face down to the right of your first choice. Set the deck down and say, "You will choose each card in a different way. This time, I would like you to cut a pile off the deck."

When he cuts the cards, take the one he cut to and place it face up on top of your second choice. Make sure you replace the cutoff pile on top so that the card you originally sighted remains on top.

Compliment the spectator on his selection and fan through the cards once more, muttering about how boring this experiment is. This time remove a card of the same color and value as the spectator's second selection and place the card face down to the right of the other two.

"Now we'll try yet another way of selecting a card," you say. Retaining the deck in your hand, tell the spectator, "Cut off a small packet, turn it face up, and place it on top of the deck." After he does so, say, "Now cut off a larger packet, turn it face up, and place it on top of the deck." This is *Double-Turnover Force* (page 39).

Explain, "Now we'll go to the card you cut to." Fan through the face-up cards and take out the first face-down card. It, of course, is the original top card, the one you sighted at the beginning of the trick. Place the card face up on top of your third face-down card.

It is important that you more or less follow the patter I have given. You don't want to put the spectators on guard by mentioning things like prediction or coincidence or any of the usual baloney.

Set the rest of the deck aside, saying, "I know exactly what you're thinking. Are there extra cards on the table? Did he slip in an extra card or two?"

Place the third set of two, the one on your right, on top of the middle set. Then place the set on the left on top of all. Now the top card matches the bottom card, and the other two pairs match each other face-to-face. I have inserted a little sneakiness into the routine here. "I can assure you that there are exactly six cards here."

Pick up the packet of six and hold it in the dealing position in the left hand. Take off the top card in your right hand with your right thumb, counting out, "One." Take off the second card in the same way, dealing it on top of the first in your right hand. You count, "Two."

Continue through the fifth card, counting aloud for each one. For the sixth card, you pause ever so slightly, saying, "And six." And place the sixth card on the bottom.

Instantly, take off the top two cards and drop them on the table. Next to them drop the next two cards. And next to them drop the last set of two. While doing this, say, "Six cards. Three sets of two."

The business of counting the cards and dropping them on the table in pairs has taken some time to explain. But the execution must be done snappily.

After a brief pause, turn over the face-down card in each pair, showing that the pairs match up in color and value. At this point it is frivolous to say anything; the climax speaks for itself. You will be delighted to hear such comments as, "But how could you know that I would pick that?"

TRANSPOSITION

Tick Tock Trick

To my delight, this trick of mine appeared in the September, 1949 issue of *Conjurors' Magazine*. This trick is always received well, and it is a nice change of pace from more conventional effects.

You deal twelve cards in a face-up circle, each card indicating an hour on the clock. Start with one o'clock and deal around to twelve o'clock, calling off each number (or time) as you deal. The card at twelve o'clock should be pushed a little above the circle so that spectators will have no trouble telling what card lies at what time. The queen of spades is placed in the middle and is dubbed "the card of mystery." A spectator mentally selects one of the cards and remembers the time at which it lies.

Turn your back and tell the spectator to quietly count from the deck a number of cards equal to the hour at which his selected card lies. If his card lies at five o'clock, he counts off five cards. These cards are placed in the spectator's pocket, or are otherwise concealed.

Now gather up the cards, apparently casually. Chat with the spectators as you do so. Pick up "the card of mystery" first and place it face up in your left hand. Pick up the rest of the cards in reverse order, starting with the card at twelve o'clock. The last one placed face up in your left hand is the card at one o'clock. Put these cards face down on top of the deck.

Now would be a good time to perform the *One-Finger Cut,* on page 26.

Have the spectator take the cards he has concealed and place them on top of the deck while you look away. You must now get rid of the top card. Riffle the end of the deck a few times, and then say, "No, I didn't do anything." Take off the top card and show it.

"See? It's not *your* card, and it's not the card of mystery." Place the card in the middle of the deck. To throw a little dust in their eyes, take the bottom card also, show it, and place it in the middle of the deck.

Deal the cards face down into a circle, starting with one o'clock. The thirteenth card is placed in the middle, and you refer to it as "the card of mystery."

Ask the spectator what time he selected. The card at that time is turned over; it is "the card of mystery." And the card in the center? Ask the spectator to name his card. Turn over the center card, saying, "Ah, your card is the new card of mystery."

Easy Aces

Every card trickster knows at least one four-ace trick, and most know several. Card performers love to do false shuffles, multiple palms, and top changes as they magically collect the aces into one pile. This version magically collects the aces into one pile, and requires no sleights.

When you hear how this one is done, you may decide that it's a little too gutsy for you. "Aw, shucks! Everyone will see how it's done." *No one* will see how it's done. The dirty work is done before anyone expects it, and with excellent misdirection.

Take the four aces from the pack, show them, and place them in a face-down row on the table. On top of each ace deal three cards face down. Set aside the rest of the deck. Place the piles one on top of the other, forming one pile.

"Obviously," you explain, "every fourth card is an ace." Fan the cards before the spectators, showing that this is true. As you fan through, say, "Three cards and an ace, three cards and an ace, three cards and an ace, and three cards and an ace." Even up the cards slowly and meticulously, demonstrating that you are performing no sleights.

From the top of the packet, deal four cards in a row on the table, saying, "Here we have one, two, three, ace." Casually take the top card of the packet in your hand. "So what's this card?" you ask, tapping the ace with the card in your hand.

The spectator will probably say that it is an ace. Regardless, you say, "Turn it over, please."

As he does so, *casually place the card in your hand on the bottom of the packet.* All attention, of course, is on the card being turned over.

Turn the ace face down. Deal a row of cards on top of the cards you just dealt, saying, "One, two, three, ace." Finish dealing the rest of the packet in the same manner, repeating, "One, two, three, ace."

The spectators are convinced that the four aces are in the fourth pile. Actually, the bottom card of the fourth pile is an ace, and the rest of the pile consists of ordinary cards. The bottom one of the third pile is an ordinary card, while the other three in that pile are aces.

Pick up piles one and two, and drop them on the deck. Take the ace from the bottom of the original fourth pile and place it face up in front of that pile. Take the ordinary card from the bottom of the original third pile and place it face up in front of that pile.

"One pile of aces," you say, "and one pile of ordinary cards." Then, suiting action to words, you add, "All we have to do is exchange the markers, snap the fingers, and the cards magically change places."

Turn over the three ordinary cards first, saying, "Now *these* are the ordinary cards." Turn over the aces, as you say, "And *these* are the aces."

Tricky Transpo

This trick is the easiest transposition trick ever—it is also a baffler. A word of warning, however. The participating spectators are required to remember both a card and a number. Do not perform this one as a part of youir regular routine; save it for times when you have bright, cooperative spectators.

Ask for the assistance of two spectators. Give the deck to the first spectator and then turn your back. Give these directions to the first spectator: "Please shuffle the cards. Now think of an even number, preferably one under twenty. Quietly count off that number of cards. When you are done, hand the deck to my other assistant."

Direct the second spectator as follows: "Will you shuffle the deck, please? Now think of an odd number, preferably one under twenty. Quietly count off that number of cards."

When the second spectator is done, continue: "Please set the rest of the deck aside; we won't be using it anymore. Now put both piles together, and I would like one of you to shuffle the new pile. Now, without changing the position of any card, I want both of you to see what card lies at the number you thought of. I would like each of you to remember your card and the number you thought of."

Turn back to the spectators and take the pile of cards. Place them behind your back, saying, "I am going to attempt to transpose the two selected cards."

When you put the cards behind your back, take the bottom card in your right hand and, starting with the top card, *quietly* deal the rest of the cards on top of it, reversing their order. While doing this, make small talk about the tremendous miracle you are attempting to perform. Bring the cards forward. Ask the first spectator for his even number. He tells you and, without changing the position of any cards (taking them one *under* the other), count down to that number. Ask the second spectator to name his card. Show that his card now lies at that number.

Replace the card in the exact same spot in the pile, and replace the cards on top so that they are in precisely the same order. Ask the second spectator what his nuber was. Count down to that number in the same way as you did previously. Before showing the card at that number, ask the first spectator to name his card. Show that it is now at that number.

The trick is a little complex, but I love it. I'm still not dead sure why it works, so every time I perform it, I am at least as astonished as the spectators.

One in Four

This trick is quite similar to the previous trick in its basic principle. But its *effect* is quite different. Roy Walton combined tricks by Al Baker and Dai Vernon; my only contribution is to add a slightly different handling.

Remove from the deck the four, three, two and ace of any suit. (Let's assume that you're using diamonds). First find the four and place it face up on the table. On top of this place the face-up three, followed by the two and the ace.

Ask Jeanine to choose a card and show it around. When she returns it to the deck, bring it to the top. (See *Controlling a Card*, page 17).

Hold the deck in the dealing position in your left hand. Pick up the four face-up cards from the table and drop them face up on top of the deck. Spread them out, along with another card or two. Say, "Here we have the ace, two, three, and four of diamonds." As you close up the four diamonds with your palm-up right hand, get a break with your left little finger below the fifth card. Immediately, turn your right hand palm down and lift off the packet of five cards, fingers at the other end, thumb at the inner end. The top, face-up card of the packet is the ace of diamonds, followed by the other three diamonds in order. On the bottom of the packet is the face-down chosen card.

"It's important that you remember the order of the cards," you say. "First, we have the ace." You now turn over the ace lengthwise and add it to the bottom of the packet. Here's precisely how: Move the packet in your right hand over the deck and hold down the ace with your left thumb as you move the rest of the packet to the right, drawing off the ace. The ace should extend over the right side of the deck about half its width (Illustration 38). From below, lift the packet in your right hand so that its left edge flips the ace over sideways. *Leave your left thumb in place, so that the ace falls on it.* Bring your right hand over the face-down ace, so that the ace is added to the bottom of the packet.

ILLUSTRATION 38

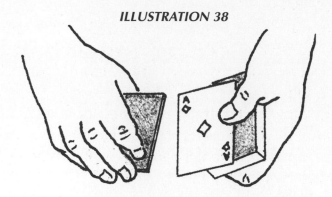

Call attention to the two of diamonds, saying, "And here we have the two." In the same way as you did the ace, turn the two of diamonds face down and add it to the bottom of the packet.

In exactly the same way, show the three and then the four. Drop the packet on top of the deck.

On top of the deck is the chosen card, followed by the ace, two, three, and four of diamonds.

Say to Jeanine, "I'd like you to choose one of the four cards— ace, two, three, or four. In fact, think of one, and then change your mind. I want you to have complete freedom of choice." She chooses one of the cards.

Suppose the ace is chosen. Deal the top card face down onto the table, saying, "All right, there's the ace. Now let's see how the two behaves." Without showing the top card, place it second from the top. Tap the top card and then turn it over. Apparently the two has returned to the top. Place the two *face up* next to the card on the table.

"Let's check the three." Place the top card second from the top. Tap the top card and turn it over. The three has returned. Deal it face up next to the two.

"And the four?" Again, place the top card second from the top. Tap the top card and turn it over, showing that the four has returned. Deal it face up to the right of the three.

Gesture towards the table. "So we have ace, two, three, four of diamonds. And you chose the ace. What's the name of your card?" The spectator names it. Turn over the face-down card. Success!

Suppose the spectator chooses two, three, or four. In each instance, the chosen number is simply dealt face down onto the table; each of the others is placed second from the top, brought back to the top, turned face up and dealt face up onto the table.

Let's suppose Jeanine chooses three, for instance. "Fine," you say. "Let's see how the ace behaves." Place the top card second from the top. Tap the top card, showing that the ace has returned. Place the ace on the table face up.

Place the top card second from the top, saying, "Let's see what the two does." Tap the top card. Sure enough, the two has returned to the top. Deal it face up to the right of the ace. Deal the next card face down to the right of the other two cards, saying, "Here's your three."

Once more place the top card second from the top, saying, "Let's see what the four does." Tap the top card; the four has returned to the top. Deal it face up to the right of the other three cards.

In all instances, you finally ask the name of the chosen card and then turn it face up.

Travelling Hearts

In concept, *Travelling Hearts* is similar to the preceeding trick.

The original of this trick, which was shown to me by Bob Stencel, required a bottom deal. I changed the trick to suit my abilities.

Look through the deck so that the spectators can't see the faces. Cut the ace of spades to the top. Then toss out these hearts, in any order, face up onto the table: ace, two, three, four, five, six.

Set down the deck and put the cards in order, the ace being at the face of the face-up packet and the six at the bottom. As you do so, say, "Try to remember what these cards are. For whatever reason, some people don't pay attention: all they can think of is the ace of spades. *Please* . . . these are hearts!"

As you speak, pick up the deck and hold it in your left hand in the dealing position. With your right hand, pick up the packet of hearts and place it face up on top of the deck. You'll now add a card to the packet, exactly as described in the previous trick. Spread out the hearts, displaying them. As you do so, casually spread out a few additional cards. As you close up the cards with your palm-up right hand, get a slight break with your left little finger under the seventh card. Turn your right hand palm down and lift off all seven cards with your right hand, fingers at the outer end, thumb at the inner end. Set the rest of the deck aside.

You're now holding the six hearts face up, with the ace of spades face down on the bottom. Take the packet in your left hand.

Say, "Try to remember these cards . . . *and* their order." Take the ace of hearts in your right hand, saying its name. Turn the card face down and place it face down on the bottom of the packet. With your right hand, turn the packet over, showing the ace on the bottom. Repeat, "Ace of hearts."

Perform the exact same procedure with the two of hearts. For the rest, you simply announce the name of the card, turn it over and place it on the bottom. The last card you place on the bottom is, of course, the six of hearts. Casually drop the packet on top of the deck.

The top six cards of the deck are, from the top: ace of spades, ace of hearts, two of hearts, three of hearts, four of hearts, and five of hearts.

Deal the top six cards into a row on the table. As you place the cards down, say, "Ace, two, three, four, five, six."

Pause. "Now watch this. We exchange the ace and the two." Change the places of the first two cards. Snap your fingers. Turn over the first card in the row. "The ace of hearts returns. Let's try the two."

Leaving the ace face up, do the same exchange with the second and third cards. Snap your fingers. "The two is back. Let's try the three."

Leave the two face up.

Perform the same maneuver with the third card, the fourth card and the fifth card. At this point, you have face up on the table the ace, two, three, four and five of hearts, along with the face-down ace of spades.

"So we have one card left. And, of course, we all know what it is." Pause. "Well, what is it?"

Most of the time, the answer will be, "The six of hearts."

Shake your head. Turn the ace of spades over. "Just as I say, some people just don't pay attention."

Once in a while, a spectator will guess the ace of spades.

"Right you are!" you say. "At least *some* people pay attention."

Joker Helps

Before I explain this Jack Avis transposition trick, I'll teach you a sleight called *Mexican Turnover*. It's a quite useful method for exchanging two cards.

Place a card face down on the table. Take another card face down in your right hand, holding it at the lower right corner with your thumb on top and your first two fingers beneath (Illustration 39). The third and fourth fingers of your right hand are curled into your palm. Presumably, you'll turn over the card on the table with the card in your hand.

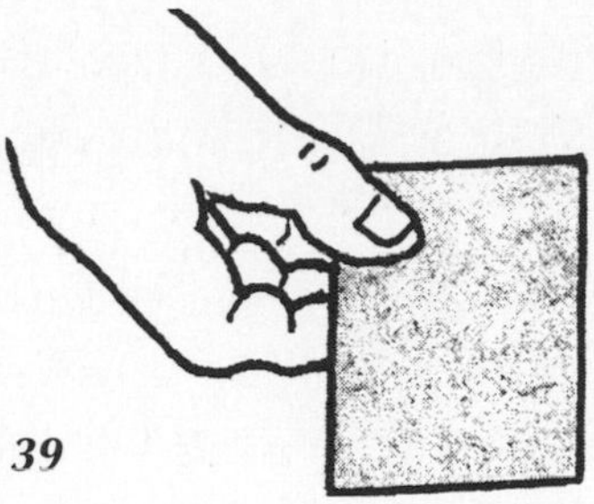

ILLUSTRATION 39

Place your left first finger on the lower left corner of the card on the table, tilting the opposite side up slightly. Slide the card in your hand under the right side of the table card, so that the bottom card extends a little less than an inch above the upper card (Illustration 40). Tilt both hands counter clockwise slightly.

ILLUSTRATION 40

As you do so, your right thumb and second finger grip the *upper* card. This card is lifted several inches at about a 45°. In that same motion, your right first finger flips the lower card face up—sideways. (Naturally, as you perform the flipping action, your left hand moves to the left, releasing the hold of its first finger on the card which was originally; on the table.) The sleight should be performed at medium speed: *don't rush it!*

You might practice by alternately performing a legitimate turnover and *Mexican Turnover.*

Now, the trick. Lay three cards out on the table, left to right: an ace, a joker, and a three. Emphasize the position of the ace and the three. Pick up the face-up joker and apparently turn the three face down. Actually, perform *Mexican Turnover.* Make sure that no one sees that the face-down three is in your right hand as you continue moving the card to the left and drop it face down on the face-up ace.

Pick up the two cards and hold them in the dealer's grip in your left hand. The three is face down on top; the ace is face up on the bottom. Turn over your left hand and push the cards through your hand with your left thumb (Illustration 41). Take them at the outer end with your right hand. Now the ace is on top face down and the three is on the bottom face up. Turn your left hand palm up and replace the two cards there. Fan the two cards, revealing the three (Illustration 42).

ILLUSTRATION 41

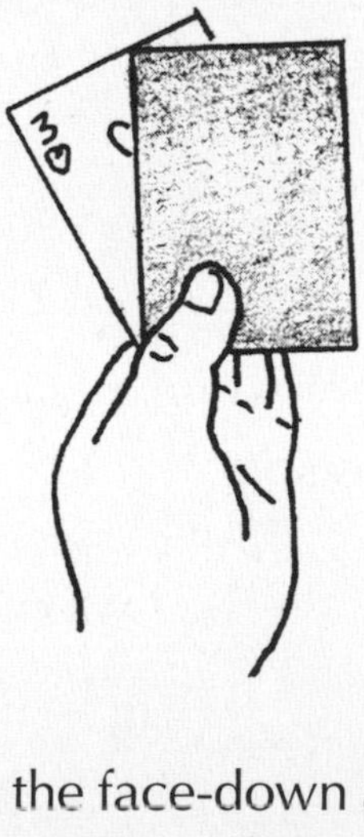

ILLUSTRATION 42

Set aside the face-up three. Now exchange the face-down ace with the face-down joker on the table, using *Mexican Turnover.* The ace and the three have changed places. Casually toss the joker face up onto the table.

Join the Knavery

Fan through the deck, faces towards yourself. Make no attempt at concealment as you cut the queen of diamonds to the top. Place the queen of spades on top of that. So, the second card from the top of the deck is the queen of diamonds; the top card is the queen of spades. Toss the two black jacks and the queen of hearts face up onto the table.

As you do the above, say, "I'd like to tell you a tale of two loving sisters, who happened to be queens, and another queen, who happened to be an evil witch."

You now do half of a legitimate one-finger cut, described in detail at the beginning of *Don't Pass It Up*, page 19. Your left first finger is pointed upwards behind the deck. In this instance, however, you revolve about *two-thirds* of the cards from the top of the deck so that they fall into your left hand. Place the part remaining in your right hand on the table to your left. "Here we have the castle in which one of the red queens lived." Touch the queen of hearts, which is face up on the table. "This queen, in fact. One day, two evil knaves came to the castle and kidnapped the queen and took her into the forest. Once there, they blindfolded her." Say to Oliver, a willing spectator, "To show that, please put her face down between the two evil knaves." He makes a sandwich of the three cards, the queen of hearts being face down between the two face-up jacks.

" 'What are you going to do to me?' asked the queen.

" 'When evening comes, we'll leave you to be eaten by wild beasts.'

" 'But besides you two, there are no wild beasts in this forest.'

" 'Then when evening comes, we'll kill you.'

" 'That's more like it,' said the queen, who was something of a perfectionist.

"And who was responsible for the kidnapping? This wicked witch, who also happened to be a queen—the queen of spades."

With the packet in your hand, now perform *Drop Sleight*, exactly as described on page 41. During the previous patter, you do the necessary preparation of letting the bottom card drop slightly and holding a break with your right thumb between this card and the rest of the packet. Then you proceed with half of a one-finger cut, and the actual sleight. As you say, "—the queen of spades," turn the top card of the left-hand packet over, using the left edge of the cards in your right hand. It is, of course, the queen of spades. Continue your patter as you complete the sleight, replacing the queen of spades with an indifferent card.

"She didn't have a castle, so she had the red queen kidnapped and took over her castle."

Place the cards in your right hand on the table, slightly to the right. With your right hand take off the top card of those in your left hand and plce it on top of the pile on the left. Apparently this card is the queen of spades.

As you proceed with the patter, place the cards in your left hand on top of those you just set on the table. Pick up the entire packet and hold it in your left hand.

The situation: On top of the packet you're holding is the queen of spades. Below it is the queen of diamonds.

"How wicked was she? Why, she'd talk with her mouth full of food. She'd cry when she didn't get her own way. And, worst of all, she'd torture her subjects by singing off-key until they begged for mercy.

"Now, with all this talk, I'll bet some of you can't remember which red queen we have in the forest. Is it the diamond queen or her sister, the heart queen?"

Pick up the three cards on the table and hold them fanned in your right hand. Meanwhile, push off the top card of the packet slightly and draw it back, getting a left little-finger break beneath it. Close up the three-card fan onto the packet, adding the additional card to the bottom of the group. Immediately lift off all four cards with your palm-down right hand, fingers at the outer end and thumb at the inner end.

"Can you remember which one was kidnapped? Was it the heart queen or the diamond queen?" Whatever the answer, with your left thumb draw the top face-up jack onto the packet. Thumb it face up onto the table. With your left thumb, draw the face-down queen of hearts onto the packet, letting it hang over the right side of the packet about half its width. Flip it over with the left side of the double card in your right hand, again letting it hang over about half its width.

"Ah, it's the queen of hearts—*not* her wonderful sister, the queen of diamonds."

With the right side of the double card, flip the queen of hearts face down, even with the top of the packet. With the same motion, drop the double card on top. Immediately fan off the top two cards, take them in your right hand, and place them on the jack on the table. The three should be spread out, forming a fan.

The queen of spades is now face down between the two face-up jacks, and the queen of hearts is on top of the packet in your hand. The second card from the top is the queen of diamonds. Do a double-lift, showing the queen of diamonds. Ask, "How many of you thought it was really the queen of diamonds?" Turn the double card face down. "Wrong, wrong, wrong!" Hold the packet from above in your right hand. Draw off the top card (the presumed queen of diamonds) with your *left* hand. "The diamond queen left her castle . . ." Move your right hand up and down slightly, indicating that the packet there is the castle in question. Place the card which is in your left hand on top of the packet on your left. ". . . and went to the wicked queen to beg for her sister's life."

Place the packet which is in your right hand down to your right.

" 'Please spare my sister's life!' she begged.

" 'Nuts to you with shells on,' said the evil queen.

" 'Then you'll be sorry,' said the diamond queen.

" 'Why should I be sorry? I'm an evil witch and I have evil witch powers.'

"And the diamond queen said, 'But I'm a good witch, and I have good witch powers—which are way stronger than evil witch powers. And now, I'll sing a magic spell (sing) When you wish upon a star, Makes no . . . Wait a minute . . . wrong movie. I've got it . . . (sing) Bibbety, bobbety, bibbety, bobbety, bibbety, bobbety boo.' And with that, both castles shook a little."

Casually show that both hands are empty. Reach out and simultaneously give each pile a little riffle.

"Instantly . . . the diamond queen was back in her castle." Turn over the top card of the pile on the right, leaving it face up on top. "And . . ." Turn over the top card of the other pile. ". . . the heart queen was back in her castle." Pause. During the following, spread the two jacks aside and turn over the queen of spades: "And the evil queen was alone in the forest with the two nasty knaves!" Before the audience has a chance to react, immediately say, "Soooo . . . they all lived happily ever after."

Quite Quaint Queens

This trick requires very little work but accomplishes an extraordinary result. This gem is the brainchild of Alan Brown.

Since you already have most of the cards you need on the table from the previous trick, you can continue the story by doing this trick. You may, however, prefer to perform this trick by itself.

Take out the jacks from the deck. Place the two red jacks, face up and fanned out, upon the table to the left; place the two black jacks, face up and fanned out, upon the table to the right. Remove the queen of spades and queen of hearts from the deck and place them near you, face up upon the table.

"The black jacks," you say, "are evil knaves. They work for this evil queen." Tap the queen of spades.

"The red jacks, however, are nice guys. They work for this very good queen." Tap the queen of hearts."

One day, the evil queen had the good queen kidnapped by her evil knaves." Place the queen of hearts face up between the two face-up black jacks, so that the lady becomes the middle card of the three-card fan. "They took her into the forest and blindfolded her." Ask Arnold to turn the queen of hearts face down, indicating that the queen's blindfolded. So the three-card fan now consists of the face-down queen of hearts surrounded by the two face-up black jacks.

Pick up the queen of spades. "While this was going on, the evil queen held the good guys prisoner with her crossbow." Place the queen of spades *face up* between the two red jacks, so that the three cards form a fan on the table.

"Why did the evil queen do this? Because she wanted this castle for herself." As you say "this castle," hold out the deck, showing that it represents the castle. "So the evil queen of spades went inside the castle with the two nice guys, the red jacks." (This is to implant the precise position in the minds of the spectators).

Hold the deck in the dealing position in your left hand. Pick up the fan of the red jacks and the queen of spades. Retaining their order (jacks on the outside), turn the three face down, and place them on top of the deck. As you close up the face-down trio, get a break with your right thumb below the top card. Double-undercut the deck, bringing the top card to the bottom. (See *Double-Cut,* page 17). "There go the red jacks and the evil queen of spades."

Gesture towards the remaining trio on the table. "The evil knaves were really stupid, and they forgot why they'd kidnapped the good queen of hearts. So they returned to the castle."

With your right hand, reach over to pick up the top black jack. As you do so, push off the top card of the deck slightly with your left thumb. Draw the card back on top of the deck, getting a tiny break beneath it with the tip of your left little finger. Place the black jack *face up* on top of the deck. "One evil knave entered the castle." Pick up the queen of hearts and place it face down on top of the deck. "When the good queen of hearts got into the castle, she slammed the door, and ran away."

You now have the queen of hearts on top, and the card below it is a black jack. Below the third card from the top, you have a little-finger break. Double-undercut the deck, bringing the top three cards to the bottom.

All the dirty work is done.

"The other evil knave finally managed to get the door open . . ." Pick up the other back jack and place it face up on top. " . . . and he immediately began searching for the queen of hearts." Give the cards a legitimate cut in the middle. Then cut off an additional small packet (ten cards or so) and complete the cut.

Snap the ends of the cards. "Now let's see what happened." Fan through the cards to the face-up black jacks and the face-down card between them. "The evil knaves finally found the queen in the dark. So they dragged her out of the castle and took her into the forest." Remove the three cards together from the deck and place the three on the table. Close up the deck.

"But they made one little mistake. They had the wrong queen." Turn the middle card of the three over, showing that it's the queen of spades.

"And what about the queen of hearts?" Turn the deck face up and fan through so that all can see. "Let's find those nice guys, the red jacks. There they are. And right between them, we have the good queen of hearts . . . just as it should be."

ESTIMATION

Easy Estimation

Tricks don't get much better than this one. Apparently you can gauge the precise number of cards a spectator cuts.

Have the deck shuffled and set down. Tell a spectator to cut off a packet of cards, not too large. Then you cut off a packet, making sure it contains several more cards than the spectator's pile. Turn your back, saying, "We'll each count our cards. Then I'll tell you exactly how many you have."

With your back turned to the spectator, count your cards as he counts his. Suppose you have twenty-two. Can you make a trick out of telling the spectator that you have twenty-two cards? It doesn't seem likely, does it? Yet that is, in effect, exactly what you do.

When you turn back to the spectator, say, "I have the same number you have, three left over, and enough more to make your pile total nineteen." Repeat the statement to make sure it sinks in.

"Now let's count our cards together." As he counts his cards into a pile, you simultaneously count yours into a separate pile. The cards should be counted deliberately, and you should count out loud.

Let us suppose he had thirteen cards. You stop dealing at the same time as he does. "Thirteen," you say. "The same number you have. And I said, three left over." Deal three cards from your pile to one side, counting aloud. "Three left over. And I said that I had enough left over to make your pile total nineteen." Point to his pile. "You have thirteen." *Count now on his pile.* "Fourteen, fifteen, sixteen, seventeen, eighteen, nineteen." You were exactly right.

So far as I know, this is the only trick based *solely* on the use of words. As I indicated, what you *really* said to the spectator was, "I counted my cards, and it turned out I had twenty-two."

Let's try another form: "I have the same number you have and enought more to make a total of twenty-two." Wouln't fool many people, would it?

Try this: "I have twenty-two cards, but I decided to subtract three from it giving me nineteen."

Still not tricky enough? Here's the actual form again: "I have the same number you have, three left over, and enough more to make your pile total nineteen."

You could also say, "I have the same number you have, two left over, and enough more to make your pile total twenty."

What you do, of course, is subtract a small number—two, three, or four—from your total number of cards. In the example, you counted twenty-two cards. Supposing that, instead of three, you decide that four should be the number left over. You subtract four from twenty-two, giving you eighteen. You now have two critical numbers, and you say, "I have the same number you have, four left over, and enough more to make your pile total eighteen." Note that these statements will work when you have a pile containing several more cards that the spectator's.

The trick can be repeated with no danger of spectators discovering the secret. To throw them off the track, use different numbers—two, three, four—for the number of cards left over.

Let's make sure you have it. The spectator cuts off a packet. Make sure it's no more than twenty cards. Cut off a pile containing several more cards than his. Turn away, telling the spectator to count his cards while you count yours. Suppose you have twenty-five. You will choose a small number—two, three, or four—to subtract from it. Let's say you choose two. You subtract two from twenty-five, giving you twenty-three. When you turn back, you state, "I have the same number you have, two left over, and enough more to make your pile total twenty-three." Then complete the trick as described above.

There are two things that throw the spectators off: the few extra cards that you count off, and the completion of the count, not on your pile, *but on the spectator's pile.*

Digital Estimation

Here's one I made up many, many years ago. I have had considerable fun with it ever since. It's a pretty good follow-up to *Easy Estimation.*

You need a complete fifty-two-card deck. Two spectators each cut off a pile and are asked to hold the packets flat in their palms. You say, "I am going to estimate the number of cards each of you is holding and break the result down to its lowest digit. Then I will find a card to verify my estimation."

The effectiveness of this trick depends on your ability to play-act. As you do the following, pause from time to time and study the piles the spectators are holding, creating the impression that you are performing a difficult feat of judgment.

What you actually do is run the remaining cards from hand to hand, faces toward you, apparently seeking an appropriate estimation card, but actually counting them. You will find you can do the counting rapidly and easily if you run the cards in groups of three. Don't forget to pause in your counting here and there to gauge the spectator's piles.

When you get the total, reduce it to a digit. Suppose the total is twenty-three; add the two and three together, giving you five. With a total of twenty-nine, add the two and nine, giving you eleven; then you add one and one, giving you a final digit of two.

Subtract your digit from either seven or sixteen, whichever gives you a single digit. Continuing to fan through the cards, find a card of that value and place it face down on the table.

For example, if you count twenty-three cards, add the digits together, giving you five. Subtract five from seven, giving you two. Find a two among your cards and place it face down on the table.

Another example: You count twenty-five cards. Add the two digits and you get seven. You are to subtract from either seven or sixteen. Since subtracting it from seven would give you zero, you subtract it from sixteen, giving you nine. Find a nine among your cards and place it face down on the table.

Now tell the spectators this: "I would like you each to count your cards carefully, and then mentally break your total down to one digit. For example, if you have fifteen cards, you would add the one and five together, giving you six."

When the spectators are done, have them each give their digit. Add these two together and break them down to a single figure. Turn over your estimation card and take a bow.

Why does it work? Let's start with a fifty-two card deck. The digits five and two add up to seven. And no matter how you divide the fifty-two-card deck, the various piles when added together and broken down to a digit will produce seven.

So, when you count your pile, presumably looking for a card to signify your estimation, you can get the right answer by reducing your total to a digit and subtracting from seven, or from any two numbers that add up to seven, like sixteen, twenty-five, thirty-four, forty-three, or fifty-two, so long as you reduce your total to a single digit.

The trick can be repeated as above, but I prefer this: "To make it even more difficult, I will try to estimate the number of cards held by *three* spectators. Again, I will break down the total and select an estimation card."

Have three spectators cut off small packets and hold them flat on their palms. Scrutinize the packets. Then fan through the remaining cards, finding your estimation card by counting and subtracting from seven or sixteen, as before. The spectators count their piles, reduce the number in each pile to a digit, add the totals, and reduce that result to a digit. Naturally, your estimation is correct. Performing this twice works out about right. No use pushing your luck.

Note: Occasionally you cannot find the appropriate estimation card in your group of cards. Sometimes you can make do by removing two cards which add up to the appropriate number. Once in a blue moon, you might have to take out three cards. If it gets worse, just *tell* them the number before they count. Most of the time, however, you'll find one estimation card.

The Perfect Pile

Long ago, while working on the same principle used in *Digital Estimation*, I came up with the idea of making an estimation using a pile of cards. I removed from the deck a pile of cards to verify my estimation, not letting the spectators see the exact number, which was eight. Then I had two specators divide the rest of the deck. Both counted their piles, reduced their number to a digit, added the digits together, and reduced the result to a digit. Naturally, the result was eight. Since the spectators had forty-four cards to divide (fifty-two minus eight), and four plus four is eight, they always ended up with eight.

So, the estimation always worked out. But the trick could not be repeated, at least not by the performer. But it certainly could be repeated by a spectator. If the spectator did exactly what the performer had done, he would duplicate the trick. So, over the years, I did not perform the trick very often. I have always liked the principle, however, and recently figured out a version that is a bit more mysterious and that will bear repeating.

Hand the deck to a spectator. "I would like you to shuffle those cards, and then cut off a pile and hand the rest of the deck to me."

After he does so, say, "I am going to try to make an exact estimation. But to make it more difficult for me, I want you to deal some cards into a separate pile, which we will not use. You can deal no cards, a few cards, or several cards."

Notice you use the word "deal" instead of "count." You don't want the spectator to think in terms of counting the cards. The reason? While feigning indifference, you *are* counting the cards he deals aside.

So the spectator deals the card, cards, or no cards into a pile, and you have surreptitiously noted the number. The situation now is this: Some cards have been set aside, the spectator has a pile, and you have the rest of the deck.

Next comes some major-league baloney. Appraising the spectator's pile, you say, "This is most difficult. Not only must I estimate the number of cards, but also reduce that number to a digit."

Remove some cards from your pile, keeping the number secret from the spectators. You may hide them under your hand or stick them under a magazine—whatever. Hand the rest of your pile to a second spectator. Explain, "I have made my estimation and have placed a number of cards under my hand to confirm my choice."

As in *Digital Estimation*, have each spectator count his pile and reduce the number to a digit. Then the digits are added together and reduced to a single number.

Have one of the spectators count your estimation pile. It is the same number as the digit arrived at by the spectators. This is a good one to do at least one more time.

How do you know how many cards to take for your estimation pile? You can work it out for yourself if you're of a mind, but basically it depends on how many cards the spectator deals off and discards. You have two numbers to remember: sixteen and twenty-five. If the spectator deals off an even number, *you* use an even number—sixteen. If the spectator deals off an odd number, *you* use an odd number—twenty-five. Note that in both instances, you use a number whose digits add up to seven. In both cases, you subtract the number the spectator dealt off, and divide by two. This give you the estimation number.

For example: The spectator deals off four cards. Since four is an even number, you will subtract it from sixteen. Four from sixteen is twelve. Half of twelve is six. So six is your estimation number, and you count off six cards as your estimation pile. Or, the spectator deals off seven cards. Seven is an odd number, so you subtract it from twenty-five. Seven from twenty-five is eighteen. Half of eighteen is nine. So there will be nine cards in your estimation pile. If your final number is in two digits, add the two together to get your estimation number.

Incidentally, with effects like these, the real trick is disguising the basic principle. So-called mathematical tricks should not appear to be so. After all, what credit accrues to the performer of a mathematical trick? He has not performed magic, but has presented a puzzle. The difference is this: With magic, you have a story.

The *Perfect Pile* trick could be presented as a puzzle. But it is far better to tell the story and act out the difficult estimation, pretending to gauge the number of cards held by the spectator. Of course it makes no sense. But it *is* magic.

FACE-UP, FACE-DOWN

Do-It-Yourself Discovery

This is one of the first impromptu card tricks I ever tried. The spectators' response told me that I had just performed real card magic. I was elated and determined to continue astonishing and mystifying.

The spectator shuffles the cards. Tell him to take half and give you the rest. "Now," you say, "while I turn my back, pick out a card, look at it, show it to the rest of the folks, and put it back on top of your pile."

Turn away and secretly turn two cards face up in your pile: the bottom card and the second card from the top.

When the spectator indicates that he is done, turn back, and tell the spectator to hold out his cards. Place your pile on top of his, even up the pile, and then direct him to place his arm behind his back, saying, "Now I want you to perform a little experiment with the cards behind your back."

Make sure of two things: that no spectator can see what goes on behind your assistant's back and that the assistant does not bring the cards forward until you are ready. To accomplish the latter, hover over the spectator, keeping alert to any premature disclosure. If he starts bringing the cards in front, say, "No, no, not until the completion of the experiment."

The position of the deck now: A card is face up second from the top, and a card is face up above the spectator's card in the middle of the deck.

"Take the top card . . . no, put that one on the bottom, so you'll know I'm not trying to fool you. Have you done that? All right. Take the *next* card, turn it face up, and stick it in the middle. Even up the cards."

Now you have the spectator bring the cards forward. Take the deck and fan through until you come to the face-up card. Ask the spectator to name his chosen card. Turn over the next card. "As you can see, you have located your chosen card yourself."

Once in a great while, the spectator will stick the card between your face-up card and the chosen card. You still have a decent trick. When you turn up the wrong card, simply say, "Oh my! You missed by one." Turn up the next card, showing that it is the selected one. When doing tricks like this, where you are trying to hide the presence of face-up cards, it is best to use a deck with a white border.

Behind My Back

This trick is clever, snappy, and mystifying.

You deal cards into a pile. When you reach twelve, tell the spectator to tell you when to stop. Wherever he says stop, make sure you actually stop on an *even number*. Call no attention to the number, however.

Set the rest of the deck aside. Pick up your even number of cards and rapidly fan through in groups of three, silently counting off half of them. Turn these face up and shuffle the pile. The pile has the same number of cards face up as face down, but in no particular order. Don't explain. Simply hand the pile to a spectator, saying, "Face-up and face-down cards. Would you shuffle them even more."

Turn away and have the spectator place the cards in your hand after he finishes shuffling. Turning back towards the spectators, quickly count off half the cards from the top and turn the bottom half over. Bring the two piles forward, one in the right hand, the other in the left. Say, "You will find the same number of cards face up in each pile." Fan through each pile, counting the face-up cards aloud and showing that you are correct.

The trick's effectiveness is dependent upon how rapidly you can do the counting behind your back, so let me offer some hints. Suppose you have a pile of eighteen cards. When you take the cards from the spectator, you must count off nine. Holding the pile in your left hand, push them from the top one at a time into your right hand, taking them one *under* the other. As soon as you have nine in your right hand, bring that hand to the front. At the same time, turn your left hand so that it is *back side up* and bring that hand forward. The hands are brought forward virtually simultaneously.

It takes a while to describe, but the actual counting and production of the cards takes only a few seconds.

The Rare Reverse

Until you try this one, you will not believe what an astonishing effect it has on spectators.

Hand a spectator the deck and tell him, "I'd like you to help me with an experiment. Please shuffle the cards. Now deal four cards face down in a row." Take the deck back.

"While my back is turned, select one of the cards and show it around."

Turn away from the spectators. Turn the top card and the two bottom cards of the deck in your hand face up. Say to the spectator, "Now I would like you to gather up all four cards on the table and mix them up a little."

Turn, holding the deck in the left hand (Illustration 43). Casually wave the hand, showing the top and bottom cards, as you say, "Now comes the difficult part of the experiment, the part where magic comes in."

Take the four cards from the spectator in your right hand. Turn the left hand over, apparently showing the bottom card of the deck. Actually, of course, it is one face-up card.

Place the four cards face-to-face with the "bottom" card, saying, "First, we need to place these cards face up in the deck. Four cards, so we must turn the deck over four times."

ILLUSTRATION 43:
Holding the deck in your left hand, casually wave the deck,
showing the top and bottom cards.

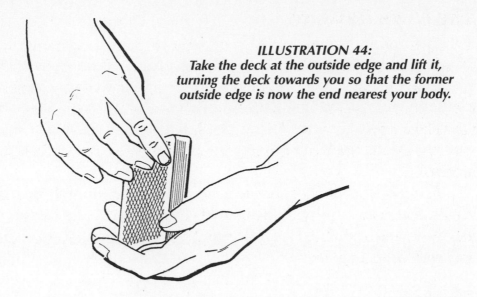

You count, "One, two, three, four," as, with your right hand, you turn the deck over four times in your left hand. Turn them over by taking them at the outside edge and lifting, turning the deck towards you so that the former outside edge is now the end nearest your body (Illustration 44). The object is to confuse spectators as to which cards are face up and which are face down.

"Now—four magical shuffles." Give the cards four brief overhand shuffles.

"Magic time! What is the name of the card you thought of?"

When the spectator names his card, fan through the facedown cards quite deliberately, tossing out each face-up card as you come to it. Fan all the way through the deck so spectators can see that there are only three face-up cards.

"The three *other* cards. And the card you thought of?" Turn the deck face up, fan through to the chosen card, and toss it out saying, "It has magically turned itself over in the deck."

My Favorite Card

When you run through this trick on your own, you may decide it is just too dumb to fool anyone. Believe me, it is effective and deceptive. What's more, althought it's over in fifteen or twenty seconds, it leaves a lasting impression.

Have a spectator shuffle the deck. Take it back, saying, "I must find my favorite card. It's my favorite card, because it never lets me down."

Fan the cards, faces toward you, noting the top and bottom cards. They must be of different suits and values. If they are not, have the cards shuffled again, saying that you want them really well mixed. It is unlikely that you will need them shuffled a third time.

You have noted the top and bottom cards. They will tell you what your favorite card actually is. Suppose that the two cards are the king of clubs and the four of diamonds. Your lucky card will be a combination of these two; it will be either the four of clubs or the king of diamonds. Find one of these and place it face down on the table. "There it is," you say, "my favorite card."

Hold out the deck to the spectator and ask him to cut off a pile. After he does, turn the remaining cards face up in your hand and place your "favorite card" face down on top of the face-up cards. Don't rush it, but do it promptly to keep the spectators from getting a good look at the face-up card. Have the spectator place his pile face up on top of all.

Place the deck face down on the table. Now is the time to give the audience a chance to forget what you just did. Any story will do, but you might want to say something like this: "Why is this particular card my favorite? Years ago I was in a big poker game, and I was way over my head. Only one card would give me the winner—a straight flush. And I got it. Ever since, that has been my favorite card. Pause. "That's a lie. But I need practice with my patter."

Tap the deck for luck. Fan through the face-down cards to your "favorite card." Let us suppose that it is the king of diamonds. Set it and the card on either side of it on the table. Place the rest of the deck aside.

"My favorite card," you say. "And on one side, a card of the same suit. And on the other, a card of the same value." As you say this, turn each of the cards over.

"Now you know the *real* reason it's my favorite card."

Ups and Downs

With this trick, a selected card is found at the precise point a spectator tells the magician to stop dealing.

For years, I tried to work out a good way to do this. There are plenty of ways, but most require advanced sleight of hand and look pretty fishy. One day a few years ago, I stumbled on a very simple method. It is not so simple, however, that it doesn't astonish spectators. A chosen card must be brought to the top of the deck. A pro would use sleight of hand; we'll try subterfuge.

As I considered various sneaky methods, I recalled a device used in an old trick called *Card from the Pocket*. Combining a variation of this device with my new idea would produce a doubly astonishing trick. A spectator looks at a card at a chosen number down in the deck. The performer causes the card to move from that number to a spot in the deck chosen completely at random by the spectator. Best of all, the working is clean and there is no sleight of hand.

Turn your back and have the spectator shuffle the deck. Say, "I would like you to think of a number from five to twenty. Now count down to that number, taking one card under the other so that you don't reverse their order. Look at the card that lies at that number, show it around, and replace the cards on top."

Turn around and take the deck, saying, "We have a chosen card which lies at a freely selected number down in the deck. Now, quick as a flash, I'm going to move your card to a much more convenient spot."

Place the deck behind your back, move the top card to the bottom, give the ends a noisy riffle, and bring the deck forward. It should take no more than a few seconds.

"All set. But first, let's make sure I *have* moved your card. What number down in the deck was it?"

When he tells you, deal the cards into a pile, one on top of the other, until you get to the chosen number. Deal that card out face up. As you place the dealt pile on top of the deck, say, "Not your card, right?"

Naturally, it is not. Pick up the card and stick it face down into the middle of the deck. The chosen card is now on top.

"I would like you to watch for your card as I deal, but don't say anything if you see it." Deal the cards into a pile. The top card is face down, the second face up, the third face down, the fourth face up, and so on. After you have dealt ten or so, tell the spectator, "Please tell me when to stop."

When he says stop, offer to deal more if he wishes. If he chooses to have you deal more, go ahead. And at the next stop, again offer to deal more. It doesn't matter to you. Just remember to continue the face-down, face-up pattern.

When the spectator stops you, pick up the pile of cards and place them on top of the deck, apparently to straighten up the pile. But by no means comment on this. Fan quickly through the cards to the last face-up card and lift them off (including the last face-up card). Set the rest of the deck down with your left hand. The top card of the deck is, of course, the selected card. As you fan through the cards and lift them off, ask, "Do you see your card among these?" Of course, he doesn't.

"Then let's take a look at the face-down ones." Deal the packet into a face-up pile. Face-down cards are turned over and dealt face up; others are simply added to the pile as they are. "Seen your card yet?" He hasn't. "Are you sure you remember the name of your card?" When he assures you that he does ask him the name. Nod knowingly and say, "Of course." Tap the top card of the deck and turn it over. "See? I told you I was going to move your card to a much more convenient spot."

Here's a minor point which could make all the difference: When you deal the cards into a face-down, face-up pile, make sure that they overlap enough to conceal that first face-down card, which, of course, is the chosen one.

SPELLING

Impromptu Speller

With this trick, a card is chosen, shown around, and returned to the deck, which is thoroughly shuffled. Nevertheless, the performer spells out the name of the card (dealing one card from the top for each letter in the spelling), and it appears on the last letter of the spelling.

That's a fairly accurate description of most spelling tricks, including this one. Spelling tricks abound. Most require setups, and many others seem cumbersome. This is one of the best, because it is quick, direct, surprising, and—add to that, easy.

A card is selected by a spectator. You must know the name of this card. I suggest you use the *One-Cut Force* (page 38), or the *Double-Turnover Force* (page 39). Have the spectator show the card around, put it back into the deck, and then shuffle the cards. You also give the cards a good shuffle.

"I know what a suspicious person you are. You know how magical I am, and you think I have sneakily removed your card from the deck. I can assure you that nothing is farther from the truth. Here, I'll show you." Turn the deck face up and begin fanning through the cards, from bottom to top.

"I want you to notice that your card is still here, but don't reveal the card to me by so much as a word or gesture. Just observe that it's still here."

As you fan rapidly through the cards, one by one, watch for the selected card. When you come to it, begin spelling the name of the card to yourself, moving one card (to the right) for each letter in the spelling. Let us say the selected card was the jack of hearts. When you come to it, count it as J, the next card as A, the next C, the next K, until you have spelled J-A-C-K-O-F-H-E-A-R-T-S. Note the very next card. Suppose it is the three of clubs. Spell out that card in the same way. Separate the cards at the point where you complete the spelling. Tap the next card with the cards in your right hand.

"See that card? I can tell you this. That card is *not* your selected card." Cut the deck at the point of the division, bringing the indicated card to the bottom, and turn the deck face down.

"Want to see another trick?" Pause. "Just kidding. No need to get upset. Now I assume you saw your card." The spectator will probably admit it. "Okay. We're going to try to find your card by spelling its name. For example, if your card had been the three of clubs (name the second card you mentally spelled out), we would spell it like this."

Spell out the name of the card, dealing out one card from the top for each letter in the spelling. On the last card of the spelling, turn the card over. It is the card you spelled—in our example, the three of clubs.

"There you are—the three of clubs. We will try to find your card the same way. What was the name of your card?"

He names it, and you spell it out, revealing his chosen card on the last letter of the spelling.

Note: When you are going through the deck, showing the spectator that his card is still there, you will sometimes find that his card is near the top. Just continue the count from the bottom, saying, "Funny, I haven't seen your card yet," or something equally inane.

Quick Speller

Ready for a paradox? In performance, this is one of the shortest tricks in the book. Naturally, it has the longest description. Stick with me on this one. The trick will seem a little complicated at first—actually it is not. You may find that this will be one of your favorites.

The trick is old but still good. Unfortunately, some versions are complicated and unnatural. All versions seem to require considerable memorization. My variation is simple and natural, and you need to remember only a few things.

First, the simple explanation. Every card in the deck can be spelled out, one way or another, in twelve cards, either by turning over the last card of the spelling or by turning over the next card. So the performer simply arranges for the chosen card to be twelfth from the top.

Here's an easy way to get it twelfth down. Have the deck shuffled. Take it back and give four cards to each of three spectators. Have each one remove a card from his group of four. A fourth spectator takes one of these three cards, shows it to everyone but you, and places it on top of the deck.

"Thus," you say, as you gather up the eleven outstanding cards, "we guarantee a card choosen completely at random." Place the eleven cards on top and proceed with a false cut (*The One-Finger Cut,* on page 26).

You ask the spectator to name his card. He does. You spell it out, dealing off one card for each letter—and there's his card. It's not quite that simple, of course, but not as difficult as some card writers have tried to make out. I will tell you exactly how I taught myself to spell out all the cards.

The most important thing to remember is that the card is twelfth from the top. This means that if the selected card spells out in twelve letters, you turn over the last card of the spelling. If it spells out in eleven letters, you spell out the card and turn over the *next* card. Exactly twenty-seven cards spell out in eleven or twelve letters. Not bad—but others you have to work at a little.

How about cards that spell out in ten letters? There are only four, and they are all clubs. Obviously, when you finish spelling out the card's name, the chosen card will still be two down in the deck. No problem. Before you start spelling, you will lose a card from the top—it's easy, as I will explain later—and turn over the next card after completing the spelling.

Seventeen cards are spelled with thirteen or fourteen letters. We eliminate the two letters in "of" by spelling out the suit and then the value. Now they can be handled exactly the same as cards that spell out with eleven or twelve letters. With twelve letters (originally fourteen), you turn over the last card of the spelling; with eleven (originally thirteen), you turn over the next card.

Only four cards, all diamonds, spell out in fifteen letters. These require special handling, as I will explain later.

Does it all sound too complicated? Actually, you need remember very little of the above. The spectator names his card, and you have it twelfth from the top. Somehow you must get to that twelfth card. This requires a quick computation. While figuring out how I'm going to spell out the card, I usually make small talk, saying things like, "Oh, the king of spades. That's one of my favorite cards. I see no reason this shouldn't work out perfectly."

How do I compute? The easiest way, I have discovered, is to first figure the suit and then the value. Clubs count five, spades and hearts six, and diamonds eight. *That* you should remember. Values count three, four or five. That you *don't* have to remember.

Let's take a few examples. The spectator names the seven of hearts. Hearts is six, seven is five. That's eleven. Add two more for "of." That's thirteen. No good. We'll have to spell out H-E-A-R-T-S and then S-E-V-E-N, and turn up the *next* card.

The spectator names the jack of spades. Spades is six; jack is four. Add two more for the "of." That's twelve. Spell out J-A-C-K-O-F-S-P-A-D-E-S, and turn over the last card of the spelling.

I will make a suggestion soon that will make all of this second nature to you. First, let's go over how you handle the spellings. As I mentioned, with cards that spell out in eleven or telve letters, you simply spell out the card. With a card that spells in eleven letters, you spell out the card and turn over the next card. With a card that spells out in twelve letters, you turn over the last card of the spelling.

With cards that spell out to thirteen or fourteen letters, eliminate the "of." Then treat them exactly like cards that spell out in eleven or twelve letters.

Let's try thirteen. The spectator says the queen of hearts is his card. You see that hearts is six and queen is five. Add two more for "of." You have thirteen. Drop the "of" and you have eleven letters. Although you have already been told the name of the card, you now say to the spectator, "Let's see—what's the suit?" He will say, "Hearts." You spell it out.

"And what's the value?" you ask. He says, "Queen." So you spell it out *and turn over the next card.*

Suppose the number is fourteen. Diamonds is the only suit in which cards are spelled out in fourteen or fifteen letters. For fourteen letters, you follow the same procedure as with thirteen, only you turn over the *last card of the spelling.*

Only four cards are spelled out with fifteen letters. You follow a procedure similar to that used for thirteen- and fourteen-letter cards. Drop the word "of," spelling out the suit and then the value. But that means you will have dealt one beyond the card when you spell it out.

So you must get rid of one letter in the spelling. You do that by getting rid of the "s" at the end of "diamonds" with a little verbal trick. It will seem perfectly natural if you follow the precise wording. Suppose that the spectator says his card is the seven of diamonds. You note diamonds is eight, and seven is five. That's thirteen—already too high. You say, "Let's see. Your card is a diamond." Spell out diamond. "And the value is what?"

He says, "Seven." Spell out seven, turning over the last card of the spelling.

Just keep remembering the card is twelfth down; the rest is easy.

But how about the cards that spell out in ten letters? As I mentioned, there are only four, all clubs. You must lose a card from the top, bringing the chosen card eleventh from the top. Now you can spell it out and turn over the next card.

How do you lose a card from the top? I do it the easy way. After the spectator names his card, and I note that it spells out in ten, I show the top card, saying, "Your card is not on top," and I bury it in the middle. Immediately, as a smoke screen, I add, "And your card is not on the bottom," and I show it and bury it in the middle. Then I proceed with the spelling.

Now for the suggestion that will make all this second nature to you. Go through the entire deck, figuring out the spelling of each card. Here's the way I do it. I count off eleven cards, look at the bottom card of the deck and place it below the eleven cards, which I return to the top. The card is now twelfth down.

I proceed exactly as though a spectator were there. I make small talk while I compute the spelling of the card, *and then I spell it out*. I discard that one. Eleven cards are already counted off, so I look at the bottom card of the deck, place it below the eleven cards, place all on top, and proceed as before.

When I finish the deck, there are still eleven cards not spelled out. I set these aside, and then take the rest of the deck, count off eleven, take a look at one of the eleven I used in the preceding spellings, place it below the new pile of eleven, and place all on top of the deck. Then I spell the card out, as before. I do the same with the remaining ten.

Incidently, the spelling of some cards differently is *not* a drawback. Since the spectator doesn't know what to expect, and since you perform the trick only once, the effect is perfect.

Review of the actual spelling: The spectator's card is twelfth from the top. The card's name can be made up of ten, eleven, twelve, thirteen, fourteen, or fifteen letters.

Ten letters. Only four cards, all clubs, spell out in ten letters. Before spelling, you must lose a card from the top. You do this by showing that the top and bottom cards are not the chosen ones and then burying them in the middle. Now you spell out the card and turn over the *next* card.

Eleven letters. Spell the card out and turn over the *next* card.

Twelve letters. Spell the card out and turn over the *last* card.

Thirteen letters. Spell out the suit (including the "s" at the end) and then the value. Drop the word "of." Turn over the *next* card.

Fourteen letters. Only five cards, all diamonds, are spelled out in fourteen letters. Spell out the suit (including the "s" at the end) and then the value. Turn over the *last* card.

Fifteen letters. Only four cards, all diamonds, are spelled out in fifteen letters. You say, "Your card is a diamond." Spell out "diamond" without the "s" at the end. Then spell out the value. Turn over the last card of the spelling.

Why have I gone into such detail with this particular trick when others seem easier? Because it is the best, the fastest, and the most direct of all spelling tricks.

A Hot Spell

An old principle is used in this trick. In fact, I use a variation of this principle in *Tick Tock Trick;* but I felt there had to be at least one more good effect using the same principle—all it would take was camouflage. I came up with this spelling trick, which gets excellent audience response.

Have a volunteer shuffle the deck as you explain, "I am going to attempt a feat of mentalism. Would you please think of a number from one to ten. Do you have one? All right. Now change your mind. This is not psychological; we must be sure you have complete freedom of choice."

"In a moment I'll turn my back, and I would like you to count two piles of cards, both containing the same number of cards as the number you thought of. For example, if you thought of four, deal two piles of cards with four cards in each pile. Do this quietly so I won't be able to hear you." Turn away while the spectator follows your instructions.

"Now lift up either of the two piles, look at the bottom card, and show it around. Please remember that card. And now place that pile on top of the deck." After your assistant is done, continue, "Please place the deck in my hand and hide the other pile you dealt."

Turn around and face the spectators with the pack behind your back and say, "I am going to find your card *behind my back,* using nothing more than mental vibrations to guide me. What's your card?"

When the spectator names his card, spell it, removing one card from the top for each letter, like this: Suppose the spectator says his card was the nine of clubs. You mentally say "N" and take the top card in your right hand. For the letter "I", you take the next card on top of the first. The card for "N" goes on top of the first two. The card for "E" goes on top of the first three. Continue on, adding one card on top of those in the right hand for each letter remaining in the spelling: O-F-C-L-U-B-S.

Naturally, you do not want the spectators to *hear* you doing this, and you do not want to give away the fact that you are doing anything tricky with the deck. The counting of one card on top of the other must be done fairly slowly; otherwise, noise will give it away. So take your time. You can do what I do: Babble while spelling out the card.

I spell the card out in three chunks. With our example, I would spell the nine of clubs like this: While spelling N-I-N-E, taking one card in my right hand for each letter, I would say something like "Nine . . . nine . . . very difficult. Really think of the value nine, so that I can feel that card vibrating." By this time, I have four cards in my right hand. I add two more for O-F, while saying something like "I'm not sure. I may have it." Then, while spelling C-L-U-B-S, I might say, "Nine of clubs is very tough. Clubs, clubs, clubs. Particularly confusing." Notice that this sort of jabbering helps you keep track of what you are doing behind your back, while creating the illusion that you are either a mentalist or a lunatic.

Bring the deck forward and say, "Presto! Here is your card, right on top." Turn over the top card. It is wrong, of course. You place the card in the middle of the deck, declaring, "Of course that isn't your card. I know what's wrong. It's what people always say about me: 'He's not playing with a full deck.' Would you please put the rest of the cards on top. I won't look."

Avert your head while your assistant puts on top of the deck the pile of cards he had hidden. Take the deck and hold it to your forehead, saying, "Concentrate on your card, please." After a moment of intense thinking, say, "I know exactly how to find your card. We'll spell it out. What is your card, please?" Yes, he has told you the name already, but there is no need to stress that.

When he names his card, spell it out, dealing one card from the top for each letter in the spelling. Turn the last card of the spelling face up; it is the spectator's card.

GAMBLING

Impossible Poker Deal

"I'd like to demonstrate a poker deal," you say, fanning through the cards. "I'll need lower-value cards. Gamblers don't want aces and face cards when they make their big killings. Those cards are so obvious that people might suspect the gamblers of cheating."

Remove all the cards from two to seven, tossing them face up on the table. Set the rest of the deck aside. Pick up the low cards and fan them out, faces towards yourself, saying, "Let's get some pairs here."

The statement is a form of misdirection. Actually, you'll remove three threes, three fives, and three sevens—three trios of *odd* cards, but you'll collect these cards in pairs. First toss out two face-down threes. On top of them, toss a three and a five. On top of the pile. toss two fives. Finally, place *three* sevens on top of all.

Turn to spectator Hal and ask, "Would you please shuffle these while I get some more pairs?" Hal shuffles the nine odd cards while you proceed.

Now gather three trios of *even* cards, using the same misdirection. Toss out two face-down twos, a two and a four, two fours, and three sixes. Put the rest of the cards back on the deck.

Have Hal set his cards aside and shuffle the packet you just collected. When he's finished shuffling, say, "Hal, you can place either packet on top of the other." After he puts the packets together, proceed by having Hal deal two hands.

I prefer, however, to give the spectators some reason to feel that, in some way, I'm exerting control. I hold out my left hand and ask the spectator to place the packet in my hand. I place my right hand flat on top of the packet and give my hands a quick up-and-down movement. "A little shake does the job," I say. In fact, I do this "little shake" before each deal.

Let's assume that you've done the "little shake." Hand the cards back to Hal and ask him to deal two five-card poker hands face down, one to you and one to himself. Hal does so, alternately dealing a card to you and a card to himself.

When he finishes, say, "Remember, you shuffled the cards yourself." Turn over the two hands, showing that you have the winner.

The two hands are on the table face up. Place your cards face up on top of his. Turn the combined hands face down. Take the undealt cards and place them face down on top of the combined packet, saying, "You might as well deal the rest of the cards into two hands."

Perform the "little shake," and have him deal again.

Once more you win. Put your face-up cards on top of his, as before. Turn the combined hands face down. This time the combined hands go *on top* of the undealt cards.

Pick up the packet and give it a "little shake." Say to Hal, "The problem is, you don't get to make any choices. The cards are dealt, and you have to accept what you get." Deal a face-up card to him and one to yourself. "But now you'll have the advantage of choosing your cards. You can decide if you want each card. If you don't want it, I get it."

Turn over the next card on the packet. "Do you want this card?" If he wants it, deal it to him face up. If he declines the card, add it, face up, to your hand. Continue until each of you has five cards. (Once Hal has five cards, you get enough more to complete your hand).

Again, you're a winner.

Place your face-up cards on top of his, asking, "Now do you want to deal, or do you want me to deal?" If *you* are to deal, place the combined pile on top of the undealt packet and deal. If *he* is to deal, place the undealt packet on top of the combined pile, and hand him the cards. In either instance, don't forget that vital "little shake."

Naturally, you win again.

Note: How does the trick work? In an older trick, only ten cards were used: three sets of three-of-a-kind with one separate card. The separate card is always referred to as the "Jonah" card—with good reason. When the ten cards are dealt out, the person with the Jonah card cannot win. (Try it out.)

This trick is subtly set up so that the same system operates. In each deal, *you* get either all odd cards or all even cards. The *spectator* gets only *four* odd cards or *four* even cards. If he gets four odd cards, he always receives one even card, the Jonah. If he gets four even cards, he always receives one odd card, the Jonah. He *cannot* win.

Freedom of Choice

I hit upon the basic principle used here some time ago, but only recently developed a trick that takes full advantage of it. This trick has been well received by magicians and laypersons alike.

Since spectator Evan likes card games, say to him, "Let's see how good a poker player you are. First, would you please shuffle the deck." After he finishes, take the deck back, and turn it face up so that all can see the cards. "Evan, I'm going to try to find you a really bad five-card poker hand. *But* I'll give you a bonus card. First, we'll take the bottom card." Name the card at the face of the deck. Suppose it is the two of clubs. Say, "So the two of clubs is your first card."

Proceed to fan through the cards, ostensibly choosing a five-card hand for Evan, along with a bonus card. As you do this, you will be placing five face-up piles onto the table. Unknown to the spectators, the second card from the bottom of each face-up pile will be a member of the spade royal flush (aces, kings, queens, jacks, tens). In other words, when each pile is turned face down, the second card from the top will be a member of the spade royal flush.

You have called attention to the two of clubs, the bottom card. "Let's find another good card for you." Fan through the cards until you come to a member of the spade royal flush. Fan off one additional card, calling attention to the card now at the face of those in your left hand. "Here's a really bad card," you say. "So this will be your second card" (Illustration 45). Even up the cards in your right hand and set them in a face-up pile on the table. In our example, the top card of this face-up pile is the two of clubs; the second card from the bottom of the face-up pile is part of the spade royal flush.

ILLUSTRATION 45

In the same way, fan through to the next member of the spade royal flush. Again, fan off one additional card. Name the card at the face of those in your left hand and make a comment about it. Even up the cards in your right hand and place them in a face-up pile next to the other pile on the table.

Do this two more times. Four face-up piles are in a row on the table. The face card of each pile is one you have selected for the spectator's hand. The second card from the bottom of each face-up pile is a part of the spade royal flush. The face card of those in your left hand is the fifth card you have selected for the spectator. "Now," you say, "I'll give you a bonus card."

Again fan through the cards, going one beyond the last card of the spade royal flush. Perform the same routine, placing a fifth pile face up on the table, next to the others. The second card from the bottom of this face-up pile is the fifth card of the spade royal flush. The "bonus card" is at the face of those in your left hand.

(If you've been following along with a deck of cards, you may have run into some trouble. I deal with this in the *Notes* at the end.)

Gesture towards the piles on the table. "These five cards are your poker hand. If you want, you can exchange one of those for the bonus card. What could be fairer?"

If Evan chooses to make the exchange, trade the card at the face of those in your left hand for the face card of the face-up packet he chooses. Set the cards in your hand aside face down. If he chooses not to make the exchange, simply set the leftover cards aside face down.

Place the top card of each pile above its pile. You now have five face-up piles in a row. Above this is another row, consisting of individual face-up cards (Illustration 46). "Now you can exchange any of your cards for any of the new cards here." Evan does so, probably enhancing his hand considerably.

ILLUSTRATION 46

"Now I'm *really* going to give you a break." Turn all five piles face down. Turn the top card of each pile face up on top of its pile. "You can exchange any of these cards to improve your hand." Now he should have an excellent hand.

Remove the leftover face-up cards from the five piles and toss them face down on top of the cards you set aside earlier.

"Do you have a good hand?" you ask Evan. Of course he does. "I agree. In fact, I think you'd win most card games with that hand. So let's see how *I* might do."

Turn over the top card of each pile. You win, for you have a royal flush in spades. "Not bad."

Notes:

(1) As you fan through the cards, two members of the spade royal flush may be close together. When you notice this, cut between the two cards and give the deck a quick overhand shuffle. Then hand the deck to a spectator and have him shuffle "so that everything is perfectly fair." The trick is not diminished, even if this occurs more than once.

(2) Sometimes you'll fan through fifteen to twenty cards without coming across a member of the spade royal flush. When this happens, comment, "I don't see anything I like here." Cut about twelve cards or so to the top and then continue the fanning procedure.

(3) Occasionally, in the fanning procedure, you'll provide the spectator some good cards—a pair of aces, for instance. When this occurs, say, "I'm feeling generous. I might as well give you a *few* good cards."

From the Land Down Under

Ken Beale created an unusual poker trick, to which I have added a strong climax and appropriate patter.

You must make a simple setup in advance. Place the four aces on top of the deck and a small straight flush on the bottom of the deck. A typical straight flush might be the five, six, seven, eight, nine of hearts. As you might know, a straight flush beats any other hand except a higher straight flush.

Look through the deck, faces towards yourself, and find the four jacks, tossing them face up onto the table. "Never play poker with a man from Australia," you say. "I met a fellow from Australia the other day. His name was Kangaroo Downs, and he invited me to play poker with him. The first thing he did was take the jacks from the deck. He said, 'In Australia, we always use the four jacks,' " Indicate the jacks on the table. "Then he said, 'In Australia, we play with just sixteen cards, so we'll need twelve more cards.' Then he counted out twelve cards like this."

Fan out the top three cards. Remove them from the deck and place them into a pile on the table, saying, "Three." Fan off two more cards and place them on top of the pile of three, saying, "Five." Deal single cards onto the pile, counting aloud: "Six, seven, eight . . . ." When you reach twelve, stop. Set the rest of the deck aside. Pick up the pile.

"Then Kangaroo Downs said, 'In Australia, we mix the cards like this.' " Turn the jacks face down so that they are in a row. Dealing from left to right, place one card on each jack. Repeat until all twelve cards are dealt out. Pick up the pile on the left. Place the pile to the right of it on top. Place the next pile to the right on top of the combined pile. And place the pile on the extreme right on top of all.

"Kangaroo said, 'In Australia, we always do a down-under deal, like this.' "

Deal the top card face down onto the table, saying, "Down."

Place the next card on the bottom of the stack in your hand, saying, "Under." Deal the next card onto the card on the table, saying, "Down." The next card goes under. Continue the deal until four cards remain in your hand. But you can stop saying "Down" and "Under" about halfway through.

"Kangaroo handed me the remaining four cards. He said, 'Here's your hand.'

"I said, 'But a poker hand should be five cards.'

"He said, 'Not in Australia. Care to make a bet?' I looked at my hand."

You are holding the four jacks. Place them face up onto the table. "A very good hand. So I makde a little wager. Kangaroo said, 'Now for my hand.'

Pick up the cards on the table and do the down-under deal until four cards remain in your hand. "I showed him my four jacks. And he showed me his four aces."

Lay the aces face up onto the table. "Then Kangaroo said, 'Let that be a lesson to you: Never play the other fellow's game.'

"I said, 'True. But in all fairness, we should play one hand of American poker, double or nothing.'

"Kangaroo said, 'Okay. You can deal, but I get to shuffle Australian style.' I agreed. He gathered up the cards like this."

Pick up the cards you dealt onto the table and put them on top of the deck. Place the four jacks face down on top of the deck. Place the four aces face down on top of them.

(You can leave out the following shuffle if you wish.) "Kangaroo gave the deck a really sneaky shuffle." You perform a riffle-shuffle as follows: Take the top half of the deck in your left hand and the bottom half in your right hand. Riffle off at least a dozen cards with your left thumb before you start interweaving the cards in your right hand. At the end, you will automatically riffle off on top a dozen or so cards from your right hand. This means that your small straight flush remains on the bottom of the deck and the four aces remain on top.

"Kangaroo said, 'Now we'll do the down-under shuffle.' "
Hold the deck from above in your left hand (Illustration 47).

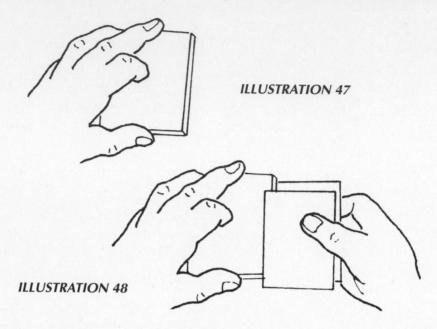

ILLUSTRATION 47

ILLUSTRATION 48

With the right thumb on top and the right fingers below, grasp the top and bottom cards together and pull them sideways from the packet (Illustration 48). Set the pair onto the table. Take the top and bottom cards again in the same way. Set this pair on top of the first pair. Continue until you have ten cards in the pile.

"Kangaroo said, 'Here are your ten cards. Deal 'em!' So I took the ten cards and dealt them like this."

Deal out two regular poker hands. The first card goes to your opponent, the second to yourself, and so on, until all ten are dealt.

"Kangaroo said, 'What do you know! I got the aces again.' "
Turn over his hand, showing the aces.

" 'Excellent hand,' I said. 'But I don't think it beats this.' "
Turn over your straight flush one card at a time.

"He was so angry, I figured the least I could do was offer some advice. I said, 'Let that be a lesson to you: Never play the other fellow's game. ' "

Two-Handed Poker

After doing a number of card tricks, you will frequently hear, "I'd sure hate to play poker with you," or, "Could you cheat at poker?" It's not a bad idea, then, to have a poker trick in your arsenal. This one is very easy and very clever.

You offer to demonstrate crooked poker dealing. But to make things easier, you will use only ten cards. Remove from the deck three aces, three kings, three tens, and a nine. Don't show them. Have the nine on top.

With an overhand shuffle, draw off the nine and shuffle the rest of the cards on top of it. Shuffle again, drawing off the last few cards singly so that the nine ends on top. If you cannot do the overhand shuffle, simply mess the cards around on the table and then gather them up, making sure that the nine ends on top. You may follow this procedure for all succeeding deals.

Deal the cards alternately to the spectator and yourself. Naturally, when the hands are turned over, you win.

This is one of the most ingenious poker effects ever devised. The fact is, the hand with the nine can never win. Is that cute, or what? Take the nine and try getting a winning hand with any four other cards of the nine cards remaining. If you take two pairs, the other hand will have three of a kind. If you take three of a kind, the other hand will be a full house. If you take a pair, the other hand will have two pairs.

Repeat the trick a few times. Then, with a shuffle, leave the nine on the bottom and let the spectator deal. He loses, of course.

Next, shuffle the nine to the top. Hand the deck to the spectator and tell him that you will try something different. "You may deal the cards one at a time to either hand in any order you wish—just so we both end up with five." If the spectator deals the first card to himself, he loses, so try the stunt again. Say, "Deal them in any order you wish."

If the first card goes to you, say, "Now *this* time, no matter what you do, *I* am going to lose."

If the spectator insists on dealing the first card to himself two or three times, you'd better hang up. You are simply destined to win. Gather up the cards, toss them on the deck, and shuffle. After all, we mustn't call attention to that nine. Don't be afraid to repeat this trick. Over the years, I've never had anyone catch on.

GAMBLER'S BONUS

Here is a routine of four gambling tricks, guaranteed to convince onlookers that you are one skilled prestidigitator. No sleight is ever involved.

When you do a gambling demonstration, you are in a paradoxical position. During most of your tricks, you are trying to convince spectators that it is all magic, that you use no sleight of hand. With a gambling demonstration, however, you attempt to show how skillfully you manipulate the cards. In the first instance, you may be using plenty of sleights; in the second, you will be using none.

When you do your tricks, what are the spectators to believe? At one level, they *know* that you are using all sorts of skullduggery, probably including sleights. But if they are to enjoy your performance, they must suspend their disbelief. In a sense, they *want* to believe in magic; often, the more skeptical a spectator seems, the more he wants to believe. To most spectators, you are Mr. or Ms. Magic; the fact that you have displayed apparent manipulative ability with the cards in a gambling routine will add to this allusion.

These tricks are arranged to facilitate going from one to the next; I recommend that you try the whole routine a few times before selecting a favorite or two.

Mind Control Poker

Ask for the help of an assistant. Tell the volunteer, "I am going to set up some cards and then attempt to control your mind in a little poker demonstration."

The setup takes very little time. Hold the card faces towards you and thumb through them, finding the appropriate cards. First, find a king; separate the cards at that point so that the king is the rearmost card of those in your right hand. Take the king behind the cards in the left hand, using the left fingers to grasp it. Thus, the king becomes the top card of the deck. Find an ace and place it on top of the king. Continue by placing on top two nines, two queens, two jacks, two tens, and a king.

From the bottom up, the eleven cards are K-A-9-9-Q-Q-J-J-10-10-K. The last king is the top card. Here is an easy way to remember this stack. I remember KANN, as in "I think I KANN." This gives me the first four cards I must put on top: K (king), A (ace), N (nine), N (nine). I have no trouble remembering the next three pairs—queens, jacks, tens—because they are in descending order. Last, a king goes on top.

Turn the deck face down and say that you're all set. "Obviously, we'll need some cards." Count off eleven cards from the top of the deck, taking them one under the other so that they retain the same order. Make no mention of the number. A good way to count them off is to take three groups of three and one group of two into the right hand. Set the rest of the deck down.

"Now you're going to choose from five sets of two cards," you say. Take the top two cards of your packet (a king and a ten) and spread them, showing them to the spectator. Make no comment about the values of the cards. Place these two cards together on the bottom of the packet, keeping them in their original order. Show the next pair in the same way. Continue on until you have shown the spectator five pairs of cards, each time placing the pair on the bottom.

"Now I am going to offer you a choice. But there really is no choice at all. I am going to control your mind so that you will end up with a *king high straight*. No doubt of it; you will choose a king high straight."

Take the top two cards and spread them slightly, face down, offering the spectator his choice of the two. "Take either one," you say, "and place it face down in front of you." After he chooses one, place the other card on the bottom.

If you have been following this with cards in your hand, take a look at your packet. You will notice that in each instance you are offering him the choice of a pair. His first choice, for instance, is from a pair of kings. Obviously, this is because you actually started with eleven cards, not ten. For whatever reason, spectators never suspect.

Again you take two cards from the top of the packet and offer the spectator his choice. Place the rejected card on the bottom. Continue on until the spectator has chosen five cards. Each time you have placed the remaining card on the bottom. This includes the last choice. Place your packet of six cards on top of the deck.

"Five different times you had complete freedom of choice," you explain, "but I still controlled your mind. Take a look at what you have."

When the spectator shows his cards, he reveals a king high straight, just as you had predicted. Give everyone a chance to verify this and then say, "That wouldn't do you much good, though. Look what you left me."

Take five cards from the top of the deck and show that you have an *ace high straight*. Before I display them, I generally adjust the cards so that they read in A-K-Q-J-10 order.

Flush of Success

You explain that you are going to demonstrate how easy it is to get a good hand when you have all the best cards to choose from. As you chat on, remove all the high cards from the deck: aces, kings, queens, jacks, and tens. You may fan through the cards and toss them out face up as you come to them. You may try this method, which is faster: Fan through the cards and when you come to one of the high cards, push it upwards about an inch so that it sticks out of the top of the deck. Do the same with all the other high cards. When done, turn the deck face down, grasp all the protruding cards at the side, and pull them from the deck.

Spread all the high cards out face up on the table. What you are about to do is lay out four hands, arranging it so that you will get a *royal flush in hearts* when the cards are gathered together and dealt.

As I will explain, you improvise with the spectators as you lay out the four hands face up. In the first hand, the second card must be a heart. Since the hands are laid out face up, we are talking about the fourth card down as the cards lie face up, or the *second card* if the hand were turned face down and dealt.

In the second hand, a heart must be placed third. In the next hand, a heart must be placed fourth. And in the last hand, a heart must be placed first and fifth.

In the first hand, a heart is second; in the second hand, a heart is third; in the third hand, a heart is fourth; and in the fourth hand, a heart is at both top and bottom.

Pick up the hands face up in this order: The fourth hand goes on the first hand; this pile goes on the second hand; that pile goes on the third hand. Turn the packet face down and give the cards a complete cut.

Spectators tend to believe that a complete cut disarranges the cards. Actually, the cards are in a never ending sequence, and a cut retains their order. If you were to cut the original top card back to the top, the packet would be in precisely the same order as before the cutting started.

Have various spectators give the cards a complete cut. For the trick to work, you must have a heart on the bottom. So after each cut is completed, grasp the deck edgeways, tilt it up so that you can see the face of the bottom card, and tap the cards on the table as though straightening them out. If the bottom card is other than a heart, have the cards cut again. Repeat this until you get a heart on the bottom.

Then deal four face-down poker hands, including one to yourself. Show the first hand, commenting on its value. Show the second and third hands the same way. Say, "It really doesn't matter. It's pretty hard to beat a royal flush." Turn your hand over and show it. Again, I like to arrange the cards from ace to ten before showing the hand.

How do you improvise with the spectators as you make up the hands? You might say something like, "Look at all these great cards. What would be a pretty good hand?"

If a spectator calls for a flush or a straight flush, you cannot oblige, for the first hand must have precisely one heart. So you might say, "Not *that* good!"

Chances are you'll be asked for two pairs, three of a kind, or a straight. Make up the hand from the spread-out cards, making sure that the second card is a heart, and that no other is. Put together the next two hands the same way. Spectators will probably want one of them to be a full house. If they again ask for a flush, say, "Sure, just watch my face if this doesn't work."

Take up the last five cards on the table; quite often they will make up a pretty good hand. Make sure you have a heart on top and a heart on bottom.

You'll have little trouble providing the hands called for; after all, the spectators must choose from the cards on the table. You can have a lot of fun improvising with the spectators.

You can also get some entertainment from the repeated cuts as you keep looking for a heart at the bottom of the stack before you deal. Sometimes the number of cuts can go to double figures before a heart finally shows up at the bottom. This can be turned to your advantage, as you say things like, "Let's try one more cut, just to make sure they're mixed." Or, "Let's try one with the left hand." You can ad-lib other equally inane reasons. When you finally get a heart on the bottom, you can say, "I don't know about you, but I'm getting sick of this." Take the cards and deal the hands.

Gambling Aces

A simple stack is required for the next trick. You can cleverly cover this up by saying, "I have to stack these cards . . . hope you don't mind." Thumb trough the cards and, following the procedure described in *Mind Control Poker* (page 118), place three nines on top. Place five spot cards on top of them. Now from the top down, you have five spot cards followed by three nines.

Mutter something like, "Now where the heck are those aces?" Find the aces and place them on top one by one in the manner described. "All set." From the top down you have four aces, five spot cards, three nines.

Commence your patter: "A cardsharp was attending a quiet party when he decided to liven things up a bit. He slapped a deck of cards down on a table . . . " Slap the deck down on the table. " . . . and said, 'Who wants to play three-handed poker?' "

"Naturally, everyone gathered around. A wise guy asked, 'Why three-handed poker?' The cardsharp told him, 'To make it easier.' The wise guy said, 'I've seen this before. Where are the four aces?' The cardsharp said, 'Right here on top—just in case I need them.' " Deal out the four aces face up.

"The cardsharp said, 'Now I'll deal a few sample hands before we start the betting.' " Put the aces back on top. Deal four hands of three cards each, including one hand to yourself.

"The wise guy said, 'You just stacked the cards so you'd get three aces.' The cardsharp said, 'Not at all. Look—one ace in each hand.' "

Pick up your hand and turn it over, showing that there is only one ace. Place the hand on top. Do the same with the third hand, the second hand, and the first hand, in that order—each time placing the hand on top.

"The cardsharp said, 'Let's try another deal.' " Again deal four hands of three cards each.

"The wise guy said, 'I've seen this. For sure, you've stacked them this time.' The cardsharp said, 'No way. Look—one ace in each hand.' " Show the hands in precisely the same way as you did the first time.

"The cardsharp said, 'Now let's get down to business. One more deal.' " Deal four hands of three cards each.

"The cardsharp asked, 'Now who wants to make a bet?' The wise guy said, "I'll make a bet. You stacked the cards, I'll bet you twenty bucks you hold three aces.' The cardsharp said, 'You're on, buddy. And you're dead wrong.' "

Move your three-card hand to one side. *Now this is important:* Place the third hand on top of the deck, followed by the second hand and the first hand.

"The cardsharp said, 'You're right about one thing—I did stack the cards.' " Turn over your hand, showing the three nines.

"The wise guy forked over the twenty and said, 'What about the aces?' The cardsharp smiled and said, 'I told you. Right here on top—just in case I need them.' " As you say this, deal the aces face up one by one. Just follow the directions; the trick works itself.

At the conclusion of the trick, replace the aces on top and give the cards a casual overhand shuffle, bringing them to the middle. You'll need them for the next trick.

Ace Surprise

You will need the four aces on top. At the end of *Gambling Aces* (page 123), you shuffled them to the middle. As you commence your patter, begin fanning through the cards, faces towards you. You will be looking for the four kings, but in your first move, simply cut the aces to the top and continue fanning through the cards.

"I'll need the four kings for this," you say as you begin going through the deck. "This is my last gambling demonstration and you may be able to catch me if you watch very carefully." Toss out the kings face up as you come to them. "Some gamblers can deal seconds, some can deal thirds, some can deal bottoms, and some can deal cards from the middle. And a good cheater makes it look as though they are all coming from the top."

You should have the kings face up on the table now. "I'm not going to tell you exactly what trickery I'm up to, but I urge you to watch closely."

Gather up the kings and place them on top. Even up the cards carefully and deal them out face down next to one another. "Are these the four kings?" Pause. "Of course they are."

As you show each one, place it back on top. Then deal the kings out again face down. "Four kings. Now watch."

From here on, do *not* describe what you are doing. Fan out four cards from the top of the deck, taking them in the right hand. Tilt the deck down slightly with the left hand and square up the cards against the base of the left thumb. Drop these four on top of the first king you dealt out, the one to your left. Even up the deck. Carefully deal the top card face down, well off to your left.

Again fan out the four top cards, taking them in your right hand and squaring them against the base of your left thumb. Drop these four on top of the second king you dealt. Even up the pile and place it on top. Square up the deck. Deliberately deal the top card face down on the one you already dealt to your far left. Follow the same procedure with the two remaining kings. Then set the deck down to your right.

"Were you watching carefully? I hope so. The question is, 'Where are the kings?' " Chances are that the spectators will say that the kings are on the pile you dealt to your left. If they do, say, "Oh, no. The kings are right here." Deal them face up one at a time off the top of the deck. "There's a much better hand over here." Deal the four-card pile face up one at a time, revealing the four aces.

If the spectators should indicate that the four kings are on top of the deck, show them that this is so by dealing them out face up. "You're right. These are the kings. But what good are kings . . ." Deal the four-card pile face-up. ". . . against four aces?"

GRAB BAG

Countdown

The principle used in this trick is old, deceptive, and applicable to any number of tricks. A card is selected and returned to the deck. The spectator locates his own card by counting off a freely selected number of cards. This is the general effect.

Actually a card is forced on a spectator. See *One-Cut Force* (page 38), *Double-Turnover Force* (page 39), or *Face-Up Force* (page 39). After the spectator shows the card around, he returns it to the deck and shuffles the cards.

Taking the deck back, you say, "Now watch how I do this." Fan through the cards, faces towards you. When you come to the selected card, count off nine cards beyond and cut the deck at that point. The selected card is now ten down from the top.

Show the spectators the bottom card, declaring triumphantly, "*This* is not your card." After the excitement dies down, add, "I could do that trick forever. But let's see how you can do."

Give him the deck and tell him to deal into a pile any number of cards from ten to twenty. Tell him to add the digits of his selected number and to deal that number back on top of the deck. For instance, if he dealt off thirteen cards, he adds one and three, and deals four cards back onto the deck.

"What is the name of your card?" you ask.

When he names it, you turn over the last card dealt back on the deck. Sure enough.

Clearly, it doesn't matter what number from ten to twenty is chosen. When the digits are totalled and the sum counted back onto the deck, the original tenth card down will be the last card dealt.

The Four Aces Again

This trick is based on the same principle as *Countdown.* The effect is so astonishing that I suspend my prejudice against setups. Besides, the setup can be done with the spectators watching.

The setup is this: You need the four aces to be tenth, eleventh, twelfth, and thirteenth from the top of the deck. If you're using your own deck, you can set up the cards in advance and make this your first trick. After I explain how the trick works, I will give you two impromptu methods of setting up the cards.

The strong point to this trick is that the spectator does it all. Tell him to think of any number from ten to twenty and to deal that number of cards into a pile. Then he is to add the digits in the number and deal that many cards back onto the deck. When he is done, take the cards remaining in his dealt hand and set them aside.

"Now I would like you to deal the remaining cards one at a time into four neat piles, just as though you were dealing hands."

The first four cards he deals are, of course, the aces; they will be at the bottom of the four piles. After he has dealt twenty or so cards, tell him, "You may deal as many more as you want and stop whenever you wish." When he stops, take the remaining cards from him and add them to the others you originally set aside.

At this point, a little review should add to the mystification. "You freely selected the original number you dealt off. And when you dealt the cards, you stopped wherever you wished. Right?"

Don't wait for an answer. Simply turn over all four piles, displaying an ace at the face of each.

"These are the markers," you explain. "If you think a card is red, we'll place it on the red marker. If you think it is black, we'll place it on the black marker. This way we'll discover whether you have any extrasensory perception."

Pick out a black card from the top portion of the fanned cards. Holding it face down, ask the spectator, "Do you think this one is red or black?" When he answers, place it face down on the appropriate marker. Continue in the same way, eliminating black cards from the top section of the deck.

Place the cards on the table in an overlapping column going away from you. From the spectator's view, the cards will look like Illustration 49.

ILLUSTRATION 49
This is the spectator's view of the two overlapping columns, with the two markers, one red, one black.

Pretend to study the cards as you pick one out for the spectator's decision. Playact. You are pleased with some of his choices; you frown slightly at others. Tell your assistant, "You're doing quite well for an amateur."

As an added fillip, you can do this: When the spectator calls black, smile, and show him the card before you place it on the black pile. Compliment him. Do this once only, of course.

When you have fifteen or more cards of the opposite color in the top portion of the deck (in our example, red), stop the deal. "I think your psychic vibrations are fading from boredom; we must try something a little different."

Hand the spectator the bottom portion of the remaining deck and keep the top portion (the cards of one color) for yourself. Tell him to shuffle his pile. While he does so, shuffle your pile.

Exchange piles with the spectator. Shuffle your pile and tell him to shuffle his. Since his are all of the same color, the shuffle will obviously not affect the outcome.

Take a red card from your pile and place it face up on the black pile. Take a black card from your pile and place it face up on the red pile. Set aside your pile without comment.

"From now on, black cards go here . . ." Indicate the new black marker. ". . . and red cards go here." Indicate the new red marker. "Now I'd just as soon you do you own dealing. I'm exhausted. Just go through one card at a time, dealing face down, and follow your instincts."

You may try another bit of byplay if you wish. When the spectator has dealt about half of the cards, stop him, saying, "Oh-oh!" Take the last dealt card from the black pile. It is, of course, a red card. Show the card and place it face down on the red pile saying, "I wish you'd be a little more careful." The cards should be lined up as in Illustration 50.

ILLUSTRATION 50
The cards should be lined up as shown above.
Two new markers have been dealt.

When the spectator finishes, one column of cards is perfect: The black cards are under the black marker, and the red cards are under the red. The other pile, however, has black cards under the red marker, and red cards under the black. In the original version, a sleight was recommended to enable the performer to show the second pile to be perfect. No sleight is necessary. The method of showing the piles given here is totally deceptive and has the added advantage of not appearing suspicious.

When the spectator finishes dealing, go to the "good" pile. Separate the reds from the blacks by leaving an inch or two at the middle marker. Remove the two markers and casually toss them aside, face down. Turn over the color group closest to the spectators, spreading the cards sideways to show they are all the same color. Then turn over the group nearest you and spread the cards sideways (nearer to you than your first spread), showing that they, too, are all of the same color (Illustration 51).

ILLUSTRATION 51
Turn over the group nearest you and spread the cards sideways
(nearer to you than your first spread).
Show that this group, too, is all of the same color.

Handle the other pile just as casually. Close it and pick it up. Turn it over so that the cards are face up and the two markers are face down. Casually discard the marker that was on top, putting it with the other two markers you have discarded. Fan the cards down to the next marker, showing them to be the same color. Remove this group, still fanned out, and place it next to the pile on the table closest to the spectators. The two groups nearest the spectators are of opposite colors (Illustration 52).

ILLUSTRATION 52
The two groups nearest the spectators are of opposite colors.

Discard the fourth marker, placing it with the other three markers. Fan the remaining cards, showing that they are the same color. Place this group, still spread out, next to the group nearest you. Everything is perfect. Reds are next to blacks, just as (presumably) they were dealt.

Pick up the markers, casually add them to the discarded pile. Give the pile a little shuffle; then congratulate the spectator on his extraordinary powers as you gather up the rest of the cards.

Go over this one several times before you try it out. You will be pleased with the reaction to "the world's greatest card trick."

The Process of Elimination

Ordinarily, I dislike tricks with a lot of dealing. But done snappily, this one has a tremendous effect.

You say, "I want you to observe how rapidly I deal these cards. It's well known that I'm among the top five percent of rapid card dealers. Which is a real money-making skill. Big call for that."

Rapidly deal six piles of five cards each, thirty cards in all. Have a spectator choose two cards from the remaining deck. set the rest of the deck aside. Take the two cards and show them to everyone, naming them and making sure to repeat their names at least twice, so that everyone will remember them.

Give the two cards back to the spectator. Tell him, "Please place one of your two chosen cards on top of one of the six piles." After he has done so, say, "Now place the other selected card on top of one of the other piles."

Take note of which two packets have the chosen cards on top. Place two other piles on top of each one. You now have two piles, sixteen cards in each one. In each pile, a chosen card is sixth from the bottom. Place either pile on top of the other.

Next, you will rapidly deal the cards alternately into two piles. Both chosen cards will be in the first pile you deal to.

You will eliminate the other pile, as I will explain later. You will repeat this procedure three times, leaving you with one pile containing two cards. They are, of course, the chosen ones.

Before we go into the elimination process, let us consider the dealing of the cards into two piles. It is not particularly deceptive if you *always* keep the pile on your left. Therefore, I recommend that on the first deal, you start with a card to your left, then one to the right, and so on. The next deal, place the first card to your *right*, the next to the left, and so on. On the third deal, start on your left; on the fourth, start on your right.

Clearly, the entire effect depends upon how you eliminate the piles. You ostensibly offer freedom of choice, while actually keeping the pile you want. Here is what I recommend.

After the first deal, tell the spectator, "Please pick up a pile." If he picks up the pile containing the two chosen cards, take the pile from him and, after brushing the other packet aside, deal the "chosen" pile into two new piles. If he picks up the other pile, take the one he leaves and rapidly deal that one into two piles. When you are done, casually take the pile from him and toss it aside.

After the second deal, tell the spectator, "Please hand me a pile." If he hands you the pile containing the chosen cards, brush the other packet aside, and deal the selected pile into two new piles. If he hands you the other pile, set it aside, pick up the pile with the selected cards, and deal it into two packets.

When you have finished the third deal, ask the spectator, "Which pile?" If he indicates the one containing the chosen cards, push the other packet aside, and deal the chosen pile into two new piles. If he chooses the other one, set it aside, pick up the pile with the selected cards, and deal it into two piles.

On the last deal, you have two packets containing two cards each. Tell the spectator to place a hand on each pile. Then direct him to lift up one hand. If he lifts the hand covering the chosen cards, take that pile and show the cards. If he lifts the other hand, take the pile he uncovers and set it aside. Then show the two selected cards.

The dealing and choosing actually take very little time. And the denouement is quite effective. But for the trick to work, I highly recommend that you follow my instructions for pile selection *precisely,* and please use the exact wording.

First: "Please pick up a pile."

Second: "Please hand me a pile."

Third: "Which pile?"

On the fourth selection, the wording is not critical. Simply tell him to place a hand on each pile.

I remember the order of selection for the first three picks with the words "pick, hand, which." Generally, I can remember the method of doing the last selection.

The Double-Match Trick

This one has to do with matches only in the sense of two things resembling each other. I wish I knew who invented this trick so that I could offer him my heartiest congratulations. It has everything: directness, cleverness, undetectability, and an astonishing climax. What's more, it's easy to execute. And since the spectator does all the work, he is completely mystified. I'm sure this trick will become one of your favorites.

Like most tricks, this one is enhanced by a little romance. "For this experiment," you say, "I need a kindred spirit, someone whose spiritual vibrations will correspond to mine." If no one volunteers, say, "I'll settle for someone who knows one card from the other."

Have your volunteer shuffle the deck. Take it back and fan the cards so that only you can see the faces. "Now I"m going to select two cards, and it's important that I concentrate." As you give the cards a casual fanning, indicating the importance of concentrating, note the top card. Find the card that matches it in color and value, and toss it out face up. For instance, if the top card is the six of clubs, find the six of spades and toss it out.

Now note the bottom card, find the card that matches it in color and value, and toss that one out face up. Have this one a little closer to you, so you'll remember to use it first.

"I would like you to look at these two cards and try to get a clear impression of them in your mind."

Hand the volunteer the deck and tell him to deal the cards into a face-down pile. After he has dealt a dozen or so cards, tell him to stop whenever he wishes. When he stops dealing, place the *second* card you took from the deck (the one matching the bottom card) face up on top of the pile he dealt from. Tell him to put the rest of the deck on top. You can also point to the second card you took and have the spectator place it face up on top of his dealt cards. This keeps the entire trick in his hands.

The position now is that in the lower portion of the deck your face-up card is face-to-face with its matching card. The bottom card of the deck matches the card on the table.

Again have the spectator deal cards from the top into a face-down pile. When he has dealt a dozen or so, tell him to stop when he wants to. Obviously, he must not deal so many that he gets to the face-up card. If he seems intent on dealing forever, simply take the cards from him and hand them to someone else to complete the deal.

When the spectator stops dealing, place the other face-up card on top of the pile he dealt, or have the spectator do so. The spectator places the rest of the deck on top.

"Now let's see if we are really *simpatico.*" Take the deck and very deliberately fan through the face-down cards. Take out the first face-up card along with the card above it and set them on the table. Fan through to the next face-up card; remove it and the card above it, placing them next to the pair on the table.

Turn over each of the face-down cards, showing how wonderfully *simpatico* you two really are. Be sure to tell the spectator, "You really did a great job. I have a feeling you must be psychic."

Note: If you have performed *Three-Card Surprise* (page 57) and spectators ask for a repeat, you can do this one. The effect is similar, but the method, as you can see, is quite different.

If you decide to do this, do *not* indicate that you are going to produce the same effect. Instead, say, "Let me show you something a little different." Then proceed with the patter above.

Astounding Appearance

This trick lives up to its title. It's as close to real magic as you're ever going to get. Occasionally you'll come across someone who knows the basic trick; don't let that hold you back. If someone says, "Oh, I know that one," or, "I do that one myself," simply give the person a conspiratorial wink and continue. The effect is worth it.

A spectator chooses a card and replaces it in the deck, which is shuffled. You show four cards individually; none is the selected card. Again you show the four cards and place them in the spectator's hand. You take away three cards, snap you fingers, and the remaining card is the chosen one.

Here's how. First, force a card. Use *One-Cut Force* (page 38), *Face-up Force* (page 39), or *Double-Turnover Force* (39). Have the card shown around and replaced in the deck. After the spectator shuffles the deck, fan through the cards, faces towards you, saying, "I'm not absolutely sure which one is yours, but I think I can locate it within four cards." Cut the deck so that the forced card is fourth from the bottom. The cut is done quite openly. "I'm sure you'll agree that narrowing it down to four cards is truly mediocre."

Before we proceed, check *The Glide* (page 15). Hold the deck in the glide grip and show the bottom card, asking, "Is this your card?" When the spectator says no, turn the deck down and deal the bottom card onto the table. Place the new bottom card on top of the deck without showing its face, remarking, "And we place the next card on top—for magical purposes." This is more effective than saying, "I place the next card on top because I feel like it." Or even worse, "I place the next card on top because if I don't, you'll soon be shown the same card twice in a row."

Tip the deck up, showing the new bottom card. "Is this your card?" Naturally, the spectator denies it. Turn the deck down and perform the glide, dealing the spectator's chosen card onto the one on the table. Place the bottom card (the one you just showed to the spectator) on top of the deck, repeating, "We place the next card on top—for magical purposes."

Show the bottom card and again ask if this is the chosen one. The spectator says no. As you place it on top of the two on the table, attempt to look crestfallen. This time, when you place the bottom card on top (to be consistent), pause after you say, "I place the next card on top . . ." Eye the spectators questioningly; they will be happy to explain that you are doing this for magical purposes.

Repeat the whole business, placing the bottom card on top of the three on the table and the new bottom card on top. When the spectator denies that the fourth one is his card, ask, "Are you sure?" Look puzzled, unless puzzlement is your natural look—in which case, look natural. "Now let's check to make sure."

There is now a pile of four cards on the table; the second one from the bottom is the chosen card. Pick up the pile and hold the cards in the glide grip. Ask the spectator to hold out his hand.

Show the bottom card. "This isn't yours?" you query. Of course he responds negatively. Turn the pile downwards and perform the glide, placing the spectator's chosen card face down on his extended palm. Place the next card on top for magical purposes.

Show the bottom card, repeating the query. Turn the pile down and place the bottom card on the spectator's palm. Do *not* shift a card to the top. Fan the remaining two cards, showing them to the spectator with the question, "And neither one of these is yours?" Add these to the face-down cards in the spectator's hand.

"Now let's check this again." Take the top card from the pile in the spectator's hand. Place it face up in your other hand, saying, "This isn't yours?" Quickly take the second card, place it face up on the first card you took, and repeat the question. And once more with the third card. Place the three cards to one side. Remaining in his hand is the chosen card.

To prevent premature disclosure, take his other hand and place it on top of the card. "Hold the card right there, please. Now tell me, what's the name of your card?" Gently hold his hand on the card so that he doesn't show it yet.

When he names his card, snap your fingers over his hands and then gesture to him, indicating that he should turn the card over.

Note: The key to this trick is performing it with some speed. No doubt you have noticed that when you place the cards in the spectator's hand, you show the same card twice. Don't worry about it—even when it is an obvious card, like an ace. If you proceed apace, no one will notice. I have done the trick for many, many years and nobody has ever called me on it.

Murder

Here's a very simple trick I came up with many years ago. It's one of those story tricks that spectators usually enjoy, and it has a surprise ending.

Put the four queens in a face-up row on the table. Also, lay the four aces, a king, and a jack to one side, also face up. A spectator selects a card and places it face up near the queens. Take the jack and place it next to the chosen card. Then use the following patter.

"I hope you all enjoy murder mysteries. The one I am about to present is challenging, thrilling, exciting, and preposterous. See if you can solve the murders. Yes, I said *murders;* this is going to be a juicy one. Now these four queens are rich, old spinsters living alone in a huge mansion. You, as symbolized by the six of clubs (name the chosen card), are their lawyer and in charge of their finances." Nod knowingly. Obviously, the spectator will be a prime suspect.

"One night you are visiting the four ladies. Also in the house is the tall, gaunt, old butler. Indicate the jack. You notice that from time to time he glares maniacally at the old ladies."

"Suddenly the lights go out, there is a shot (snap your fingers), and when the lights go on again, one of the ladies has been murdered." Turn one of the queens face down.

"You are a good friend of the chief of police (indicate the king), so you phone him and ask for help. He immediately sends out four of his best detectives to surround the house." Put the four aces in a face-up square around the queens, the jack, and the choosen card.

"If the detectives had been sensible, they would have gone *inside* the house. But that might have prevented any more murders, and would have spoiled this engrossing murder mystery. Somehow they must have known that.

"Sure enough, the lights went out, a shot was fired (snap your fingers), and another lady was murdered." Turn down another queen.

"Before the detectives could get to the house, the lights went out again, and two shots rang out (snap your fingers twice), and both remaining ladies were murdered." Turn the last two queens face down.

"The chief was infuriated when he learned of this, so he came to the house personally and gathered up all the suspects and took them to the station for a lie detector test." Gather up the cards so that they will read, from top to bottom: chosen card, ace, ace, jack, ace, ace.

"Yes, the chief was even suspicious of his own detectives. For the lie detector test, he decided to use the word 'murder.' Whoever reacted positively to his word would be the guily party. So let's spell out 'murder.' "

See *The Glide* (page 15). Hold the cards in your left hand in the glide grip and transfer one card from the top to the bottom for each letter as you spell out the word "murder." Show the ace at the bottom. Turn the cards face down and deal the ace face down on the table with the right fingers.

"We eliminate one of the detectives." Repeat the spelling, and the chosen card appears at the bottom. Show this card as before, but when you turn the cards down, perform the glide, drawing off the second card from the bottom and placing it face down on top of the ace you have eliminated.

"And—surprise!—you too are eliminated." Continue the elimination until only two cards remain.

"This leaves only two suspects: one of the ace detectives and the butler. Naw, it couldn't be the butler."

As you say this, separate the two cards, holding one face down in each hand. When you bring them back together, put the former bottom one on top. Spell out "murder" again. Show the bottom card, the jack, and deal it into the elimination pile.

"I *knew* it couldn't be the butler. So who do we have left? That rotten, vicious, conniving, sneaky, criminal . . ."

Look at the remaining card.

"Oh, no. There must be some mistake."

Turn the chosen card face up.

Quaint Coincidence

This one should be reserved for times when you have two bright, cooperative spectators, helpers who are capable of following directions.

This is similar in some respects to *Tricky Transpo* (page 64), so it would not be advisable to perform both in the same set, but it is different enough to include here, since it has an excellent climax.

Hand the deck out to be shuffled. Turn your back and have one spectator think of an odd number from five to twenty-five. Another spectator thinks of an even number from five to twenty-five. Each spectator is to count off the number of cards equal to the number he thought of. The rest of the deck is put aside. The two piles are put together and shuffled.

Turn around and take the pile. Tell the two assistants to note the two cards that lie at the numbers they thought of. Once they have noted the cards, they need not remember the number. Slowly deal the cards into a face-up pile, counting aloud as you do so. When you complete the deal, pick up the cards and turn them face down.

"Now don't forget your cards," you smilingly caution, "or this effect goes right up in smoke. We've dealt the cards only once, and, as you know, three is the magic number. So let's try deal number two."

Before you deal, give the cards a false cut—see the *One-Finger Cut* (page 26)—to throw off spectators.

Now hold the cards face down in the left hand and, starting at your left, deal them alternately into two face-down piles.

"Now for the third and magical deal." Take the left-hand pile face up in your left hand, and the other face down in your right hand. "Stop me immediately if either of you sees his card."

Simultaneously thumb off cards into two piles. Deal from the top of each pile. Make sure that you have exactly the *same* number of cards in each pile. Clearly, the pile on your left is dealt face up and the one on your right, face down. When one of the spectators tells you to stop, set the cards in your hands aside. Point to the face-up card and ask the spectator if he is certain that it is his. Then ask the second spectator to name his card.

When he does so, turn over the top card of the other pile, revealing the quaint coincidence.

MIND READING

A Word About Mind Reading

There are three ways in which the card artist can read minds:

1. *Force* the selection of a card on a spectator.
2. Learn the name of a card after a spectator has thought of it.
3. Actually use telepathy.

If you can do number three, you may as well skip this section. Most often the mind reader uses method one. Four of the five tricks in this section are actually *forces*. Some might be applicable to other tricks where it is necessary for you to know the name of a selected card, but the *forces* on pages 34 through 40 are quicker and more direct. Obviously, you can decide for yourself.

If you are going to do mind reading, I recommend that you program a number of tricks. Besides the tricks in this section, you might choose among the various prediction tricks.

If you are doing several mind-reading tricks, a spectator might naturally wonder, "Why can't I just think of a card and then you name it?" Before the issue comes up, I like to explain, "I am better able to see the card in your mind if you actually look at a card and then concentrate as you visualize it." Sure, it's nonsense. But if you *can* read minds, it's semilogical. There will be more tips on the techniques of mind reading as you go along.

In the Palm of Your Hand

Don't be frightened by this one. It's as close as you can come to real mind reading.

First, let's practice. Hold the deck in your left hand. Push off the top card and, with the aid of the left middle fingers, take it into the palm of your right hand, trying to conceal it (Illustration 53).

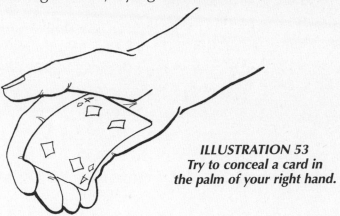

ILLUSTRATION 53
Try to conceal a card in
the palm of your right hand.

Don't worry; I'm not going to ask you to palm a card in plain sight. Put the cards behind your back and try the same palm. Now place your right hand on your left wrist as in Illustration 54. Practice this a few times. You're ready to roll.

ILLUSTRATION 54
Place your right hand on your left wrist.
The card should now be completely hidden.

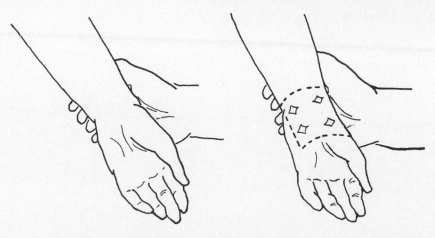

To start, you must know the top card. See *The Peek* (page 14). Now ask a spectator to come up and help you. For this trick, you cannot be surrounded by spectators, as you will see. Have the spectator stand by your side as you put your hands behind your back, deck in the left hand. Palm the top card and place your right hand on your wrist, as described above. Obviously, no one should be in a position to observe this.

Turn your back to the spectator, offering the deck, and say, "Cut off a pile of cards, please." After he has done so, turn towards him, add the palmed card to the top of the deck, and reclasp your wrist, saying, "Is that enough?" Again, no one can be behind you to observe.

The answer to your question is invariably yes. If he says no, say, "Sure, it is," and proceed. Turn you back to the spectator again and proffer the cards in your hand, saying, "Look at the card you cut to, show it around, and replace it."

After he has done this, say, "Now put the rest of the cards on top and take the deck."

Apparently, the spectator has cut the deck, looked at the card he cut to, and replaced the cutoff cards. What's more, he then took the deck into his own hands, eliminating the possibility of your trying any funny business.

Turn to face the spectator. It is time for a little psychological smoke screen. "I would like you to give the deck one complete shuffle." The spectator shuffles the deck.

"Aha!" say the spectators to themselves, "He must know the card above or below the selected card." They know a trick that works like that.

You continue to foster the misapprehension by saying, "Now if I go through the deck and find your card, would that be a good trick?" Usually the spectator agrees.

"Well, I don't want to do a trick. Instead, I am going to attempt to read your mind."

Take the deck from the spectator and hold it to your forehead. "Please concentrate on your card. I see red clouds. I would say your card is a red—a diamond. Let me see—it looks like a four—no, no—an ace. The ace of diamonds."

Equally, you could see dark clouds, of course, for a spade or a club. I like the idea of almost naming the wrong value, briefly mistaking a four for an ace, a queen for a jack, a three for an eight—any two cards that look somewhat alike. All of this enhances the illusion that you are actually mind-reading.

Crisscross

One piece of advice: Just because a trick is easy, don't give it short shrift. Just because the secret is simple, don't hurry through your presentation. A simple method of mind reading, for instance, can be just as effective as a complex one—maybe even more so. Consider this trick, which appears in most elementary magic books. When I teach magic, I use this to provide insight on presentation.

To begin with, you must know the top card of the deck. See *The Peek* (page 14). Set the deck down and ask a spectator to cut off a pile of cards. He is to set the pile down and put the rest of the deck on top of it crosswise.

The former top card of the deck is now on top of the lower pile; you know it, and if the spectators think about it, they know too. They aren't going to think about that, because you're going to do this absurdly simple trick like a real pro. You're going to take their minds and eyes off the cards.

Touch this card. ➔

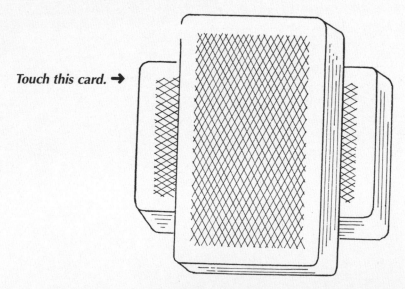

ILLUSTRATION 55
*The spectator cuts off a pile of cards, sets down the deck,
and then places the rest of the deck on top of it, crosswise.
Then, touch the top of the card of the lower pile with your forefinger.*

152

To do this, you merely speak for a moment. I usually say something like this: "You had complete freedom of choice as to where you cut the cards. You could have cut off a big pile, a little pile, whatever you chose. Now I want you to take a look at your card." Here you *touch* the card he is to look at so there will be no mistake (Illustration 55).

You do *not* say, "I want you to look at the card you cut to." This might bring up nasty thoughts, like, "Which one *did* I cut to?"

Have him show the card around. Now add more tinsel to the tree by having him replace the card from where he took it and even up the deck. He is to give the deck one shuffle of his choice, but only one shuffle.

Again, you hold the deck to your forehead and gradually reveal the color, the suit, and the value.

Yes, the trick is elementary. So what? Does it fool people? With proper presentation, it certainly does. Toss this in occasionally among the more subtle mind-reading tricks and check out the spectator reaction. I think you'll be pleased.

The Big Deal

To begin with, you must know the second card from the bottom of the deck. You may choose among the methods offered in *The Peek* (page 12). I recommend this variation of number four.

You say, "The vibes just aren't right. I'd better remove my bad-luck card."

As you fan through the deck, note the second card from the bottom. Continue on to the queen of spades, or some other "bad luck" card, and remove it from the deck. If you can, shuffle the deck, retaining at least the bottom two cards.

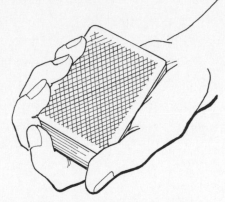

ILLUSTRATION 56
Hold the cards in your left hand, in the dealing position, with your thumb along the left edge.

Hold the cards in the left hand in the dealing position, with the thumb along the left edge (Illustration 56). Run the thumb down the side of the deck, riffling all the cards. Do this a few times and then say, "I want you to select a card. Just tell me when to stop as I riffle through."

Now the spectator is going to get the bottom portion of the deck, and you want him to have less than half the cards. So start your riffle just above the middle, and riffle *slowly*. Make sure you stop *exactly* where the spectator indicates. Keep the top portion and give the bottom portion to the spectator.

"Now let's deal them into piles, one card at a time." Deal your pile in front of you, as he deals his in front of him. Match him card for card. Stop dealing when the spectator runs out of cards. Set the rest of your cards aside.

Tell the spectator, "Place your top card in the middle. Now put your bottom card in the middle. Next, look at the new top card and show it around."

Suiting action to words, you have shown the spectator the way by placing the top card in the middle of your pile and the bottom card in the middle of your pile. You have also lifted the top card of your pile, *definitely not looking at it,* and returned it to the top. The card the spectator has looked at is, of course, the card which was originally the second card from the bottom of the deck.

Tell the spectator to shuffle his packet. Hand him your packet and tell him to shuffle it in with the others. It is a mistake, I believe, to simply name the chosen card. I like to stress the mind reading. Granted, there may be a hint of a twinkle in my eye. While it is true that the spectators, at one level, *know* you cannot possibly read minds, it is just possible that you may be able to. And how *could* you have done it if you had not read the spectator's mind?

I tell the spectator to concentrate on his card as he shuffles. Then, as with the other mind-reading tricks, I gradually reveal the suit and the value.

Pretend to concentrate. You might tell the spectator something like this: "You may or may not believe in mind reading, but I would like you to do as I ask. Please concentrate on the color of your card. Actually think of the color." Then reveal the color.

"Now please think of the suit." As you concentrate, tell the spectator that you are getting mixed signals, that you can't be quite sure. Then tell him the suit. Do something similar in revealing the value.

Believe me, all of this razzmatazz enhances the trick. The spectators are not quite sure whether you have actually performed mind reading. Regardless, they know you have done a great trick.

The Three Piles

I invented this trick by combining two well-known principles. You will like this one, I think, when, after you have finished, you hear spectators comment on how "you didn't even touch the cards."

Again, you must know the top card. You can use one of the methods listed under The Peek (page 14). Then, if you can, shuffle the cards, making sure that the top card stays there.

Hand the deck to a spectator and tell him to deal out a pile. After he has dealt seven or eight cards, tell him to stop when he feels like it. Ask him to deal another pile next to it. Again, after several cards have been dealt, tell him to stop when he wishes. Tell him to deal a third pile next to the second one. When the spectator has finished dealing to the third pile, take the rest of the cards from him and set them aside.

The spectator now has three piles in front of him. The *bottom* card of the first pile he dealt is the original top card of the deck.

Tell the spectator, "Put your hand on a pile, please."

1. If he places his hand on the first pile he dealt, gather up the two remaining piles, placing them on top of the deck. Tell him to look at the bottom card of his pile.

2. If he places his hand on a different pile, say, "And place your other hand on a pile."

Suppose he places his *other* hand on a different pile. Don't *say* anything. Gesture with your two hands that he is to hand you the two piles he is covering. If he doesn't catch on, say, "Hand me the two piles, please." Put the two piles on top of the deck and tell the spectator to look at the bottom card of his pile.

Suppose he places his *other* hand on the pile containing the force card. Pick up the uncovered pile. Tell the spectator, "Lift a hand, please."

If he lifts the hand covering the pile containing the force card, gesture that he is to hand you the covered pile. If his eyes glaze over, point to the covered pile and say, "Hand me the pile, please." Have him look at the bottom card of the remaining pile.

If he lifts his other hand, the covered pile is the one containing the force card. Pick up the uncovered pile and have him look at the bottom card of the remaining pile.

The above *sounds* complicated, but just run through it a few times and you will find that, in practice, it is quite simple.

After the spectator has looked at the bottom card of the pile and has shown the card around, have him place the pile (with the chosen card) on top of the deck. Even up the deck and set it aside. Then, as with the previous three effects, read the spectator's mind as convincingly as you can.

The Three Location

The previous mind-reading tricks were variations of forcing a card on a spectator. This trick, however, is quite different.

Since I first came across *The Three Location* many years ago, I have included it nearly every time I have displayed my so-called mental powers. In the original version, the spectator was offered only nine cards to choose from. As a slight improvement, I developed a method of offering thirteen cards.

Fan through the deck, saying, "I want to find a suitable card for you to choose mentally." Find a three, count six cards beyond it, and cut the cards at that point so that the three becomes the seventh card from the top.

"I'm going to show you some cards, and I want you to think of one. I won't watch your face, and I don't want you to say anything when you have thought of one."

Slowly show the cards one by one to the spectator, taking them one under the other so that they remain in the same order. Keep your head averted. Show the spectator exactly thirteen cards and return them to the top, saying, "Do you have one?"

If his answer is no, say, "I'll go slower this time", and go through the thirteen cards again. When the spectator has one, say, "Now I'll try to find your card."

Put the deck behind your back, count off six cards and turn the seventh card (the three you found) face up. Replace the six cards on top, cut the deck, and bring the cards forward.

"I have located your card in the deck. What's the name of your card?" If he names the three, you have a miracle. Show him that it is face up in the middle.

If it is another card, fan through the cards, faces towards you, saying, "Note that there is a face-up card in the middle." As you fan to the three, showing the face-up card, spread the cards on either side, so that you can see where the chosen card is in relation to it.

Turn the cards face down, leaving them spread out. If his card is either directly above or below the three, say, "And with the face-up card, I have located your card." Pull out the face-up three with the chosen card, either above or below it. "What's the name of your card?" you ask. The spectator repeats the name. Turn the two cards over, revealing the mentally selected card.

If his chosen card is second from the three on either side, say, "Note that the face-up card is a three." In fact, you make this statement in all ensuing instances. Now you start on the three and count to the selected card, like this: Touch the three, saying, "One"; touch the second card, saying, "Two"; touch the selected card, saying, "Three." Pull the selected card from the deck. As before, and in all other instances, ask, "What is the name of your card?" When he repeats the name, turn the card over.

If the thought-of card is three cards from the three on either side, count over three, as above, starting with the *next* card. Pull the selected card from the deck, and finish as before.

Suppose his selected card is four cards from the three. As before, say, "Note that the face-up card is a three." Then, starting with the three, spell out T-H-R-E-E, landing on his selected card.

If the selected card is five cards from the three, spell out T-H-R-E-E, starting with the card next to your face-up three, again landing on his selected card.

If it is six cards from the three, again spell out T-H-R-E-E, starting with the card next to your face-up three, but, at the completion of your spelling, pull out the *next* card.

Why do you ask the spectator to name his card twice? Nothing but good can come out of it. It helps build to the climax. Also, some spectators will forget that you asked the first time; thus, you have a genuine miracle. What's more, you create the impression that you paid no attention when the thought-of card was named the first time.

When you fan the cards, showing the face-up three to the spectators, they see only the backs of the cards and they are looking at the face-up card you are displaying. They do not realize that at the same time, you are looking at the faces of the cards.

Despite my labored explanation, this is quite a snappy trick. Need I add, do it only once?

Either/Or Force

You must know the top card. Deal cards into a pile, telling a spectator to tell you when to stop. As soon as he says stop, start dealing another pile to the right of the first one. Again, the spectator tells you when to stop. Immediately, start dealing a third pile to the *left* of the first one. Once more the spectator tells you when to stop. Place the remaining cards in your hand to the far right.

Four piles are in a row on the table. You know the bottom card of the second pile from your left. Cover the two piles on the right with your outstretched right hand and the two piles on the left with your outstretched left hand. Ask, "Right or left?" Whichever is chosen, push aside the two piles on your right.

"Pick up a pile, please." If he picks up the pile containing the force card, push aside the remaining pile and tell him to look at the bottom card. If he picks up the other pile, take it from him and place it aside with the other discarded piles. Tell him, "Please look at the bottom card of your chosen pile."

This business is called the *equivogue* or the *magician's choice,* of which there are many versions. Try it out; it's quite easy and totally convincing.

PREPARATION

Two-Faced Card Trick—1

For the next two startling tricks, you'll need a double-faced card. Such cards can be purchased at your local magic shop. But for our purposes, you can just as easily make up your own. Simply take two cards and glue them back to back, making sure they're precisely even.

This first trick was reported by Harry Riser in *MUM*, the publication of the Society of American Magicians.

Let's say that your double-backed card has the jack of spades on one side and the ten of hearts on the other. You'll also need a regular jack of spades and ten of hearts. Have the double-faced card in your pocket, with the ten of hearts side facing out.

To start, take the legitimate jack of spades and ten of hearts from your pocket and show both sides of both. "I'd like to try an experiment with these two cards— the jack of spades and the ten of hearts." Place the two cards back to back and square them up. Still keeping them squared, turn over the two, displaying first one side and then the other.

Ask spectator Sean to assist you. Place the two cards into his pocket, with the ten of hearts facing out.

"Sean, where's the ten of hearts?" Naturally, he replies that it's in his pocket. "And the jack of spades is in the same pocket, right?" Of course. "So if I take the ten of hearts from your pocket, like this . . ." Remove the ten of hearts from his pocket. ". . . then you would still have the jack of spades in your pocket. And now *I'll* have the ten of hearts in *my* pocket." Suiting action to words, place the ten of hearts *face out* into your pocket, *behind the double card.*

With a laugh, say "I think we all understand now that the jack of spades is in your pocket and the ten of hearts is in mine. But let's check to make absolutely sure." Remove the jack of spades from Sean's pocket and hand it to him. Remove the double-faced card from your pocket, displaying the ten of hearts side. (Make sure no one sees the other side of the card).

Holding the ten of hearts in the dealing position in your left hand, take the jack of spades from Sean with your right hand. Turn it face down and place it under the double faced card. Apparently the jack of spades and the ten of hearts are now back to back. Even up the cards and dispay both sides. Put both cards into Sean's pocket, with the legitimate jack of spades facing out. Behind it, of course, is the double card with the ten of hearts side facing his body.

Now comes a very sneaky piece of business based on an ambiguity in the expression "Pick a card for me." It can mean either "Do me a favor and pick a card," or "The card you name will become my card." So say to Sean, "Pick a card for me, Sean—ten of hearts or jack of spades." If he chooses the jack of spades, say, "Okay, you picked the jack of spades for me." If he chooses the ten of hearts, say, "You picked the ten of hearts, so I get the jack of spades."

Reach into Sean's pocket and remove the double-faced card, showing the jack of spades. (Practice this move. Needless to say, it's vital that no one see the other side of the card). Place the double card into your pocket behind the legitimate ten of hearts.

Pause a moment, staring into space. Shake your head. "I keep forgetting. What card do you have?" He says that he has the ten of hearts. Ask him to remove the card from his pocket. It's the jack of spades. You remove the legitimate ten of hearts from your pocket.

Casually show both sides of the two cards and put them away.

Two-Faced Card Trick—2

Let's try another stunt with a double-faced card. Reported by Martin Gardner, this was a specialty of Bert Allerton's.

Again, assume that the double-faced card has the jack of spades on one side and the ten of hearts on the other. You'll also need a regular jack of spades and ten of hearts. Place the jack of spades face up on the table. On top of it, place the ten of hearts face up. On top of all, place the double-faced card, with the jack of spades side up.

Place all three in your pocket with the two-faced card on the outside, jack of spades side facing out.

Start by removing the two outermost cards from your pocket, making sure that spectators don't see the other side of the double-faced card. Fan the two out, showing the jack of spades on top and the ten of hearts below it (Illustration 57).

ILLUSTRATION 57

The jack of spades, of course, is the double-faced card. "As you notice, we have the jack of spades and the ten of hearts." Close up the two cards and turn them over, showing the back. Ask, "Can you remember what the two cards are?" Turn the two face up once more. "That's right, the jack of spades and the ten of hearts." Move the jack of spades below the ten of hearts. Move it back on top again. Close up the two cards and turn them over, showing the back. "What are they again?" Turn them face up and fan them. "That"s right."

Ostensibly, you've shown the backs and fronts of both cards.

Place the double-faced card on the table; naturally the jack of spades side is up. Now perform an easy sleight known as *Wild Card Turnover.* With your right hand, hold the ten of hearts at the lower right corner with your thumb on top and fingers beneath. Place your left first finger on the lower left corner of the card on the table. (See Illustration 40, page 71). Slide the card in your right hand beneath the right side of the card on the table and, with a counterclockwise move, flip both cards over. Release your grip on the ten of hearts as you complete the move. Logic tells us that both cards should now be face down, but (as you'll discover) logic doesn't prevail. On the table now is a face-up ten of hearts (the other side of the double-faced card) and a face-down ten of hearts. In your pocket is the jack of spades, facing outward.

With your right hand, pick up the face-up ten of hearts (the two-faced card) and place it *behind* the card in your pocket. Make sure no one sees the other side as you place it in the pocket with the ten of hearts side out. In what seems to be an attempt to fool the spectators, as you place the card in your pocket, say, "Now I'll put the jack of spades into my pocket." As you say this, look as shifty-eyed and sneaky as you possibly can.

With your right hand, point to the card on the table. "So what's this card?" The group won't be deceived by your miscalling of the card you placed in your pocket. Someone's bound to say, "*That's* the jack of spades."

"No, no," you say, pulling the outermost card from your pocket and tossing it onto the table. "*This* is the jack of spades. The other card is the ten of hearts." Turn it over. Pick up the jack of spades, casually show its back and drop it face up onto the ten of hearts. Pick up the two and place them, faces outward, in the pocket *behind* the double-faced card. (You'll recall that the double-faced card has its ten of hearts side facing out).

165

Apparently, you're done. "Did you like that?" Pause. "Maybe you'd like to see it again."

Remove the two outermost cards from your pocket. This time, simply fan them face up without showing the backs. On top is the ten of hearts side of the double-faced card; below it is the face-up jack of spades. Drop the double-faced card on the table, ostensibly the ten of hearts. With the jack of spades, perform *Wild Card Turnover* (page 165). On the table the spectators see the jack of spades side of the double-faced card and a face-down card. Pick up the double-faced card, saying, "Now I place the ten of hearts in my pocket." Place the card *behind* the ten of hearts in your pocket. Point to the card on the table. "What's the other card?" You'll be told that the other card is actually the ten of hearts. Pull the outermost card from your pocket, saying, "No, no. *This* is the ten of hearts." Turn over the other card. "This one is the jack of spades." As before, casually show the back of the ten of hearts, drop it on top of the jack of spades, and place the two, faces outward, in your pocket behind the double-faced card.

Again, pretend briefly to be done. Then say, "Would you like to see how it's done?" They will. "Actually, I use three cards."

Remove the two outermost cards from your pocket and separate them on the table. Spectators will see a jack of spades and a ten of hearts. Actually, they're seeing the jack of spades side of the double-faced card.

Explain, "I actually use *two* jacks of spades." Pull the jack of spades about halfway out of your pocket so that all can see it. Push it back into your pocket.

Pick up the ten of hearts and turn both tabled cards over, using *Wild Card Turnover*. Spectators now see the ten of hearts side of the double-faced card and a face-down card. Pick up the double-faced card, apparently the ten of hearts, and place it in your pocket behind the other card as you say, "I actually put the ten of hearts in my pocket, but I call it the jack of spades to confuse you."

Pause a moment, saying, "It's really quite easy. You see, I just reach into my pocket and take out the *other* jack of spades." Take the outermost card, the jack of spades, from your pocket and toss it onto the table.

Someone's bound to say, "But what about the jack of spades that's still on the table?"

Shake your head. "I'm afraid you're really not paying attention. That isn't the jack of spades . . ." Turn the face-down card over. ". . . That's the ten of hearts."

Casually show both sides of both cards and put them away.

Lucky 7

I developed a slight variation of a Lin Searles trick.

There's an easy setup: You have a face-down seven on top, followed by seven face-up cards.

Spectator Charlene should be willing to assist. Say to her, "Charlene, I'd like you to choose a card, but let's make sure that you choose one completely by chance. When I give you the deck, I'd like you to place it behind your back." (If you're seated at a table, she should take the deck under the table). Give her the deck, making sure no one is behind her to see what goes on.

When the deck is behind her back, continue: "Now please cut off a good-sized pile from the top of the deck and turn the pile over so that it's face up on top."

Turn away and continue the directions: "Even up the cards. Now bring the deck forward and fan through the face-up cards to the first face-down card. Set down all the face-up cards for a moment. Next, look at that first face-down card, the one you cut to. This is your chosen card, so you must remember it. After you look, leave it face down on top of the packet. Now pick up that pile you cut off and place it *face down* on top of the deck." Make sure you give all the directions slowly and clearly so that Charlene understands every step.

Turn back and take the pack from Charlene. With your right hand, take off the top card, making sure no one sees its face. Say, "Behind my back, I'll stick this card face up somewhere in the deck." Your left hand takes the deck behind your back, while your right hand takes the card behind your back.

"Let's see. I'll put it in face up right about . . . there." Actually, you simply place the card face down on top of the deck. Bring the deck forward. Turn it face up. Start fanning through the cards.

"With the deck face up, the card I stuck in should now be face down." Fan through to the face-down card. Set aside all the cards you fanned through to arrive at the face-down card.

"Ah, here's my card. Let's see what it is." Turn it face up and drop it on the table. "Perfect! A seven. That's my lucky number. Let's count down seven cards. What was your card?" Charlene names it. You deal off seven cards, and hers shows up as the last card in the count.

Color Confusion

Don Smith created this trick; I adjusted the handling somewhat. You'll need a red-backed deck and a blue-backed deck. Remove seven cards from the blue-backed deck. Make sure there are at least three spot cards on the bottom of the blue-backed deck. Take eight assorted face cards from the red-backed deck. Place one of these in your pocket. The rest go on the bottom of the blue-backed deck.

The situation: You have a blue-backed deck from which seven cards have been removed. At the bottom of this deck are seven red-backed face cards. Directly above these are at least three blue-backed spot cards. In your pocket is a red-backed face card. Place the deck into the blue-card case. (Get rid of all other cards).

In performance, remove the deck from it's card case. Hold the deck face down and casually fan through about two-thirds of the cards, saying, "Let's try an experiment with these cards." Make sure you don't get to the red-backed cards. Don't call attention to the color of the backs. The fanning should be sufficient to establish this.

Close up the deck. Turn it over. "On the bottom, I have a group of face cards." Fan through them, showing them, and fan a few cards past them. As you close up the fan of face cards with your palm-up right hand, add a spot card at the back. Lift the packet off with your right hand as you set aside the balance of the deck face down. Even up the packet.

You're about to perform the *flustration count*, a sneaky maneuver attributed to Brother John Hamman. It isn't a difficult sleight. In fact, it's not a sleight at all, but an easy, subtle move which is totally deceptive. In performing the *flustration count*, you'll casually demonstrate that all the cards in the packet you're holding have blue backs, even though only one of the cards actually does have a blue back.

Now you're holding the packet from above in your right hand, fingers at the outer end and thumb at the inner end. (If you have shorter fingers, your right first finger may be resting on top near the outer end). Turn your right hand palm up, displaying the blue back of the top card. Turn your right hand palm down. With your left thumb, draw off the card on the face of the deck (Illustration 58).

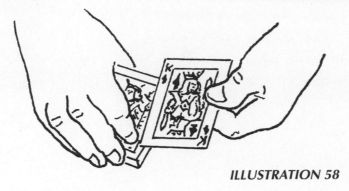

ILLUSTRATION 58

Hold this card in your left hand. Draw off another card from the face of the deck with your left thumb, letting the card land face up on top of the other card in your left hand. Casually turn over your right hand, showing the back of the top card again. Draw off two more cards individually. Once more show the back of the top card. Turn your right hand palm down and place the packet in your right hand face up on the table. Take the face-up cards from your left hand into your right hand and place these face up on top of those on the table. Pick up the packet with your right hand and place it face down in your left hand.

"Let's add a card." With your right hand, remove the red-backed face card from your pocket, showing only the back. "This one should be easy to tell from the others." Insert the card face down into the middle of the packet. Turn the packet face up and cut it several times.

Fan out the cards so that all can see the faces. Ask, "So what was the card we added?"

Spectators notice the spot card and name it.

"And do you remember the color of its back?"

The answer is "Red."

"Oh, how quickly we forget," you say. Take the spot card out and turn it over. It has a blue back. Pause a moment. "And you probably forgot that all these are red." Turn the packet over and spread it out, showing the red backs.

DISCOVERY

Discovery is the theme of some of the most imaginative card tricks, yet the basic idea is one of the simplest. A card is chosen, and the magician locates it.

No Touch, No Feel

Long, long ago, magician George Sands, came up with this superb, puzzling trick. I have added a few wrinkles.

Since spectator Ginny is quite bright, ask her to assist you. Hand her the deck of cards, saying, "Throughout this experiment, Ginny, I'm not going to touch the cards. To start with, I'd like you to give the deck a good shuffle." When she finishes, say, "Now I'd like you to deal the cards into a pile." Make sure you *don't* say, "Count the cards into a pile." At this point, you don't want her thinking about numbers. You, however, are counting the cards to yourself—as casually as you can. When she has dealt ten cards, say, "You can stop whenever you wish."

Continue to count the cards silently until she stops dealing. Turn away, saying, "Please set the rest of the deck aside. Now I'd like you to think of a number . . . say, less than ten. Remember that number. Next, look at the card that lies at that number from the top of your pile. For instance, if you thought of the number five, you'd look at the card that lies fifth from the top of your pile. Please remember that card and leave it at that number."

When she's ready, continue, "Ginny, set your packet down and pick up the rest of the deck. Remember that number you thought of? Please deal that same number of cards from the deck on top of your pile. So, if you thought of the number five, you'd deal five cards from the deck onto your pile. Then set the deck down again and pick up your pile.

"The first person to try this experiment was an Australian, so we must honor him by doing a 'down-under' shuffle. Deal the top card of your pile onto the table. Now put the next card underneath your pile. Deal the next card onto the table and place the next card underneath your pile. Continue like this until all your cards are on the table."

When she's done, say, "Pick up your entire pile and place it on top of the deck. Even up all the cards."

Turn back to the group. "Ginny, at no time have I touched the cards, and I'm not going to touch them now. Neither you nor I know exactly where your card is in the deck. Still, there is a certain aura which is attached to the card you've chosen, and I'm going to try to detect that aura. Please deal the cards slowly into a pile."

Ginny deals the cards down. "Slow down," you say, as she nears the selected card. "I feel that it's very close." Finally, you say, "Stop! What's the name of the card you thought of?" She names it; you point to the last card she dealt onto the pile. She turns it over and, of course, it's that very card.

You should be ashamed of yourself, bamboozling Ginny with a trick that's as easy to do as this one. As I mentioned, before you turn away, you note the number of cards that are dealt. With a very easy calculation, this number tells you at what number from the top the assistant's card will be when she slowly deals the cards out.

You divide by two the number of cards dealt out. If you end up with a number followed by one-half, you take the next whole number. This is the number at which the card will lie near the end of the trick. But if you divide by two and end up with a whole number, you divide *that* number by two. And you continue to divide by two until you do get a number that ends in one-half. When you finally get one-half at the end, take the next whole number.

For instance, suppose the assistant deals out fifteen cards. Divide fifteen by two, getting seven and one-half. Take the next whole number, eight. When the assistant deals out the cards at the end, the selected card will be eighth from the top.

Suppose the assistant dealt fourteen cards at the beginning. Divide this by two, getting seven. But you must get a number with one-half at the end, so divide the seven by two. This gives you three and one-half. Take the next whole number, which is four. The chosen card will end up fourth from the top.

Let's take an extreme example. The assistant deals out twenty-four cards at the beginning. You divide this by two, getting twelve. You divide the twelve by two, getting six. You divide the six by two, getting three. You divide the three by two, getting one and one-half. At last, a number with one-half at the end! Take the next whole number greater than one and one-half, which is two. At the end, the assistant's card will be second from the top.

Sheer Luck

This is my version of a trick of unknown origin. In some respects, it is similar to *No Touch, No Feel*, but the overall effect and the climax are quite different.

The trick works best when you display a sense of curiosity and wonderment throughout. You and the audience are participating in an experiment; heaven only knows what will happen!

"I'd like to experiment with something I've never tried before," you explain, smiling engagingly to prove that you're not lying through your teeth. "Mel, would you please help out."

Hand the spectator Mel the deck, asking him to shuffle the cards. "Now what? Oh, I have an idea. Why don't you cut off a good-sized bunch of cards and shuffle them up? I'll turn my back while you're doing it."

Turn away. Continue: "Let's see . . . maybe you should look at the top card of that bunch. Yeah, that's a good idea. In fact, show that card around and then put it back on top of the bunch.

"Hey, I've got an inspiration! Mel, set that bunch down and pick up the rest of the deck. Now we all know that seven is a lucky number, so think of a number from one to seven. Got one? Then deal that many cards from the deck onto your pile . . . right on top of your card." As he does this, you might mutter something like, "This is really getting good."

Continue: "Okay, Mel. Set down the rest of the deck and pick up the pile containing your card. Put that pile right on top of the rest of the deck and even up the cards." Turn back to the group and pick up the deck. "All I have to do is find your card. Now we're getting to the part that I haven't quite worked out yet." Casually fan off eight cards from the top of the group. (Don't count these aloud; you make it appear that any small number will do). Hold this packet of eight cards and set the rest of the deck aside. "Maybe it'll work better if we have fewer cards." Riffle the group of eight next to your ear. "Sounds like your card's here, all right."

Have Mel pick up the rest of the deck. Set the packet of eight on the table. "You know what might help, Mel? Remember that number you dealt on top of your card? I'll turn away again, and you deal that same number on top of the pile again." Point to the pile of eight cards so that he'll know exactly what to do. Turn away while he does his dealing. Turn back and have Mel set the deck aside and pick up the pile containing his card.

"It's pretty obvious what we have to try now, Mel. We have to eliminate lots of cards. Please put the top card on the bottom. Then deal the next card onto the table. Next, put the top card on the bottom. And again deal the next card onto the table." Have him continue this deal until only one card remains in his hands.

"What was your card, Mel?" He names it. It's the one he's holding.

Note: The deal used at the end of this trick is the opposite of the "Australian shuffle." In the latter, the *down-under* deal, a card is dealt onto the table and then one placed on the bottom, and so on. This is an *under-down* deal. The first card goes on the bottom, the next on the table, and so on.

Double Discovery

Whoever discovered the clever principle used here should be very proud, for it has been incorporated into any number of excellent tricks. This is my favorite.

You'll need a complete fifty-two-card deck and two willing assistants—Wendy and Grant, for instance.

Hand Wendy the deck. "We're going to have both you and Grant choose a card, Wendy. But we want to be absolutely fair. So each of you should have exactly half the deck. Would you please count off twenty-six cards and give them to Grant."

After she does so, turn your back. Give the following instructions, with appropriate pauses: "I'd like each of you to shuffle your cards. Look at the bottom card of your group and notice its value. Now very quietly deal off that many cards from the top of your group. Just deal them into a pile on the table. If the bottom card is a six, for example, you'd deal off six cards from the top of your group. A jack counts as eleven, a queen as twelve, and a king as thirteen.

"Once you've dealt off the cards, you don't need to remember the number. Just look at the top card of the pile you dealt off. Please remember it; that's your chosen card.

"Wendy, you're holding a group of cards. Please place this group on top of the cards that Grant dealt off.

"Grant, place the cards that you're holding on top of the pile that Wendy dealt off.

"One more job, Wendy, and then we're done. Put either pile on top of the other, and even the cards up."

When she finishes, turn back to the group. "It's pretty obvious that no ordinary human being could locate the two selected cards. But I am no ordinary human being. As a matter of fact, I'm from Krypton . . . or is it Mars? I can never remember."

Pick up the deck and hold it face down. You will deal the entire deck into a face-up pile, spreading the cards from left to right as you deal them (Illustration 59).

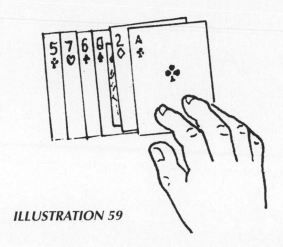

ILLUSTRATION 59

Deal out twelve cards face up. As you place the thirteenth card face up onto the pile, think to yourself, "King." As you deal the next card onto the pile, think, "Queen." As you deal the next, think, "Jack." Continue all the way down to ace. As you do this, at some point the card you're dealing will match the card you're thinking. For instance, you might think to yourself, "Six," and the card you're placing onto the pile is a six. Don't stop or pause at this point, but continue on as though nothing had happened. The fact is, however, that six tells you everything you need to know about the two chosen cards. The card following it is one of the chosen cards. Furthermore, the six tells you that the other chosen card is sixth from the bottom of the deck.

So you have dealt a six, and it matches the number you were thinking. Deal the next card (one of the selected cards) slightly out of line to mark the position of the six. This is important, as I will explain later.

You now continue dealing the rest of the deck face up. Spread out the cards. As you do this, mentally count backwards from the face of the deck to the sixth card from the bottom. Pass one of your hands back and forth over the cards. Let your hand fall on the first chosen card that you noticed, the one that followed the six. Push this card forward. "I believe that this is one of the chosen cards. Whose is it?"

Let's say that Grant admits that it's his. "Good. Now I must find Wendy's card." Again you pass your hand over the cards. This time, let it fall onto the sixth card from the bottom. Push this card forward. "And this must be your card, Wendy."

Another Example: You deal twelve cards one at a time into a face-up pile. When you deal out the thirteenth card face up, you think to yourself, "King." You continue the sequence, mentally counting one card lower each time you deal a card. Suppose that you're thinking, "Nine," and you deal out a nine at the same time. This means that the next card you deal will be one of the chosen cards, and that the other chosen card will be ninth from the bottom of the deck.

Sometimes, as you go through the backward sequence from king to ace, more than one card will match up. Suppose, for instance, that you mentally match both jack and three. The card after the jack might be one of the chosen cards, but so might the card after the three. What do you do?

After you come to each match, you move the next card a bit out of line. This eliminates the possibility of any later confusion. After you finish dealing out the entire deck, you can easily go back and look at the two possibilities. So a jack matched, and suppose that right after it came the seven of clubs. And a three matched, and let's say that right after it came the ace of diamonds. You'll have to eliminate one of the possibilities. The best way is the most direct way. Simply say, "Did one of you choose an ace?" If the answer is no, say, "I didn't think so." You now know that one of the chosen cards is the seven of clubs (the one that followed the jack), and that the other chosen card is eleventh from the bottom.

If one of your assistants *did* choose an ace, you say, "I thought so." Push the ace of diamonds forward. "I think it's this one." The matching card just before the ace was a three, so you now know that the other chosen card is third from the bottom.

Four Times Four

Years ago, I read a trick in a magic magazine in which four spectators each think of a card, and the magician discovers all the chosen cards. Unfortunately, I couldn't figure out the explanation. Either something was wrong with the write-up, or I was extremely dense. Since I preferred the former theory and I very much liked the plot, I worked out my own method.

Ask a spectator to shuffle the deck, take four cards for himself, and distribute four cards to each of three other spectators. The rest of the deck is set aside.

Tell the four spectators, "Please look through your cards and figure out one card that you like. Remember that card. Then mix up your four cards so that even you don't know which one is your card."

Mentally number the spectators from left to right as one, two, three, and four. Take Spectator Four's packet. Place Spectator Three's packet on top of it. Spectator Two's packet goes on top of the combined packets. And Spectator One's packet goes on top of all.

"If you don't mind, I'll mix the cards a bit. In fact, I'll give them the famous *holy-moley-what-the-heck-kind-of-a-shuffle-is-that?* shuffle."

Take the top card into your right hand, just as though you were going to deal it. Take the next card on top of that card, grasping it with your right thumb. Push off the next card with your left thumb. Grasp it with the right fingers, taking it below the two in your right hand. The next card goes on top of those in your right hand. The next card goes on top of those in your right hand. Continue alternating like this until all the cards are in your right hand. "Let's try that again."

Perform the same peculiar shuffle. "That should do it."

With your right hand, take off the top four cards of the packet, dealing them *one on top of the other,* so that their order is reversed. Set the rest of the packet down. Fan out the four cards so that the four spectators can see the faces. "Does anyone see his card here?"

Whatever the answers, close up the cards and deal them out from left to right—in a special way. From your left to right, consider that there are positions one, two, three, and four on the table—matching the positions of the four spectators. When any spectator sees his card displayed, that card is dealt face down at the appropriate position; the others are dealt face up. Suppose that, on your first display, Spectators One and Four have seen their cards. Deal the top card (signifying Spectator One) face down at Position One. Deal the second card (signifying Spectator Two) face up at Position Two. Deal the third card (signifying Spectator Three) face up at Position Three. Deal the fourth card (signifying Spectator Four) face down at Position Four.

Since Spectators One and Four saw their cards, you dealt the first and fourth cards face down at Positions One and Four; the others were dealt face up (Illustration 60).

ILLUSTRATION 60

Pick up the packet, which now contains twelve cards. Fan out the top four cards of the packet. Take them from the packet, *retaining their order.* Set the rest of the packet down. Hold the four cards so that the four spectators can see them. Again ask if anyone sees his card. Let's suppose that Spectator Three sees his card. Deal the first two cards face up on top of the cards at Positions One and Two, respectively. Deal the third card face down on top of the card at Position Three. The fourth card is dealt face up on top of the card at Position Four. In other words, since Spectator Three saw his card, it is dealt face down; the others are dealt face up (Illustration 61).

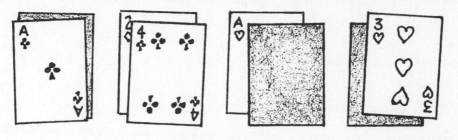

ILLUSTRATION 61

Pick up the packet, which now contains eight cards. With the right hand, take off the top four cards, *one on top of the other,* reversing their order. Set the remainder of the packet down. Show the four cards you counted off, as before. If a spectator should see his card, that card would be dealt face down at the appropriate number; the others would be dealt out face up on their respective piles. But no one sees his card, so all four are dealt face up on the appropriate piles.

Pick up the remaining four cards and fan them out, showing them. In this instance, you know that Spectator Two will see his card. So, as you go ahead and deal the cards onto their piles from left to right, you deal the second card face down on the pile at Position Two. The others are dealt face up.

With your right hand, pick up the face-up cards at Position One and place them, still face up, into your left hand. Pick up the face-down card at Position One. Ask Spectator One for the name of his chosen card. When he names it, turn the card over and hand it to him.

Do the same for the remaining three spectators, working from left to right. You have managed to identify all four chosen cards.

Note: You show a group of four cards four times. The first and third times, you take the cards one on top of the other, reversing their order. The second and fourth times, you fan out four from the top and take them in the right hand, retaining their order.

Sixes and Nines

Are you ready for a trick that has fooled some of the most know-ledgeable card experts in the world? This is it. And Wally Wilson is the performer. He says that the basic trick is very old. But I was not familiar with it. Of course Wally has added a few wrinkles, along with his own special performance magic.

Preparation: Take the sixes and the nines from the deck. Place the sixes on top and the nines on the bottom.

Start by giving the deck a casual riffle shuffle. Let's assume you have the bottom half in your left hand and the top half in your right hand. Riffle off at least a half dozen cards with your left hand before you start meshing in the cards. This pretty much guarantees that a half dozen or so cards from your right hand will fall on top. It also guarantees that the sixes will still be on top and the nines on the bottom.

Spectator Lana will be delighted to assist you. Hand her the deck and say, "Lana, I'd like you to deal out the entire deck into four piles, going from left to right. Just deal them as though you were dealing out four hands in a card game—only neater."

When she finishes, continue: "Please pick up any one of the piles. Fan through the cards and take out any one you want. Put it aside for a minute while you set the pile back down. Now look at your card and show it around, but don't let me see its face."

After everyone but you has had a chance to see the card, go on: "Lana, put the card on top of any one of the piles." She does so. "Now if you want to, you can cut that pile. Or, if you prefer, place one of the other piles on top of it." If she cuts the pile on which her card sits, have her then stack all four piles in any order she wishes. If she does not cut that pile, have her proceed directly to the stacking of the piles.

The deck is now given at least two complete cuts. "You're the one who's been handling the deck, Lana, so it's certain that I have no idea of where your card is." Spread the deck face up onto the table so that all the cards can be seen. "Nevertheless, some people suspect that I sneak cards out of the deck. I want you to notice that your card is still there. I'll look away while you check it out." As you say this, spread through the cards as though further separating them to provide a better view. Actually, you're looking for the sixes and nines. In one instance, you will find a six and a nine separated by one card. That card is the one chosen by the spectator; remember it.

Mostly you'll find a six and a nine side by side. If Lana cut the packet before stacking the cards, you'll find a lone six and a lone nine somewhere. Just keep in mind that you're looking for the card that separates a six and a nine.

After you note this card, which will take just a few seconds, avert your head. "When you're done, Lana, gather up the cards, please, and give them a good shuffle."

At this point, you can take the deck from Lana and reveal the card any way you wish. You could read her mind, for instance. Wally Wilson prefers this startling conclusion that includes an easy sleight I'd never seen before:

Fan through the cards, faces towards yourself. Cut some to the top. Fan through more cards and cut another small group to the top. Eventually, cut the cards so that the chosen card becomes the third card from the top. As you do all this, mutter things like, "It has to be here somewhere. I don't know. I should be able to figure this out." After the last cut, turn the deck face down. "I think I have it, Lana. But this is very difficult, so I want four guesses. I probably won't need all four guesses, but you never know . . ."

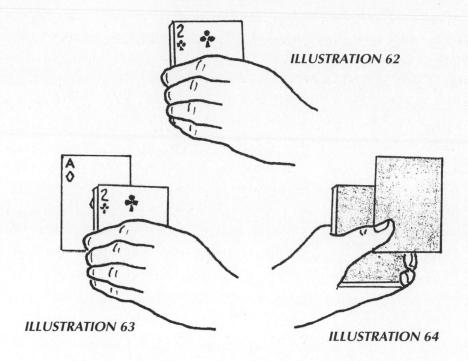

ILLUSTRATION 62

ILLUSTRATION 63

ILLUSTRATION 64

The deck is in your left hand in the dealing position. Lift your left hand so that the bottom card faces the group (Illustration 62). With your right thumb, pull up the top card diagonally. Move your right hand away so that about half the card is displayed (Illustration 63). The left thumb holds the bottom left corner of the card (Illustration 64). "Here's my first guess. Is this your card, Lana?" No, it isn't.

With the right hand, push the card back so that it is even with the others. At this point, you're still holding the cards in a vertical position. Lower the left hand to the regular dealing position. Deal the top card face down onto the table to your right.

Again raise the deck to a vertical position. Show the next card in the same way as before. Wrong again! Push the card back, turn the deck to a horizontal position, and deal the top card onto the table to the left of the first card.

Once more raise the deck to a vertical position. This time, you'll perform a deceptive move that I call the *thumb glide.* Move the right hand up to the deck, as though to display the next card. As you chat with the spectators about your hopes for your third guess, move the top card down about half an inch with your right thumb. This is easily accomplished by using *very light* pressure (Illustration 65). Then pull up the *second card from the top* and display it as you did the others (Illustration 66). You're wrong again, of course. Push the card back with the right fingers and push the actual top card back into position with the right thumb. *Now* lower the deck and deal the top card onto the table to the left of the other two cards. You have cleverly and successfully managed to switch the card you showed for the chosen card.

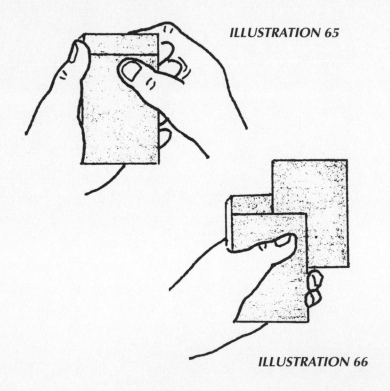

ILLUSTRATION 65

ILLUSTRATION 66

You want to show a fourth card, but the spectators just saw the present top card. So you say, "Lana, this doesn't seem to be working. Maybe I'll have better luck if you cut the cards." Place the deck on the table and let her cut it. Pick the deck up and show a fourth card in the same way as you did the first two. Failure! Give Lana a look of mock disgust, saying, "Thanks a lot, Lana." The fouth card goes face down to the left of the others.

Place your right hand on the two cards on the right, and your left hand on the two cards to the left. Say, "Left or right, Lana?" Whatever she replies, lift your left hand. Pull the two cards beneath your right hand towards you. Turn one of them over. "So you say that this is not your card, Lana." Right. Turn the other card over. "And this isn't your card." Again, right.

"Hand me one of these cards, please." Indicate the two face-down cards on the table. If she hands you the card on your left, turn it over, saying, "And this isn't your card."

If she hands you the card on your right, take it, and set it in front of her. Turn over the other face-down card, saying, "And this isn't your card."

In either instance, the chosen card remains face down on the table. "So, what is your card, Lana?" She names it. Make a few magical gestures over the chosen card and then ask Lana to turn it over. At last you've located the chosen card.

SETUP

These tricks, in one way or another, require some preparation. In some instances, only a card or two must be placed in position. In others, a number of cards must be set up in advance. I believe that a really good trick is worth the bit of extra trouble.

Blind Chance

I have seen versions of this principle used by both Nick Trost and Ed Marlo, so it's hard to know whom to credit. Regardless, it's a wondrous trick. My variation differs somewhat in order to create what I think is a stronger climax.

You may make the necessary preparation ahead of time, but I find it just as easy to do this: Turn away from the group, saying, "Excuse me for just a moment. I have to pick out a proper prediction card, and this requires extreme concentration." Turn over any card about sixth from the bottom of the deck. Find its mate—the card that matches it in color and value. Remove this from the deck. Turn back to the group, the deck face down in one hand and your prediction card face down in the other.

Let's say that you have turned the ten of spades face up so that it's several cards from the bottom of the deck. Your prediction card, then, is the ten of clubs. Place this face down on the table, saying, "Here's my prediction. But its accuracy will depend on someone else." Single out spectator Dorothy. "Will you help me, Dorothy? If we're on the same wavelength, this should work perfectly."

Hand her the deck. "Please place the cards behind your back. I want you to be able to choose a card without being influenced by me or anyone else in any way at all."

Make sure that Dorothy stands so that no one can see the cards.

"Reach into the middle of the deck, Dorothy, and take out any card. Turn it face up and set it on top of the deck. Now give the cards a cut and even them up."

When she is done, have her hand you the deck.

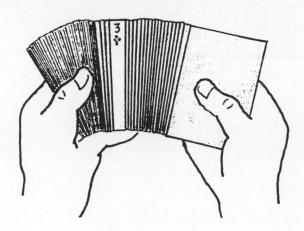

ILLUSTRATION 67

Fan through the cards so that all can see. When you come to a face-up card, fan a few cards beyond (Illustration 67). Next, fan back so that the face-up card is on top of the face-down cards in your left hand. Separate your hands; the face-up card remains on top of those in your left hand, while the balance of the deck is in your right hand. Place all the cards that are in your right hand *below* those in your left hand. You are now holding a face-down deck with a face-up card on top. "So your card is . . ." Name it. Naturally, it's the card that *you* previously turned face up. Place the card face up next to your prediction card.

Turn the deck face up. Murmur, "Let's see if you accidently turned over more than one card." Casually fan through about four-fifths of the deck, showing the faces. "No, I guess not." Close up the deck and set it aside.

"Dorothy, we'll now find out whether we're on the same wavelength. If we are, these two cards should match each other in color and value." Turn over your prediction card, showing that it matches her choice.

Note: At the end of the trick, you have a face-up card near the top of the deck. You have several options. You could make this your last trick, and simply put the cards away. Or you could do a few tricks where the face-up card will not show up. Then, at a break in the action, step aside and turn the card over. My favorite is to do a "take-a-card" trick. Turn away while the assistant shows the card around. Naturally, while your back is turned, you turn the face-up card over.

The Ideal Card Trick

Here's the ideal card trick: A card is selected, you do something miraculous with it, and no skill is required. Here we have the invention of U. F. Grant, a creative giant in the field of magic.

Preparation: Place any four face-up fourth from the bottom of the deck.

Spectator Daphne may have a funny name, but she sure is a good sport, so fan the cards out and ask her to select a card. Make sure, of course, that you do not spread the cards out near the bottom; no need to disclose the face-up four. Have her show the card around and then replace it on top of the deck. Give the deck a complete cut and set it on the table.

"Daphne, I am going to attempt a feat that is nearly impossible. I am going to try to turn a card face up in the middle of the deck. Will it be your card? Oh, no, that would be too easy. Instead, I will try to turn over a card that will tell us where your card is. I can't believe how tough this is going to be."

Pick up the deck and give it a little riffle at the ends. "I hope that works." Fan through the cards until you come to the face-up four. "Ah, here we have a face-up card, a four." Set the cards above the four onto the table. Lift off the four and place it, still face up, on the table. "So let's count off four cards." Deal off four cards, counting aloud. Place your finger on the last card dealt off. "What was the name of your card, Daphne?" She names it, and you turn it over.

Seven for Luck

Len Searles created this superb trick. Here's my variation.

Preparation: Place a seven on top, followed by seven face-up cards.

Address spectator Richard: "I'd like you to select a card completely by chance, so we should follow a certain procedure." Extend the deck towards him on the palm of your hand. "Richard, please cut off a substantial group of cards, turn the group face up, and set it back onto the deck."

When he finishes, even up the cards, and hand him the deck. "Now just fan down to the card you cut to and take a look at it . . . I'll look away." Avert your head while he looks at his card. "Done? Okay, then turn those face-up cards face down again and put them back on top of the deck, right on top of your chosen card."

Take the deck from Richard and show that the cards are all evened up. Take off the top card with your right hand, but don"t let anyone see it. Glance at it. It doesn't matter what the card is because you're going to miscall it anyway. Put the deck behind your back with the left hand and the card with your right hand, saying, "Okay, I'm going to stick this seven face up into the middle of the deck and hope for the best." Actually, you simply place it back on top of the deck and bring the cards forward.

"Seven! That's definitely good luck. Let's see where the seven is, and then we'll count from there." Turn the deck face up and fan through until you come to the face-down card, which, of course, is a seven. Take the cards you fanned off and set them aside. Pick off the seven and turn it over so that all can see. "There's the seven," you declare, for those who are farsighted. Set the seven aside. "So we'll count off seven cards. Richard, what was your card?" He names it. You count off seven cards and there it is . . . on the seventh card.

What Do You Think?

A spectator merely *thinks* of a card and, in practically no time, you—with your incredible magical powers—locate it.

Preparation: First, unknown to all, put all the eights and nines on the bottom of the deck. The order of these placed cards doesn't matter.

Ready? Say to spectator Greta, "I'd like you to think of a number *between* one and ten." (Be sure to say "between," because you don't want her to choose one or ten). "Now I'll show you ten cards one at a time. Please remember the card that lies at the number you thought of."

Avert your head as you hold up the top card, face towards Greta. At the same time, say, "One." Take the next card in front of the first and show it to Greta, saying, "Two." Continue through the tenth card. Replace the ten cards on top of the deck. They are, of course, in the same order.

"Greta, I'm going to put these cards behind my back and perform an astonishing feat. I'm going to put your chosen card in a position where you yourself will locate it with a randomly chosen card."

Put the deck behind your back. Take off the top card and put it on the bottom. Turn the deck face up. To yourself, *very quietly* count off the nine bottom cards, one on top of the other. Place this packet on top of the deck. Turn the deck face down and bring it forward. You now have an indifferent card on top, followed by the eights and nines.

"Okay, Greta, everything is ready. All I need to know is the number you thought of." She names the number. Let's say the number is six. Count aloud as you deal five cards onto the table. When you say "six" aloud, lift off the sixth card, turn it over, and continue to hold it. It will be either an eight or a nine. Whichever it is, announce its value, and say, "Let's hope that this card will help us find your card."

If the card is an eight, place it face up onto the pile you dealt off. In another pile, deal eight cards, counting aloud. Ask Greta to name her card. Turn over the last card dealt. It is the one she thought of.

If the last card you lift off is a nine, call attention to it, and then turn it face down on top of the deck. Deal off nine cards, counting aloud. As before, the last card will be the one chosen.

Summary: When the spectator gives the number she thought of, you deal off one less than this number, counting aloud. When you name the last number of the count, you hang on to the card. Turn it over, still holding it. If it's an eight, drop it on top of the pile you just dealt; deal off eight cards from the rest of the deck and turn over the last card. If it's a nine, replace it face down on top of the deck; deal off nine cards from the deck and turn over the last card.

A Face-Up Miracle

Doug Maihafer developed an astonishing trick which would ordinarily require considerable skill at sleight of hand. His trick, however, requires only a bit of preparation.

Ahead of time, note the bottom card of a blue-backed deck of cards. Go through a red-backed deck and find the duplicate to this card. Place the red-backed duplicate *face up* second from the bottom.

So the situation might be this: You have a blue-backed deck. The bottom card is the blue-backed jack of hearts. The second card from the bottom is a red-backed jack of hearts, which is face up.

In performance, approach spectator Hector, fanning the cards face down from hand to hand. (Make sure you don't get too close to the bottom and tip off the red-backed card.) "Hector, I might spread the cards like this and have you choose a card. But this might give you a better choice."

Place the deck on the table and do the *Crisscross Force* (page 40). There's a difference, however. After the spectator cuts off a portion and places the other portion on top crosswise, you stall for a moment. Then you pick up the *top pile* of the crisscrossed cards. Take off the bottom card of this group and, without looking at its face, hand it face down to Hector. In our example, this is the blue-backed jack of hearts. "Take a look at your card, Hector and show it around."

Meanwhile, put the pile you're holding on top of the other pile. Even the cards and pick them up. Hold the deck in the dealing position and tell Hector, "Push your card into the deck, please." He probably won't be able to push it all the way in, so you might have to push the card even with the others.

"I will now attempt an almost impossible feat. I'm going to try to make your card turn face up in the deck. What was your card, Hector?" He names it. Riffle the ends of the deck. Fan through to the face-up jack of hearts. "There it is—face up!" Take it from the deck and place it face up on the table. When the murmurs of approval die down, say, "What more could a magician do?"

Spread the deck face down next to the face-up jack of hearts. "Maybe I could change the color of the back!" Snap your fingers and turn the jack of hearts over, displaying its red back in contrast to the blue-backed deck.

Immediately pick up the deck; you don't want anyone going through it just now. Pick up the red-backed jack of hearts and put it into your pocket. Proceed with other tricks. If, as you're doing your routine, someone points out the blue-backed jack of hearts, say, "Oh, yes, I brought it back. *And* I changed it back to a blue-backed card." Then move right along.

FOUR ACES

It's Out of My Hands

How about yet another trick in which the spectator does all the work? Sprinkled among others, such tricks seem to be especially magical.

Spectator Edgar is an excellent card player, so you might ask him to take the deck and shuffle it. Continue: "Please go through the cards and take out the four aces.

When Edgar turns the deck face up, take note of the bottom card and remember it; this is your key card. Then you banter with the group, paying no particular attention as he tosses the aces out. (If he somehow manages to change the bottom card, however, take note of the new bottom card. This is your key card).

The aces are face up on the table. Ask Edgar to turn the deck face down. "Now, Edgar, put the aces in a face-down row, and then deal three cards on top of each ace." When he finishes, say, "Gather the piles up, one on top of the other, and put them on top of the deck."

Then: "Please give the deck a complete cut." Make sure that, as he begins the cut, he lifts off at least sixteen cards. Usually, the completed cut will leave the aces somewhere around the middle of the deck.

"In a moment, we're going to make some piles, Edgar. Which pile would you prefer—pile one, pile two, pile three, or pile four?" Whatever he replies, repeat his choice so that everyone will remember.

"Please deal the cards slowly into a face-up pile. If all goes well, I'll get a strong feeling as to when you should stop."

At a certain point (described below) you tell him to stop. Then: "Deal the next four cards into a face-down row. Then deal the next four cards into a row, right on top of the first four cards. Do the same with the next four cards, and then four more." Make sure he deals the cards across in a row each time. As he deals each group of four, count, "One, two, three, four."

Call the group's attention once more to the number of the pile that Edgar chose. "Don't forget. At no time have I touched the cards. Would you please turn over the pile you picked." He does so, and there are the four aces.

How you do it: When Edgar deals the cards out face up, you know exactly where to stop him. You watch for your key card, the original bottom card of the deck. To make sure the aces get into the proper pile, you simply subtract the number of the chosen pile from four. For instance, if Edgar chooses pile four, you subtract four from four, getting zero. After he turns over the key card, you allow no more cards to be dealt out face up. He immediately begins forming the four piles.

If he chooses pile three, you subtract three from four, getting one. So you let one more card be dealt face up after the key card.

If he chooses two, you subtract two from four, getting two. Therefore, two more cards are dealt after the key card.

If he chooses one, you subtract one from four, getting three. So three more cards are dealt after the key card.

An Ace Collection

I particularly enjoy tricks in which the "dirty work" is over before you've barely begun. This old four-ace trick, which I have modified somewhat, is a good example.

Fan through the deck, faces towards yourself, looking for the aces. "I'll need four aces for this experiment," you explain. As you find each ace, slip it to the face (bottom) of the deck. Spread out the aces on the bottom, showing them. "Here are the aces. And I can assure you that these are the only aces in the deck." Continue fanning through the cards. After you fan off three more cards, hold all seven cards slightly apart from the rest with your right fingers (Illustration 68). Don't pause, but continue fanning through several more cards.

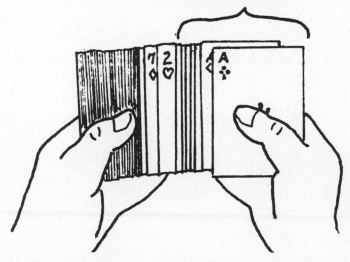

ILLUSTRATION 68
*Seven cards are held apart
from the rest of the deck.*

Casually close up the cards, letting your right fingers slide under all seven cards at the face of the deck. Immediately lower your left hand and flip the rest of the deck over with your left thumb.

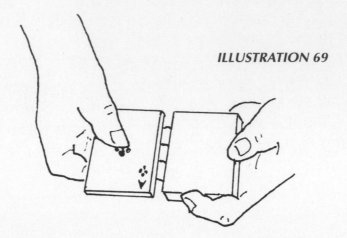

ILLUSTRATION 69

Place the left side of the face-up packet that's in your right hand on the tips of the left fingers (Illustration 69). Flip this packet over with the tips of your *right* fingers, so that it falls face down on top of the deck. This whole casual sequence takes just a few seconds.

As you go through the moves, say, "Now what we're going to do is . . ." By this time you should have completed the sequence. ". . . mix the aces . . ." Tap the top of the deck. ". . . throughout the deck."

Set the deck on the table and turn to spectator Hedda. "I'll need your help, Hedda. Would you please cut the deck into two fairly even piles. But don't forget which is the top bunch."

She cuts the deck into two piles. Point to the original top group. "And this is the top group, right?"

Right. "Now would you cut each of *those* piles into two fairly even piles." She does. Again, point to the original top group. "And this is the group that was on top."

Pick up that pile. "Now let's distribute the aces." Deal one card from the top of the pile you're holding onto each of the other three piles. (Presumably, an ace is now on top of each pile; actually, all four aces are on top of the pile you're holding). Set this pile down, alongside the other three.

"Let's make sure those aces are separated. Hedda, I'd like you to put these piles together in any order you wish. Just put one pile on top of the other until you have one pile."

After she finishes, have Hedda, or other spectators, give the deck any number of complete cuts.

Pick up the deck, saying, "It's magic time!" Riffle the ends of the cards. Turn the deck face up and fan through the cards, showing that the aces are all together.

Double or Nothing

I believe that the basic principle used here was developed by Stewart James, and Ray Boston adapted it to a four-ace trick. My version creates great spectator interest and has an extremely strong climax.

Start by tossing the four aces face up onto the table. "Here we have the four aces, as you can see. Now I'm about to play a game of *Double or Nothing.* I'll give out real money to the winner. Whoever volunteers will risk nothing whatever. Do I have a volunteer?"

You choose Hannibal from the multitude of eager volunteers.

"Congratulations, Hannibal. Just by volunteering, you have already won. To win even more, you'll have to keep track of the aces."

Arrange the aces in a face-down row. Fan off three cards from the top of the deck and place them on top of one of the aces. Tap the pile of four cards. "For double or nothing, keep track of this ace, Hannibal."

Place the pile of four cards on top of the deck. As you do so, get a break with your left little finger beneath the top card of the four. Double-cut this card to the bottom of the deck. (See *Double-Cut,* page 17).

"Where's that first ace, Hannibal? Is it on the bottom?" Turn the deck over, showing the bottom card. "No. Is it on top?" Turn over the top card, showing it, and then turn it face down again. "No. So where is it?" You coach Hannibal by saying, "Somewhere in the mmmm . . . somewhere in the mid . . ." Whatever he responds, you say, "Right! Somewhere in the middle of the deck. You've doubled your money! You now have *two . . .* pennies." This should get a chuckle. "Double or nothing, Hannibal. Let's try four pennies." Fan off the top three cards and place them on another ace. Pick up the four cards and place them on top of the deck. Double-cut the top card to the bottom of the deck.

"Where's that ace, Hannibal? Is it on the bottom?" Show the bottom card, as before. "No. Is it on top?" Show the top card and replace it. "No. So where is it?" Hannibal should have no trouble this time. "That's right," you say, "somewhere in the middle of the deck. You now have eight pennies. Let's try for sixteen."

The procedure this time is a little different. Fan off three cards from the top of the deck and place them on top of one of the two remaining aces. Pick up the four-card pile. Carefully even it up; you're going to turn the pile face up and you don't want anyone to get a glimpse of the other aces in the pile. *Now* turn the pile over, showing the ace on the bottom. Place the pile face down on top of the deck. "You *must* know where that ace is. Obviously, it isn't on the bottom." Show the bottom card of the deck, as before. "And it isn't on top." Show the top card and return it to the top.

At this point, double-cut the top card to the bottom. "So, for sixteen pennies, where is it?" As usual, it's somewhere in the middle of the deck.

"The last double-or-nothing." Fan off the top three cards and place them on the last ace on the table. Place the four cards on top of the deck. "For thirty-two pennies, Hannibal—where are all four aces?"

Chances are he'll say, "In the middle of the deck." If he does, say, "Not exactly. They're right here." Deal off the top four cards face up. They are the aces. (Whatever he responds, proceed the same way).

Pause a moment for audience appreciation. "But that was close enough, Hannibal. You still win the thirty-two pennies." Take out your wallet. "Do you have change for a big bill?"

Wally's Wily Ace Trick

Wally Wilson was kind enough to give me permission to use his simplified and surprising version of an excellent four-ace trick. What's unique about this effect is that no one knows it's a four-ace trick until the very end.

In the original version, some preparation was necessary. I have changed things a bit so that the trick can be done impromptu. (You may prefer to do the other version, which I fully explain in the *Note* at the end). We will assume that some time earlier you performed a four-ace trick so that the four aces are together somewhere in the deck. Casually fan through the deck and cut the four aces to the top.

Spectator Estelle enjoys a good card trick, so approach her, saying, "Believe it or not, Estelle, I've just memorized the position of every single card in the deck. Let's see if I can prove it to you." As you say this, fan the cards face down from hand to hand, counting them. When you reach the twelfth card, hold it, along with the cards above it, separate from the rest; continue fanning through the cards. "Please pick one out, Estelle." After she takes a card, close the cards up, getting a break with your left little finger beneath the twelfth card. (It's best to count the cards in groups of three, thinking to yourself, "Three, six, nine, twelve.")

"Show the card around, please."

Grip the deck with the right hand from above, transferring the left little-finger break to the right thumb (Illustration 70). The thumb break is on the right side of the deck. The first finger of the right hand is holding the cards down so that no separation will be apparent to the spectators.

Riffle your left thumb down the left side of the deck all the way to the bottom (Illustration 71). Start to riffle the cards again, but stop when your thumb reaches a point about a third down in the deck. Lift off the top twelve cards with your right hand.

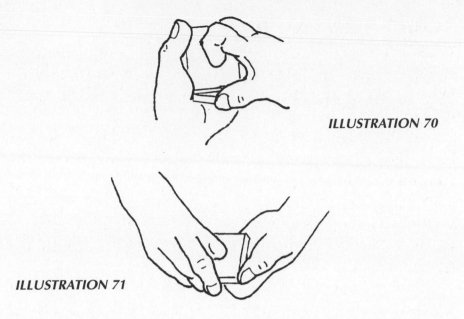

ILLUSTRATION 70

ILLUSTRATION 71

Hold out the lower portion with your left hand for the return of the chosen card. If Estelle hesitates, say, "Just put it right there, please." After she places her card on top of the pile, replace the twelve-card packet. This time you don't hold a break. Her card is now thirteenth from the top of the deck.

"Contrary to what you may have heard, Estelle, I'm a very observant person. For instance, I happen to know that your card is in the top half of the deck. So we won't need all these cards."

Deal three cards from the top of the deck, one at a time, into a pile. To the right of these, deal another pile of three cards, also one at a time. Go back to the first pile and deal a card on top of it. Do the same with the pile on the right. Continue alternating until you have two thirteen-card piles. (Count silently, of course.) At the end, you are holding half the deck. Turn over the top card of these. Let's say that it's a red card. If you choose, you may now use one of Wally Wilson's clever lines. Say to Estelle, "Your card was a red card, was it not?" If she says yes, fine. If she says no, say, "Well, I said it was not."

Regardless, replace the card face down and set down the half deck you're holding so that it's well out of the way.

At this point, the pile on your left has three aces on the bottom; the pile on your right has one ace on the bottom. You must arrange it so that the left pile has *two* aces on the bottom and an ace second from the top. And the right pile must have its ace on top. Here's how you manage it: Point to the two thirteen-card piles. "So, Estelle, I know that your card is in one of these piles." Pick up the pile on the left. Hold it from above in the left hand (Illustration 72). With the right thumb on top and the right fingers below, grasp the top and bottom cards together and pull them sideways from the packet (Illustration 73).

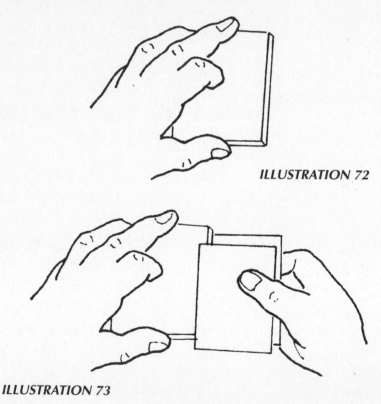

ILLUSTRATION 72

ILLUSTRATION 73

"Your card could be the top or bottom card of this packet," you say. *"Apparently*, I have no way of knowing." Place the two cards on top of the deck. Fan the cards out. "More than likely, your card is somewhere in the middle. *If* it's in this pile." Close up the packet and set it onto the table. That pile is set. What's more, the chosen card is in proper position.

Pick up the packet on the right. Casually give it an overhand shuffle, shuffling off the last few cards singly so that the bottom card ends up on top. "Of course, your card might be somewhere in here." Fan the packet out. "Who knows?" Close the packet up and return it to the table. This pile is also set.

Place one hand above each pile, twitching your fingers and staring into the distance. Pick up the pile on the right and place it to one side. Indicate the pile under your left hand. "It must be in this pile."

Pick up the pile and, going from left to right, deal it one card at a time alternately into two piles. The pile on the left contains seven cards, and the pile on the right six cards. Toss in appropriate patter about trying to sense which pile contains the chosen card as you again place your hands over the two piles. Eventually, you pick up the pile on the left and place it right next to the first pile you discarded. Indicate that the small pile remaining under your right hand contains the chosen card.

Pick up this six-card pile and deal it into two piles, as before. This time each pile contains three cards. This time, you eliminate the pile on the right. Place it near the other two discarded piles.

"So we're down to three cards." Deal them out alternately from left to right. On your left is a two-card pile, which, after the usual rigmarole, you place aside with the other discarded piles. On your right is one card. "This must be the one you chose, Estelle. What's the name of your card?"

She names it, and you turn it over. You're absolutely right. But you may not receive the praise and applause you're entitled to. After a pause, you say, "Well, if you didn't care for that demonstration, perhaps you'd like to see something with the four aces."

Turn over the top card of each of the discarded piles. They are, of course, the four aces.

It's easy to remember which pile you must set aside: The first time, you set aside the pile on the right; next, the pile on the left; then the pile on the right; and finally the pile on the left. In other words, you first discard the pile on the right, and then alternate.

Wally's Setup Version: You may prefer to have the deck set up in advance. If so, the four aces must be distributed like this: on top of the deck, third from the top, twenty third from the top, and twenty sixth from the top.

Approach Estelle, fanning the cards and saying, "I could offer you the choice of a card by letting you pick one from the deck, Estelle. But let's do something a little different." As you fan the cards, count off the top *eleven*. When you reach the eleventh card, close the cards up, getting a break with your left little finger beneath that card. (Count the cards in groups of three, thinking to yourself, "Three, six, nine, and two more.")

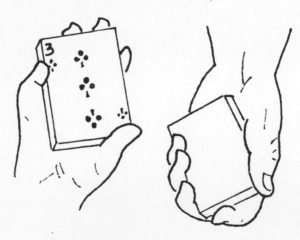

ILLUSTRATION 74

Still holding the break, grasp the deck with the right hand from above (refer to Illustration 70). Riffle your left thumb down the left side of the deck all the way to the bottom (refer to Illustration 71). "Just tell me when to stop, Estelle," you say, starting to riffle your thumb down again, slowly this time. If she says stop somewhere in the top third of the deck, fine. If not, riffle rapidly all the way down. "Let's try again," you say with a smile. When Estelle does stop you in the top third of the deck, lift off the top eleven cards with your right hand. Show the card to her (Illustration 74), saying, "Please remember this card, Estelle." Replace the packet on top of the deck. This time you don't hold a break. All the "dirty work" is done.

You do not shift the aces around as in the first version. Simply deal the cards into two piles of thirteen cards each, alternating from left to right. As in the first version, first eliminate the pile on the right, then the pile on the left, and so on, alternating.

Sneaky Aces

This is another trick shown to me by Wally Wilson, who felt it was the invention of Harry Lorayne.

Unknown to the spectators, you have the four aces on top of the desk. False-shuffle the cards, leaving the aces on top. Set the deck on the table. Ask spectator Myra to cut the deck in half, and then to cut each half in half.

There are now four piles on the table. Make sure you keep track of which pile has the aces on top. Pick up that pile.

Say to Myra, "Let's see how you did." One by one, take the top card of ech of the other piles and place it face down on top of the packet in your hand.

"We have to build suspense here. You cut to four cards." Count aloud, as you deal off the four top cards onto the table, one on top of the other. Pick up the four and place them back onto the packet, getting a break beneath them with your left little finger.

You should be holding the packet quite close to the pile which is on the table to the right. Turn over the top card and set it squarely on the packet. "Ah, an ace!"

With your palm-down right hand grip the top four cards, fingers at the front, thumb at the back. Lift off the four cards and place them on top of the pile which is on the right on the table. Apparently, you've placed only the ace on the pile.

Turn over the next card on top of the deck. "Another ace!" In precisely the same way as you gripped the four-card pile, grip the ace and place it face up on top of one of the other piles.

Do the same with the next ace. Finally, turn over the top card of the deck. Evidently, Myra has cut to all four aces. Gaze at her in wonder and say, "My, I'd hate to play cards with you!"

Grand Illusion

Fr. Cyprian is credited with the subtle move used in this trick.

Start with two aces on top of the deck and two on the bottom. (You might do this: After performing a four-ace trick, make sure the four aces are together somewhere in the deck. Perform a few more tricks. Then casually fan through the deck and cut between the aces, bringing two to the top and two to the bottom.) Give the deck a riffle shuffle, keeping two aces on top and two on the bottom. Set the deck on the table.

Spectator Joe's a good sport, so ask him to help out. "Joe, would you please cut the deck in half."

After he does, pick up the packet with the aces on top and give it a false shuffle, retaining the aces on top. (See *Controlling a Group of Cards,* page 32.) Set the pile down.

Pick up the other packet and shuffle the bottom two aces to the top. (See *Bringing the Bottom Card to the Top,* page 31.) Set this packet down near you, at a diagonal from the other packet. The positions of the two halves on the table:

A

B

Cards will be cut from these packets and placed on the table. Packets will then be at these positions:

A   C
D   B

This is how it comes about: Have Joe cut off some cards from the packet at A. Point to position D and have him place the cards there. Have him cut off some cards from the packet at B and have him place these at position C.

The situation: Two aces are on top of the packet at position D and two aces are on top of the packet at position C.

Say, "Joe, I wonder how well you did."

Simultaneously grasp the top card at position C with your right hand and the top card at position D with your left hand. Grasp the card at position C at the *far end*, and the card at position D at the *near end*. Turn these aces face up at the same time. Place the ace from position C face up on top of the packet at B; place the ace from position D face up on top of the packet at A.

Again you'll grasp the top card at position C with your right hand and the top card at position D with your left hand. This time, however, you grasp the card at position C at the *near end* and the card at position D at the *far end*. Simultaneously turn these aces face up and place them on the piles from which you just lifted them.

This entire business of turning over the aces takes but a few seconds. If you follow with the cards, you'll see how simple it actually is. The illusion is that the top card of each packet was an ace.

"Good job, Joe! You cut the aces."

MISCELLANEOUS

I Guess So

Wouldn't it be wonderful if you could tell exactly how many cards a spectator cuts from the deck? Of course. But surely it would take years of practice. Yes. *Unless* you're willing to resort to treachery and deceit. Certainly *I* am.

I derived this trick from one by Norman Houghton, which required a trick deck. My method can be done impromptu with any deck. But it must be a complete deck of fifty-two cards.

Ask spectator Lauren to shuffle the deck. Take the cards back. Hold them face down as you begin fanning them from hand to hand. Count the cards in groups of three as you fan them. When you have fanned out twelve cards, push one more into the right hand. Hold this packet of thirteen separate from the rest as you continue slowly fanning the cards. Say to Lauren, "I'd like you to take any three cards from the deck. It doesn't matter which three you take. As you'll see, these are just 'confusion cards.' " Make sure she takes the cards from below your packet of thirteen.

"The values don't matter," you say. "Just set the three cards face down onto the table." While saying this, close up the deck. But with the tip of your left little finger get a small break below the thirteen cards.

Grasp the deck from above with the right hand, transfering the break to the right thumb (Illustration 75). Casually, with your left thumb, riffle down a dozen or so cards on the left side of the deck (Illustration 76). With your right hand, lift off the thirteen-card packet and hand it to Lauren. "Shuffle these, will you, Lauren?"

Since spectator Bret isn't busy, hand him the rest of the deck. "And you might as well shuffle these, Bret."

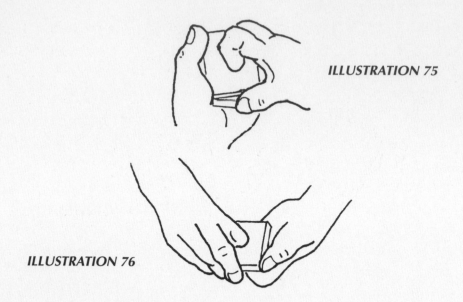

ILLUSTRATION 75

ILLUSTRATION 76

Have Lauren set her pile onto the table. When Bret is done shuffling, have him set his pile down also. "Bret, would you cut some cards off that pile that you just shuffled and set them down on the table."

The situation: Three piles are on the table. One pile contains thirteen cards, and you know which one. Three other cards are face down on the table.

"Lauren, I'd like you to place the 'confusion cards' on any piles you wish. Place them all on one pile, or two on one pile and one on another, or one on each pile—whatever you want."

These really *are* "confusion cards." You're using them to confuse the spectators as to what you're really up to.

It doesn't matter where Lauren places the three cards. All you have to do is keep track of the original pile of thirteen cards. If Lauren adds cards to it, remember the new number.

"Over the years, I've developed some skill at estimating the number of cards in a pile. Let me show you what I mean. Bret, pick any one of the three piles."

If Bret chooses the first pile you handed out, simply stare at the pile for a few seconds and then say, "The pile contains exactly thirteen cards." Or name the new number if Lauren added any cards to it. Have either of your assistants check the count. Gather up the cards and proceed to do something else.

ILLUSTRATION 77

If, however, Bret chooses one of the other two piles, have him pick it up. "I'd like to demostrate something. Bret, would you please count those out." He counts them aloud. "Now do you see how long that took?" Hold out your two hands palm up and flat. Have Lauren place one of the remaining piles on your right hand and Bret place the other remaining pile on your left hand (Illustration 77). You eye the two piles, and then give your estimate for each pile. "In this hand, I have (so many), and in this hand I have (so many)." Be sure to repeat your estimate. When Lauren and Bret count the piles, they discover that you were exactly right.

Let's assume that in your right hand is the original pile you handed out, the one containing thirteen cards. Further, let's assume that Lauren added one of the "confusion cards" to this pile. You know that the pile now contains fourteen cards.

When Bret counted his selected pile aloud, he came up with say, twenty-one cards. You add twenty-one to fourteen, getting thirty-five. So the cards on the table and the cards in your right hand add up to thirty-five. There are fifty-two cards in a full deck. Clearly, you subtract thirty-five from fifty-two to get the number of cards in your left hand—seventeen. You need not be a lightning mathematician. Most of the figuring can be done as you stare at the piles resting on your palms, ostensibly trying to make an accurate estimate.

Oily Water

There are probably more four-ace tricks published than any other type. I would guess that a close second would be the old-time trick "Oil and Water." The reason for the title is that oil and water don't mix, and neither do red and black cards. No matter how you mix them, black cards gather together, and so do red cards. Every version I've come across requires a fair amount of sleight of hand. My version depends on a swindle and bare-faced lying.

Hand the deck to a spectator, saying "Please remove four red cards and four black cards from the deck. Then arrange them so that they alternate black and red." The rest of the deck is set aside.

Take the eight cards from the spectator and fan them out face up, showing the alternating order. "You've probably heard the ridiculous theory that oil and water don't mix. Here we have red and black cards alternating. The black cards are oil, and the red cards are water. As you notice, they certainly do mix."

Turn the packet face down. "What happens if I move one card to the bottom?" Move the top card to the bottom. Turn the packet face up and fan it out. "Nothing. The cards still alternate." Turn the packet face down.

"How about two cards?" Move two cards to the bottom, one at a time. Turn the packet face up and fan it out. "They still alternate." Turn the packet face down.

"How about this?" Lift off two cards from the top, hold them to one side so that all can see that there are two, and then place them together on the bottom. Again turn the packet face up and fan it out. "Same thing." Turn the packet face down.

"What if I deal off a bunch of cards?" Take off five cards with the right hand, dealing them one at a time and one on top of the other. Do *not* count them aloud. Place this bunch on the bottom of the packet. Turn the packet face up and show it, as before.

Still holding the packet face up, say, "What happens if I remove a pair together from this group?" Pull two cards out. "Obviously, I always get a red and a black. And notice that the *remaining* cards still alternate red and black."

Replace the two cards in their original position. Pull out another pair, again demonstrating that a pair taken together from anywhere in the group will consist of a red and black. Again, point out that the remaining cards alternate red and black. Replace this pair in their original position. "So, obviously, oil and water *do* mix."

Turn the packet face down. "Now a little demonstration." Take off *four* cards with the right hand, dealing them one at a time and one on top of the other. Don't count them aloud. Casually fan out the group so that all can see that it consists of alternate colors. Place this bunch face down on the bottom of the packet. "What happens when we deal off a bunch of cards? You know the answer." Make a motion as though to turn the packet over.

"Does it matter if we transfer them one at a time?" Move three, one at a time, from the top to the bottom. "Of course not." Take off the top two cards together and place them face down onto the table at your left. "And here's a pair of red and black."

Move two cards, one at a time, from the top to the bottom. Take off the top two cards together and place them face down onto the table at your right. "Another pair of red and black."

Move one card from the top to the bottom. Take off the top two cards together and place them face down onto the two at your *right*. "Another black and red pair." Drop the last pair onto the pair at your left. "And the last pair of red and black.

"So here we have proof positive . . ." Turn over the pile on the left and spread out the cards. Turn over the pile on the right and spread these out. "Hmm . . . Don't tell me that everybody else is right . . . that oil and water *don't* mix."

More Oily Water

T. S. Ransom adapted an old principle to the "oil and water" theme. I have added the ideas I developed in *Oily Water*. The trick may be done separately, but let's assume you're doing it as a follow-up to *Oily Water*.

"Let's try that again," you say, still skeptical. "First, we alternate the colors." Hold the four reds in a face-up packet in the left hand and the four blacks in a face-up packet in the right hand. Thumb off the card at the face of each packet so that it falls face up onto the table. On your right, a black card lies face up on the table; on your left, a red card lies face up on the table. Cross your hands so that the left hand can thumb off a card onto the card on the right, and vice versa (Illustration 78). Uncross your hands. Thumb off a card from each hand onto the piles where you started. Cross your hands and thumb off a card from each hand, as before.

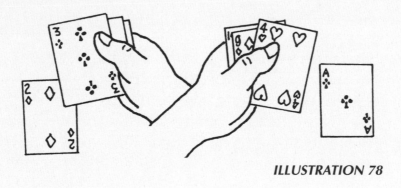

ILLUSTRATION 78

Clearly, each pile alternates red and black cards. Place either pile on top of the other. Pick the combined pile up and turn it face down. Apparently, the packet alternates reds and blacks. Actually, the fourth and fifth cards from the top are of the same color.

You now go through the same procedure as in *Oily Water*, except that you do not count off the four cards at the beginning. Fill in with appropriate patter as you proceed:

Move three, one at a time, from the top to the bottom. Take off the top pair and place them face down onto the table at your left, saying, "A pair of red and black."

Move two cards, one at a time, from the top to the bottom. Take off the top pair and place them face down onto the table at your right. "Another pair of red and black."

Move one card from the top to the bottom. Take off the top pair and place them face down onto the pair at your right. "Another black and red pair." Drop the last pair onto the pair at your left. "And the last pair of red and black.

"*Now,* let's take a look." Show that each pile consists of the same color. Shake your head. "I guess I'm just not a good mixer."

Most Oily Water

In this final "oil and water" demonstration, we have another T. S. Ransom idea. I have changed it slightly to make it less obvious.

Feeling brave? This swindle works perfectly when done rapidly and with aplomb. If, however, you feel less than confident, don't bother trying it.

This works best as a follow-up to the previous trick, More *Oily Water.*

Turn the four red cards face down and hold them in the left hand. Turn the four black cards face down and take them in the right hand.

Now proceed rapidly! Cross your left hand over your right and thumb off each top card face down onto the table. Uncross your hands. *Immediately* cross your right hand over your left and thumb each top card onto the card already there. Uncross your hands. Repeat your first move, in which you placed your left hand over your right. You now have three cards of the same color in each pile, and you are holding one card in each hand. As you uncross your hands this last time, turn the two cards face up. One is red and the other is black. Take them in one hand and proudly display them, saying, "See? Oil and water *do* mix."

Toss the two cards to one side. In eager anticipation, turn the three-card piles over. Each pile contains the same color. Shake your head ruefully. "Or not!"

Big Turnover

A card is chosen. The magician causes it to turn face up in the middle of the deck. This is one of the strongest tricks you can perform. Tom Ogden developed a patter theme, which makes the trick even more entertaining. I have expanded on the theme somewhat.

Fan through the deck, asking spectator Troy to choose a card. When he returns the card to the deck, fan one card on top of it. Get a small break with your left little finger at this point. The chosen card is now the second card below the break. Perform one of the moves listed under *Control* (starting on page 17). The selected card is now second from the top of the deck.

"Troy, I will now magically cause your card to turn face up in the deck."

Tap the top of the deck. Tip the deck down so that all can see as you fan through the face-down cards. Clearly, no card is face up.

"But it may take a minute. I know what I did wrong. I should have riffled the cards." Riffle the ends of the deck. Fan through the cards as before. Again, failure.

"Okay, Troy, then I'll do it the easy way." Tap the top card. "I'll just turn your chosen card over . . . like this!"

Grasp the top card at the outer end with your right hand and turn it over so that you're holding it a few inches to the right of the deck. As you do this, push off the next card slightly with your left thumb. As you draw this card back onto the deck with your left thumb, get a small break beneath it with your left little finger. Immediately place the face-up card in your right hand squarely on top of it.

The situation: You have a face-up card on top of the deck. Beneath it is the chosen card. And below this card, you're holding a small break with your left little finger.

As you place the card face up onto the deck, say, "That *is* your card, isn't it, Troy?"

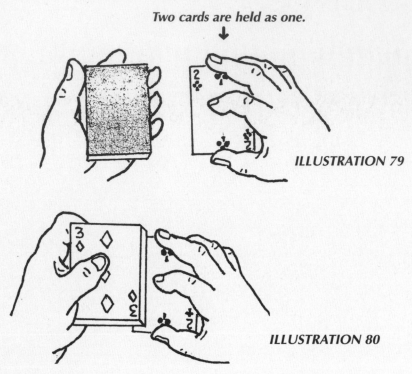

Two cards are held as one.

ILLUSTRATION 79

ILLUSTRATION 80

No, it isn't.

With your right hand, lift off the top two cards as though they are one. Your first finger rests on top, the other fingers are at the outer end, and the thumb is at the inner end (Illustration 79). With your left thumb, flip over the remainder of the deck so that it is face up. Slide the double-card under the deck as though you are replacing the face-up card on top (Illustration 80). Raise the right first finger to facilitate the placement.

The entire deck is now face up, except for the chosen card, which is face down at the rear of the deck. Since the deck is apparely face up, it's perfectly logical for you to say, "Now I *know* that your card is face up. It *has* to be one of these face-up cards." Tip the cards down and fan through about half of the face-up deck. Close up the cards and casually give them a cut. Turn the deck face down.

Easy Match

Simple is good. In this instance, simple is not only good, but extremely deceptive. This fine trick by Cy Keller has fooled some of the best.

The original trick called for two decks. I have arranged a one-deck version which is totally impromptu.

Spectator Rex will be delighted to assist you. "In this experiment, Rex," you say, "we'll each need about half the cards." Turn the deck faces towards you and note the bottom card. You're going to fan through the deck, looking for its mate—the card that matches it in color and value. Fan through several cards and place them *face down* in front of yourself, saying, "Some for me." Fan through several more. If the mate is not in sight, place these cards face down on your pile, saying, "Some more for me."

Fan through to the mate of the original bottom card. Lift off is batch, including the mate. Even up the group and place it *face* in front of Rex, saying, "And some for you." You now have a all face-down packet in front of you, the bottom card of this pile g the original bottom card. In front of Rex is a face-up pile; the rmost card is the mate to your bottom card.

f the pile in front of Rex is fairly small, add cards from the o his pile and to yours until each consists of about half the Naturally, the cards go on his pile face up and on yours face As you add cards to the piles, keep saying, "Some for you" me for me."

e pile in front of Rex is quite large, put the rest of the deck r pile. If his pile is still larger than yours, take some cards turn them face down, and put them onto your pile.

ds a little complicated, but the bottom line is this: Once down the first two piles, you make sure that each con- ut half the deck.

"See, Troy? I told you I'd turn your card face up." To the
the group: "Thank you so much. I hope you enjoyed th
demonstration."

Pause, looking slightly angry. "Did I hear someor
word 'putrid'?" Since spectator Francine is very good-n
turn to her, saying, "Was that you, Francine?" Don
chance to answer. "Shame on you. Do you think *i*
magic? Let's see you give it a try."

Make her take the deck. "What was your
names it.

"All right, Francine, let's see *you* be magic
the deck and then fan through the cards."

She does. And of course, the chosen c?

"Good heavens! She got it!" Paus
Francine, I could really use a good assist?

Easy Match

Simple is good. In this instance, simple is not only good, but extremely deceptive. This fine trick by Cy Keller has fooled some of the best.

The original trick called for two decks. I have arranged a one-deck version which is totally impromptu.

Spectator Rex will be delighted to assist you. "In this experiment, Rex," you say, "we'll each need about half the cards." Turn the deck faces towards you and note the bottom card. You're going to fan through the deck, looking for its mate—the card that matches it in color and value. Fan through several cards and place them *face down* in front of yourself, saying, "Some for me." Fan through several more. If the mate is not in sight, place these cards face down on your pile, saying, "Some more for me."

Fan through to the mate of the original bottom card. Lift off this batch, including the mate. Even up the group and place it *face up* in front of Rex, saying, "And some for you." You now have a small face-down packet in front of you, the bottom card of this pile being the original bottom card. In front of Rex is a face-up pile; the lowermost card is the mate to your bottom card.

If the pile in front of Rex is fairly small, add cards from the deck to his pile and to yours until each consists of about half the deck. Naturally, the cards go on his pile face up and on yours face down. As you add cards to the piles, keep saying, "Some for you" and "Some for me."

If the pile in front of Rex is quite large, put the rest of the deck onto your pile. If his pile is still larger than yours, take some cards from his, turn them face down, and put them onto your pile.

It sounds a little complicated, but the bottom line is this: Once you've put down the first two piles, you make sure that each consists of about half the deck.

"See, Troy? I told you I'd turn your card face up." To the rest of the group: "Thank you so much. I hope you enjoyed that little demonstration."

Pause, looking slightly angry. "Did I hear someone say the word 'putrid'?" Since spectator Francine is very good-natured, you turn to her, saying, "Was that you, Francine?" Don't give her a chance to answer. "Shame on you. Do you think it's easy doing magic? Let's see you give it a try."

Make her take the deck. "What was your card, Troy?" He names it.

"All right, Francine, let's see *you* be magic. Tap the top card of the deck and then fan through the cards."

She does. And of course, the chosen card is face up.

"Good heavens! She got it!" Pause briefly. "You know, Francine, I could really use a good assistant . . ."

Pick up your pile and casually give it an overhand shuffle as you tell Rex, "Please pick up your pile and turn it face down." Near the end of your overhand shuffle, draw off the last few cards singly, bringing the bottom card to the top. The top card of your pile now matches the top card of Rex's pile.

"Now for the experiment. Rex, let's see what happens when we perform the identical actions. Please do exactly what I do."

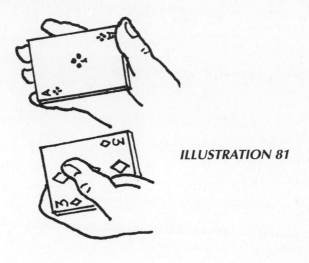

ILLUSTRATION 81

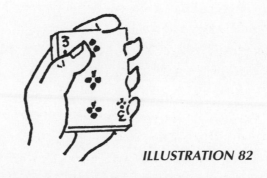

ILLUSTRATION 82

With Rex following your example with his cards, you cut off the top half of your packet. You place this top half face down onto the table. Turn the cards in your hand face up and give them several overhand shuffles (Illustration 81). Even up these cards and hold them face up in your left hand in the dealing position (Illustration 82). Lift off the top card of those you placed on the table and place this card face down on top of the face-up packet you're holding. Turn this packet face down and place it on top of your pile on the table. Rex, of course, has gone through the identical routine with his cards.

In case Rex and others are not sufficiently disoriented, you now use a bit of "time misdirection" so that they will forget precisely what has occurred. "Very often, Rex, when two persons perform identical actions, they get similar results. When this happens, some people call it coincidence, others call it fate. I think of it as good luck, especially if I'm conducting the experiment. So we performed the same actions; let's see the result."

Spread your cards out face down and have Rex do the same. His face-up card matches yours.

List to One Side

Time is hanging heavy on your hands. Why not telephone Nola and perform a card trick for her?

All you need is a pencil and paper, along with enough persuasive power to convince Nola to cooperate.

Start by asking her to get a deck of cards. When she returns to the phone, ask her to shuffle the deck. Then: "Nola, deal the cards from the top of the deck into a face-up pile. Please name the cards as you deal them out."

As she names the cards, jot down the name of each one, using this conventional shorthand:

9C

10S

JH

QD

(These stand for nine of clubs, ten of spades, jack of hearts, and queen of diamonds.)

After Nola deals ten-plus cards, tell her that she can stop whenever she wishes. Have her set the deck aside. "Pick out any card you want from those you dealt off. Remember that card and stick it into the middle of the main deck. Now shuffle up the main deck."

When she's ready, say, "Shuffle up the rest of the cards that you dealt off and put them on top of the main deck. When you're ready, give the deck a complete cut."

These are your final instructions: "Again, would you deal the cards from the top into a face-up pile and name the cards as you deal them." As she names the cards, keep your eye on the card names you jotted down. As soon as she names one, put a check mark by it. Continue checking off cards from the group. (Because she shuffled these cards, they will not be in order. But the checked-off cards *will* be together in a bunch.) Eventually, you will check off all the cards in the group except one. That is her chosen card. Stop Nola and tell her the name of her chosen card.

Sometimes the spectator will name a card from the group you wrote down but then will name cards that are *not* in the group. That first card she named from the group is her chosen card.

Note: When Nola names the cards for the second time, you might want to make a second list which you can use after she gets well down in the deck. This eliminates the possibility of your failing to check off one of the cards on your initial list.

Pop-Up Card

While chatting with the spectators, hold the deck in the dealing position in your left hand. Grip the deck from above with your right hand, fingers at the front, thumb at the rear. With your right thumb, riffle the top few cards slightly, separating the top two cards from the rest of the deck. Hold a break below these two with the tip of your left little finger.

Even up the cards at the ends with your right hand. Now simply *lift off* the top two cards with your second and third fingers at the front and your thumb at the rear. Hold the double card straight up so all can see it; then bend it almost in half so that the top of the face of the double card almost meets the bottom. Replace the double card on the deck, holding the center down with your left thumb. Take the top card in your right hand, thumb on top and fingers below. Hold this card sideways so all can see that it's bent downwards at the ends. Slide the card into the middle of the deck. Incidentally, as you take off this card, make sure your left thumb continues its pressure, holding down the center of the next card.

Grip the deck from above with your right hand, curling your first finger under so that it, rather than your left thumb, is now holding down the top card at the center. Move up the deck in your left hand, holding it at the sides between thumb and fingertips. Squeeze at the sides to prevent the top card from popping up, Take your right hand away and hold the deck up sideways so that all can see.

Say, "One, two, three." On "three," release the pressure of the fingers and thumb on the sides, and the card will visibly pop up at the middle about a quarter-inch or so. As I say, "Three," I usually snap the fingers of my right hand to add emphasis. With your right hand, carefully lift off the card, showing that it's risen from the middle of the deck.

Don't repeat the trick.

Those Mysterious Ladies

A card is chosen and replaced in the deck. Four queens are dealt out face down. The spectator chooses one, and it mysteriously changes to his chosen card.

"I'm going to need four mysterious cards," you say. Fan through the deck and remove the four queens, placing them face down in a pile on the table. Do this without showing their faces. First remove a red queen, then another red queen, followed by the black queens. So, from the bottom up, the pile on the table consists of two red queens and two black queens.

Have spectator Evan select a card as you say, "You need to choose a card to represent you." The card is taken, shown around, and replaced in the deck. You cleverly bring it to the top. The way I cleverly do it is with a double-cut (see *Double-Cut,* page 17), but you may use any other method. (See *Controlling a Card*, starting on page 17.)

Turn the deck face up and fan the cards from the bottom somewhat (not revealing the top card, of course), saying, "You could have chosen any of these cards to represent you." Close up the fan. "Now it's time to examine the mysterious cards." Place the deck face up on the queen pile. Pick up all the cards with your right hand, turning them over and placing them in your left hand.

"Four mysterious cards," you say. "And what could be more mysterious than four lovely ladies?"

Fan out the four face-up queens with your right hand, pushing off an additional card below them. As you push the queens back, obtain a little-finger break beneath the fifth card. With your right hand, from above, take the cards with your thumb at the near end and fingers at the outer end. Draw off the top queen onto the deck with your left thumb. Using the left edge of the remaining cards in your right hand, flip it face down. "Here we have a lovely red-head," you say. Turn the next queen the same way, saying, "And another gorgeous redhead." Flip it face down as before. Turn over the next queen, saying, "A mighty pretty brunette." As you flip this queen face down, drop the two cards remaining in your right hand (presumably one card) on top of the deck. "And yet another attractive brunette." Push this last queen to the left with your left thumb and then, with your right fingers, flip it face down.

From the top down, the top four cards are black queen, chosen card, black queen, red queen. (The other red queen, irrelevant to the rest of the trick, is the fifth card down.) Spread out the top four cards and take them from the deck in your right hand. Set the rest of the deck aside.

Say to Evan, "Now you're going to have to choose one of these beautiful young ladies."

You're about to perform an easy maneuver known as *The*

ILLUSTRATION 83

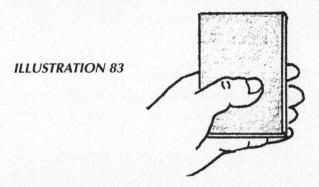

Olram Subtlety. Place the packet of four cards into your left hand so that they're considerably forward of the regular dealing position (Illustration 83). (This is so that when you turn your left hand palm down, the bottom card can be easily seen.)

ILLUSTRATION 84

Draw the top card off the front end of the face-down packet with your right hand. The instant it clears, turn both hands over. Your right hand displays the card just drawn off (a black queen), and your left hand displays the bottom card of the three card packet (a red queen) (Illustration 84). Turn both hands palm down, immediately dropping the card from your right hand face down and—*at the same time*—thumbing off the top card of those in your left hand, letting it land to the left of the card that comes from your right hand.

With your right hand, draw off the top card of the two remaining cards. Again, turn both hands over, displaying the faces. Turn your hands palm down. Simultaneously drop the card in your right hand to the right of the two on the table while dropping the card in your left hand to the left of those on the table.

Apparently, you've shown all four queens. Actually, you've shown a red queen twice. From your left to right, the cards on the table are red queen, chosen card, black queen, black queen. Let's assume that the chosen card is the seven of clubs. The layout could be this, as you look at it:

QH   7C   QC   QS

You now do an *equivoque* or *magician's choice* similar to that described in *Either/Or Force* (page 161). Say to Evan, "Pass your hands over those cards, and when you feel ready, let each hand fall onto a card." He covers two of the cards with his hands. If one of the two is the chosen card, pull the other two cards towards you, saying, "Now please hand me one of those." If he hands you the chosen card, say, "So this is your free choice." Set the card face down directly in front of him. If he hands you the other card, drop it down with the others which you pulled out of line. Point to the card under his card, saying, "Your choice."

Suppose he covers two cards other than the chosen card. Indicate that he is to lift his hands. You pull the two cards towards you. As before, ask him to hand you one of the remaining two.

In all instances, Evan gets his chosen card. Turn the queens face up one by one, saying, "Here we have the poor ladies who weren't chosen." Toss them face down onto the deck.

"So you've chosen a red-haired lady. The question is, would she choose you? What was the name of the card representing you?" Evan names it, and you have him turn it over. "Excellent. You *were* chosen, and everyone lives happily ever after."

If performing the trick for a woman, use the four kings. In the patter, they become two redheaded men and two darkhaired men. When you pick up the kings so that they are face up on the face-down deck, fan them out, as with the queens. The patter changes slightly, however. "We have four mysterious men."

Good Choice

Here's a fast, clever trick requiring only nerve and a bit of practice.

In your pocket, you have four kings. The king of spades and the king of clubs have blue backs. The king of hearts and the king of diamonds have red backs. The order doesn't matter.

ILLUSTRATION 85

Remove the four cards from your pocket, making sure spectators cannot see any of the backs. Hold them face up in your left hand. Spread the kings out and ask spectator Ted to name one (Illustration 85). After he does so, say, "You can change your mind if you want to, Ted—it doesn't matter." When he finally decides on one, remove it from the group, saying, "This one." Replace it so that it's the lowermost of the face-up cards. Maneuver the other cards about so that the king that's of the same color as the one chosen is at the face of the packet. As you do this, say, "You could have chosen this one, or this one, whatever one you wished." Tell him that he can still change his mind. If he does, maneuver the cards so that they're in the appropriate position described.

You are about to perform a variation of the *flustration count,* previously described in the trick *Color Confusion,* page 170.

Close up the face-up packet and hold it from above in your right hand, fingers at the outer end and thumb at the inner end. Turn your right hand palm up, displaying the back of the top, chosen, card. Let's assume he has selected the king of clubs. Say, "It's amazing that you should choose the king of clubs, which has a *blue* back." Turn your right hand palm down. With the left *fingers,* draw the king of clubs from the back of the packet into your left hand. (This first maneuver differs from the standard *flustration count.*) Turn your right hand palm up again, displaying a red-backed card. Turn your hand palm down and, with your left thumb, draw off the card at the *face* of the packet so that it comes to rest on top of the king of clubs. (This is the standard move in the *flustration count.*) Perform the action again. Then display the back of the last card, turn your right hand palm down and drop the card face up on top of those in your left hand.

Ted has chosen the only card with a different-colored back.

Note: If you wish, repeat the trick several times. Simply put the cards into your pocket. Chat for a moment about what a coincidence has occurred. Then say, "I have another set of kings in my pocket." Dig into a different pocket. "No luck. Maybe they're here." Take the same set of kings from your pocket and repeat the trick. You might even put the kings away again and then go through the same routine. The basic trick is so deceptive that there's little danger that spectators will catch on, and it becomes quite amusing when spectators suspect that you're using the same kings.

Spin-Out!

Reinhard Muller created this quick, simple, startling effect.

Remove from the deck the two red aces, setting them aside face down without showing them. Have a card chosen and bring it to the bottom of the deck. The easiest way is to secure a little-finger break below the chosen card and then do a double-cut. (See *Double-Cut*, page 17.)

Hold the deck from above in your left hand, fingers on one side, thumb on the other side. Pick up one of the aces, show it, and place it face up on the bottom. As you reach out with your right hand to pick up the other ace, draw back the ace on the bottom slightly with your left fingers (Illustration 86).

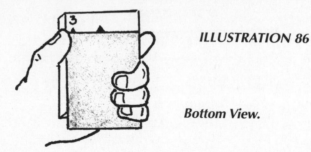

ILLUSTRATION 86

Bottom View.

Place the second ace face up on top of the deck. Still retaining the left-hand grip, grasp the front of the deck with your right hand. Your right thumb is on top, your right first finger on the selection, and your right second finger on a red ace (Illustration 87).

ILLUSTRATION 87

Bottom View.

The following move sounds a bit difficult; in fact, you'll master it after a few tries. Let loose of the left-hand grip. Simultaneously, with the right hand revolve the deck forward, and, in a snappy dealing motion, toss the cards onto the table, but not *all* the cards. You cling to the three cards you're gripping with your right thumb and first and second fingers—the two aces and the selected card.

ILLUSTRATION 88

Fan the three cards with your right hand (Illustration 88). Turn the fan over, showing that "the selected card, hidden in the middle of the deck, has been captured by the aces!"

GOTCHA!

Most so-called "sucker" tricks should be reserved for times when you have an obnoxious spectator. You can do only one sucker trick for a particular group, obviously, because your victim is unlikely to take the bait twice.

"Second Deal"

For this one, you must have an odious onlooker who's eager to catch you. Apparently you show the top card and then deal off the second card from the top in an extremely sloppy "second deal." The victim *knows* that the card on the table is not the card you claim it is.

The method is quite simple. You apparently show the top card. Actually, you perform a double-lift. (See *Double-Lift,* page 42.) You name the card. Then you make sure full attention is paid to your sloppy deal by saying, "I will now deal the card onto the table."

Very obviously push off the top card with your left thumb and pull the second card out with your right thumb (Illustration 89).

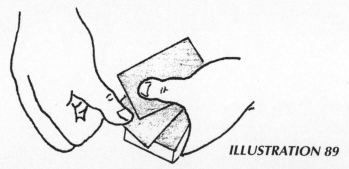

ILLUSTRATION 89

Pull the top card back with your left thumb. Actually, you're performing a "legitimate" second deal, only you're making it as sloppy as possible.

Look as smug as you can. Turn to the obnoxious spectator and say, "Can you remember what this card is?

Don't let anyone turn the card over. Put your hand over it if you have to.

The intended victim will probably say that it's not the card you claim it is. But if he doesn't, simply say, "Does everyone agree that this is the seven of hearts?" Or whatever card. If no one disagrees, say, "You're right." Show the card and continue with something else.

But it's your lucky day. The victim caught it all; he knows exactly what happened. This is definitely not the card; you dealt a second. Show the card and pause for a few seconds before the next trick so that you can enjoy the other spectators complimenting your dupe on his perspicacity.

No Wonder

Have spectator Karen select a card, show it around, and return it to the deck. Bring it to the top. (See *Controlling a Card,* page 17.)

Say, "Let's see if we can locate your card, Karen."

Double-lift, showing the second card from the top. (See *Double-Lift*, page 42.) Suppose this card is the three of hearts. Say, "Let's use the three of hearts to help us." Turn over the double card on top of the deck. Take the top card (the chosen one) and hand it face down to Karen. Say, "Just stick it face down partway into the deck."

After she does so, fan through to the partially inserted card (the one selected). Set aside the cards above it, remove the inserted card, and put it face down near Karen. Turn over the next card, asking if it's the one selected. Naturally, the answer is no.

Have Karen pick up the face-down (selected) card and insert it partway into the deck face down again. Once more it fails to locate the chosen card. You might even do it a third time. Finally, hand Karen the face-down card and say, "What was your card?" When she names it, say, "Well, no wonder it didn't work." Indicate that she is to turn the card face up.

If Karen should turn over the card sometime during the procedure, ask her why she seems startled. When she points out that it is her card, say sardonically, "Wonderful! Now this will *never* work."

Spectators will be amused by either conclusion.

Dunbury Delusion

Your potential victim, Mervin, has been trying to spoil your every trick. Have him select a card and show it around. Mervin is quite capable of lying about his chosen card just to goof you up, so it's vital with this trick that all spectators know the name of the card. When the card is returned, bring it to the top. (See *Controlling a Card*, page 17.)

Now give a lengthy speech. Near the end, you'll prepare for a sleight.

"This is the only experiment I do with cards which never fails. *Never* fails. And why? Because I've learned to tell when a spectator is lying and when he's telling the truth. Now, Mervin, I am going to cut the cards three times. The first time I'll cut a card of the same suit as your card, the second time a card of the same value, and the third time a card that will help us find your card.

"When I cut the cards, Mervin, I'll ask you a question which you are to answer yes or no. Nothing more. You may lie or tell the truth. It doesn't matter, because I'll be able to tell if you're lying or not. That's why this experiment never fails. If something has gone wrong, I'll be able to tell and can make an adjustment. Remember, just yes or no. And you can lie or tell the truth."

As you near the end of the speech, casually perform an overhand shuffle, in-jogging the first card and shuffling off. The card above the chosen card is now in-jogged. (See *Controlling a Group of Cards*, page 32.)

You're about to perform *Drop Sleight* (page 41). The preparation is slightly different from that described, however. Hold the deck in dealing position in your left hand. Grip the deck from above with your right hand, fingers at the front and thumb at the rear. Lift up at the jogged card with the right thumb so that you're holding a break above the chosen card with the tips of your left fingers along the right side and your right thumb at the rear (Illustration 90).

The cards above the break should be bent up slightly at the rear with your right thumb, letting a card drop off. With the aid of the third and fourth fingers of your left hand, adjust the cards so that your right thumb grips the top section along with the card which has been dropped at the rear (Illustration 91).

ILLUSTRATION 90

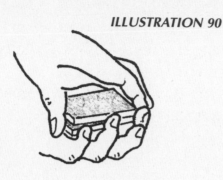

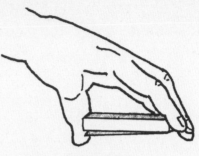

ILLUSTRATION 91:
For clarity, the left hand isn't shown.

You say, "Now the first card I cut will tell me the suit of your card."

Lift off the cards above the break with your right hand. Shove over the chosen card with your left thumb. (Let's assume the card is the four of hearts.) Flip it face up with the left edge of the cards in your right hand.

"See, the four of hearts."

As you continue talking, perform the drop sleight.

"This tells me that your card is a heart. Yes or no?"

As Mervin answers, thumb the card face down onto the table. Place the lower packet on *top* of the pile in your right hand, lifting the first finger to permit passage. The chosen card, presumably on the table, is now on top.

Chances are, Mervin's answer will be yes. It doesn't matter. If he says no, smile confidently and say, "Sure."

Cut the deck at random and flip over another card (the eight of clubs). Name the card and flip it face down. Thumb it face down next to the first card, and return the packet *below* the one in your right hand, so that the chosen card remains on top.

Meanwhile, comment, "This means that your card is an eight. Yes or no?" If he says yes, say, "Of course it is." Chances are he'll say no, to which you respond, "I can tell you're lying by that almost undetectable, sneaky little smile." In either instance, reassure him that this is the one trick you do which never fails.

Again you cut off a pile of cards and flip over the card you cut to. Name it, flip it face down, thumb it off onto the table next to the other two. The pile in the left hand is returned below the one in your right so that the chosen card remains on top.

Let's assume that the third card you cut to was the seven of spades. "Ah, here we have the seven of spades. This means that your card is seventh from the top. Yes or no? No need to answer. Of course it is. Now watch this as I magically move it from the seventh position to the very top of the deck." Give the cards a false shuffle or a false cut.

Lift off the top card and hod it face down. "And now the key question. Here we have your chosen card. Yes or no?"

Whatever the response, ask, "What is your card?" When he names it, turn the card over, announcing, "See? The one effect I achieve that never fails."

Watch them dive for that first card you dealt on the table!

Notes: Sometimes when you cut the second card, it's the same suit or value as the chosen card. This won't do. If it's the same suit, you're saying that this *is* the chosen card. If it's the same value, you're saying that you know that the first card you ostensibly placed down is the chosen one. So simply say, "Whoops, wrong card!" Continue cutting until you get one of a different suit and value.

Save the "sucker" tricks for severe cases. The best response to most irritating spectators is simply to perform your tricks well.

RECOVERY

An Out

The spectator names his selected card; you turn over the one in your hand, and it's the wrong one. Here's a way out.

Show the card and return it to the deck, asking, "Are you sure the five of spades was your card?" Fan through the cards so that no one else can see the faces. "It must be here somewhere."

What you want to do is bring the chosen card second from the top. Fan several cards from the bottom and transfer them to the top in a bunch. Continue doing this until you come to the chosen card. Fan one card beyond it and put that group on top. Confess, "No luck."

Turn the deck face down in the dealing position in your left hand. Take the top card and turn it face up. As you do so, push off the second card (the chosen one) slightly with your left thumb and then draw it back, taking a slight break under it with your left little finger.

Immediately place the card in your right hand face up on the deck. Square the ends of the deck with your right fingers and thumb. The two cards are now as one, separated slightly from the rest of the deck by the tip of your little finger.

"Obviously your card isn't on top." Grasp the double card with your right hand from above, thumb at the rear, second finger at the front, and first finger resting on top. Dig your left thumb beneath the deck and flip the deck face up. Place the double card underneath, presumably replacing on top the card you've just shown (Illustration 92). Carefully even up the deck, saying, "And equally obviously, your card isn't on the bottom. Watch for your card."

Fan ten or so cards from the bottom. "It's not among these." Turn these cards face down and put them on the back of the deck (Illustration 93). Continue this way all through the deck.

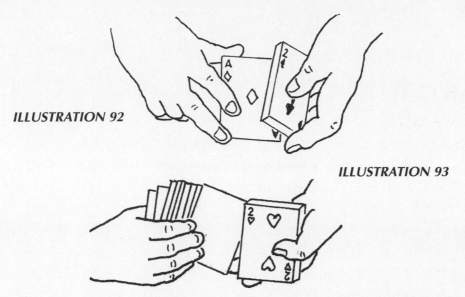

ILLUSTRATION 92

ILLUSTRATION 93

The last group you take includes all the cards up to the first face-down card. Presumably, you've shown every card in the deck, and the chosen card isn't among them. Actually, it's at your disposal on top of the deck.

How do you reveal it? You might do *Sneaky Slide*, in which you double-lift the top card, showing that the chosen card is still not there. Then you lift off the top card, slide it through the deck edgewise, and turn it over, showing that it has changed to the chosen card.

A second possibility is one which is also a good trick on its own merits. Put the deck into your pocket. Remove a card from the bottom and place it on the table. *Rapidly* continue doing this, saying, "Tell me when to stop." Make sure you get your hand back to your pocket when the spectator says stop, so that you can pull out the top card and flip it over face up.

A third possibility is to force the chosen card on your assistant, causing him to choose the same card again. You may use the standard force or one of the surefire forces. (See *Forces*, page 34.)

Clever Card
Tricks for the
HOPELESSLY
CLUMSY

MOVES AND MANEUVERS

Preposterous Patter

Here we have some patter lines that many find funny. Some are original, but most have been concocted by others, and are quite ancient. Obviously, a joke isn't old to someone who hasn't heard it before, so you may find some of these useful.

But that is not my main purpose in presenting them to you. I hope that you'll observe the *sort* of lines that have found success. As with all humor, you'll find here the unexpected, the well-turned phrase, or the just-plain-silly. Perhaps some of these will give you some ideas on how to develop lines of your own to use with your tricks. In all of the tricks presented here, you will find patter suggestions that may inspire you to devise original comical lines to enhance your performance.

On the other hand, depending on your nature, you may decide to make a more serious presentation. Regardless, here are the lines, most of which are very familiar to experienced magicians.

(1) "Would you like to see a card trick? All right, then I'll have to get out my trick cards. I'm kidding. This is an ordinary deck of marked cards. Yes, they're marked. See the marks? This is a queen of spades. This is a seven of hearts. This is a five of clubs. They're all marked."

(2) "Take a card, any card . . . " The spectator does. " . . . except that one."

(3) "We have here an ordinary deck of 57 cards."

(4) Point up one sleeve. "Nothing here." Point up the other sleeve. "Nothing here." Point to your head. "And very little here."

(5) "I believe your card is a cherry-colored card."

"No, it isn't."

"You've never heard of black cherries?"

(6) "Your card is a licorice-colored card."

"No, it isn't."

"You've never heard of red licorice?"

(7) "Do you know one card from the other?"

"Sure."

"Okay. Name one card. Come on . . . you can do it."

"Six of spades."

"Excellent. Now for something really tough. What's the other?"

"Jack of spades."

"Right! You *do* know one card from the other. Terrific job!"

(8) "I am the most amazed person when one of my experiments happens to work. The magical result just astonishes me. When I do this stunt, however, I seldom have to worry about that."

(9) With the right spectator, you might even be moderately insulting: "Hold out your hand, please . . . No, the clean one. Just kidding. Heck, my hands are almost as dirty as yours."

(10) "Take a card. Now show it to your friends. This shouldn't take long."

(11) "This is the first time I've ever made that mistake . . . again."

(12) "I can't believe it! This entire deck of cards is printed upside down. Of course it's kind of hard to tell."

Control

Every magician who does card tricks must have some way of controlling a card after it has been chosen. Most methods require considerable skill. Here's one that's very easy.

Simplicity Itself

In some instances, this control works best. For example, you might want to bring the chosen card to a fairly high number from the top. This would do perfectly, as I'll explain.

Before the spectator chooses a card, sneak a peek at the bottom card of the deck. You can do this as you separate the deck in two, preparing to do a riffle shuffle (Illustration 94). Then, when you shuffle, keep the card on the bottom. Easier yet, look at the bottom card as you tap the side of the deck on the table, apparently evening up the cards (Illustration 95). More suggestions for peeking at the bottom card can be found near the beginning of the tricks "The Way Back," on page 266, and "Piles of Magic," on page 61.

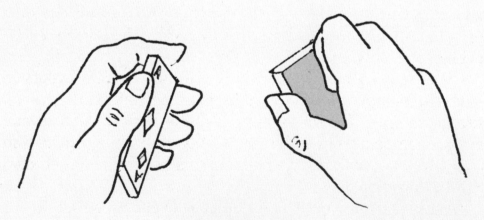

ILLUSTRATION 94

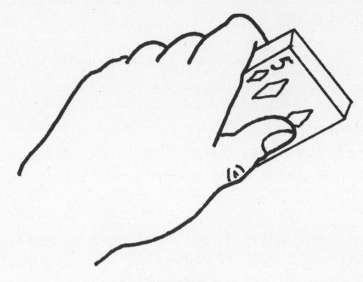

ILLUSTRATION 95

So you know the bottom card of the deck. Fan out the deck, and a spectator selects a card. Close up the deck. From the top of the deck, lift off a small packet and drop it onto the table. Lift off another small packet and drop it on top of the first one. After dropping several packets like this, say to the spectator, "Put your card here whenever you want." After you drop one of your packets, he places his card on top. You put the rest of the deck on top of it. Even up the cards and pick them up. The card that you peeked at is now above the chosen card.

Start fanning through the cards, their faces toward yourself. Mutter something about, "This is going to be really hard." Fan off several cards. Cut them to the rear of the deck. Fan off several more. Again, cut them to the rear. You're establishing a pattern so that it won't seem so odd when you finally cut the chosen card to a key position.

Let's say you simply want the card available on top of the deck. Continue fanning groups of cards and placing them at the rear until you see that you'll soon arrive at the key card. The card on the near side of the key card is the one chosen by the spectator (Illustration 96). Cut the cards so that the key card becomes the top card of the deck (Illustration 97). Just below it, of course, is the chosen card. Turn the deck face down.

"I can't seem to find your card." Turn over the top card of the deck (the key card). "This isn't it, is it?" No. Turn the card over and stick it into the middle of the deck. Turn the deck face up. "How about this one?" No. Take the bottom card and stick it into the middle of the deck. Turn the deck face down. The chosen card is at your disposal on top of the deck.

Suppose, for purposes of a specific trick, you want the chosen card to be 10th from the top. Again you start by fanning off small groups and cutting them to the rear of the deck. When you get to the chosen card, you start counting to yourself. You count the chosen card as "One." Count the next card as "Two." Cut the cards so that the card at "Ten" becomes the top card. The chosen card is now 10th from the top.

ILLUSTRATION 96

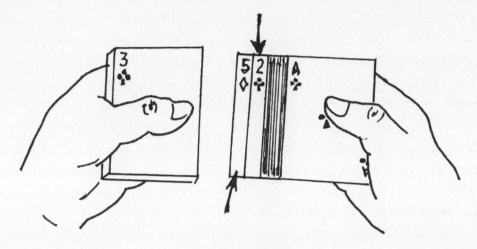

ILLUSTRATION 97

False Cuts

An efficient false cut should be done casually, just as a genuine cut would be performed. Often magicians manipulate the cards back and forth between their hands, rapidly shifting piles here and there, and finally end up with a single pile. Naturally, spectators don't know exactly what happened, but they sure as heck know that *something phony was done*. This is not always bad; sometimes it's all right to show that you're skillful. But many of us prefer to keep our skills—however minimal—secret. I recommend this.

Just a Casual Cut

Hold the deck in your left hand. With your right hand, lift off the top portion of the deck and place it face down onto the table. Make some casual remark. At the same time, *without looking at the card*, take the rest of the deck with your right hand. Place this pile *to the right* of those on the table.

Continue commenting. Glance down at the cards on the table. Pick up the pile on the right and place it on top of those on the left. Pick up the combined pile.

The cards retain their original order.

And Another

With the left hand, take the bottom portion of the deck. The left hand should be palm down, and the packet should be grasped with the second finger at the far end, the first finger on top and the thumb at the near end. The top portion of the deck is retained in your right hand (Illustration 98). Gesture with the left hand as you make a comment. At the same time, drop your right hand somewhat, so that it becomes lower than the left hand.

Place the left-hand portion onto the table. Put the right-hand portion on top of it (Illustration 99). Pick up the entire deck with the right hand.

The cards are back in order.

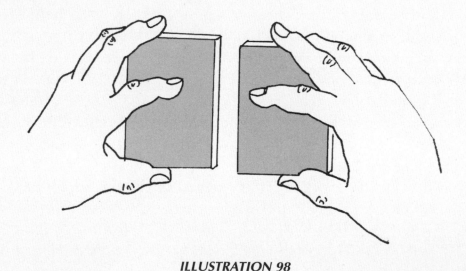

ILLUSTRATION 98

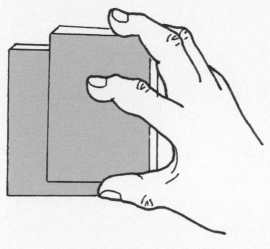

ILLUSTRATION 99

Roll-Up Cut

I designed this cut specifically for the gambling trick "Really Wild," which appears in my book *World's Greatest Card Tricks*. There is no sleight of hand, and the deck is kept in order.

Since the cut does not appear ordinary, it can work well if you just give it a fancy name. For instance, you might say, "I'll just give the cards my 'inside-outside over-and-out cut.'" Or, "Here's my famous 'whoop-dee-doo and row-dee-dow cut.'" Actually, you can give it any extravagant name; I generally call it something different every time.

Hold the deck in the dealing position in your left hand. With your left thumb, flip the deck face up. (For an example of this move, see Illustration 108, page 268.) If the move is too difficult, simply grip the ends of the deck between the right fingers and thumb, and turn it over (Illustration 100).

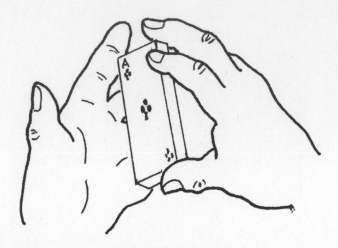

ILLUSTRATION 100

With your right thumb, grip about a quarter of the face-up deck on the left side (Illustration 101). Lift this packet, pivoting it to the right, as though opening a book from the back (Illustration 102). Let the packet fall face down onto your right hand. Place it face down to your left.

Flip the rest of the deck over with your left thumb so that the cards are now face down. As before, if this is too difficult, just turn the cards face down with your right hand.

With your right thumb, lift about a third of the face-down cards on the left side. Pivot these over, as before (as though opening a book from the back). Let the packet fall face up onto your right hand. Set the packet onto the table a few inches to the right of the first packet.

Again, flip the rest of the deck over with your left thumb, or turn it face up with your right hand. With your right thumb, pivot off about half of the cards and set them face down on the table to the right of the other two packets.

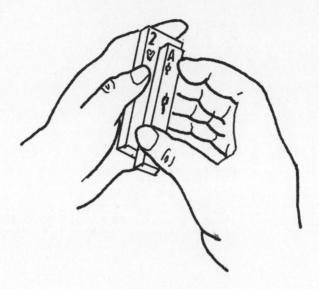

ILLUSTRATION 101

Remaining in your left hand is a packet of face-up cards. Take the packet into your right hand and set it face up to the right of the others. Pause, saying, "Now comes the hard part."

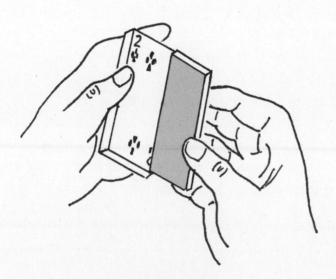

ILLUSTRATION 102

With your right hand, grasp the right side of the packet you just placed down. Turn this packet over on top of the packet to its left, as though closing the back portion of a book (Illustration 103). In the same way, turn the combined packet over and place it on the packet to its left. Once more, turn the combined packet over and place it on the packet to its left— the first packet you placed down.

Even up the cards. The deck is face down and in the precise order it was at the beginning.

If you follow the instruction with a deck of cards, it will seem that the cards can't possibly be in their original order. It just doesn't seem logical. Maybe I should have called it the "illogical cut."

Note: When lifting off the packets to place them onto the table, you may prefer to grasp them at the ends with the palm-down right hand, fingers at the outer end and thumb at the inner end. As with the other method, you pivot the packet in an arc to the right, as though opening a book from the back. Then place the packet onto the table.

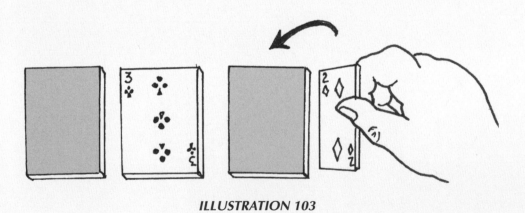

ILLUSTRATION 103

Milking the Cards

This is actually a fairly simple procedure with a small packet of cards. The idea is to slide off the top and bottom cards together and place the two together onto the table. Again, you slide off the top and bottom cards together and place these two on top of the first two. You continue like this until the pile is exhausted. The move is important in quite a few tricks.

Let's get more specific. Hold a packet of cards from above in your palm-down left hand, thumb at the inner end, first finger resting loosely on top, and the other fingers at the outer end (Illustration 104). Your palm-up right hand lightly grips the top and bottom cards, thumb on top and fingers on the bottom. The right hand pulls the top and bottom cards to the right until they clear the packet (Illustration 105).

The two cards are set onto the table. Draw off two more cards, dropping them on top of the first two. Continue until all the cards are in a pile on the table.

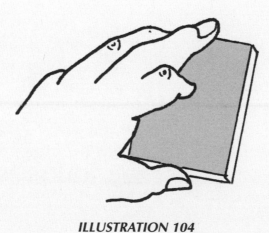

ILLUSTRATION 104

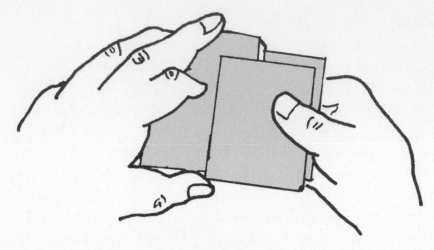

ILLUSTRATION 105

The Up-and-Down Shuffle

Anytime you perform this maneuver, you refer to it as a shuffle. Actually, it is not. It's a subtle method of rearranging the cards to your advantage. Usually, it is performed with a packet of cards—somewhere between 10 and 25.

Start by holding the packet in the left hand in the dealing position. Push off the top card with your left thumb and take it with your right hand. Push off the next card with your left thumb. Move your right hand forward (away from you) a bit. Take this second card below the first card in your right hand. This second card should be two inches or so below the first card.

Move the cards in your right hand back toward you. Push off a third card with your left thumb. Take it below the first two cards, so that it is even with the first card you drew off.

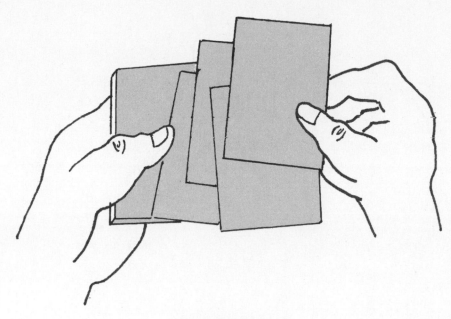

ILLUSTRATION 106

Move the cards in your right hand back toward you. Push off a fourth card with your left thumb. This card goes on top of the others and is even with the second card you drew off (Illustration 106).

Continue alternating like this until the packet is exhausted. Hold the upper group with your left hand as, with your right hand, you strip out the lower group from the others (Illustration 107). This group goes on top of the cards remaining in your left hand.

Notes: (1) Depending on the trick, in the first move of the shuffle you may move the top card *down* or toward you, the next card up, the next card down, and so forth.

(2) Depending on the trick, when you strip out the lower group (the cards nearest you), these will sometimes go *below* the cards you hold in your left hand.

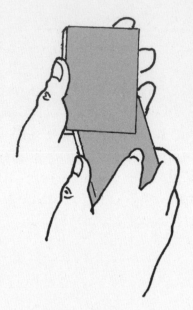

ILLUSTRATION 107

(3) Speed is not needed for this maneuver. If you take your time, you can do it quite easily.

What If Things Go Wrong?

You have the wrong card! For some inexplicable reason, the trick simply didn't work.

There are two cardinal rules: (1) Under no conditions try the trick again. (2) Don't blame the spectators.

You failed; accept it. Why did you fail? The possibilities are unlimited. Try one of these excuses, for instance:

"Just what I thought, the deck was too slippery."

"Well, the score is now one to nothing, your favor."

"What was your card?" She names it. "Just as I suspected. That's my 'bad luck' card."

"I'm not surprised. That trick never works. Let's try one that does."

"You have to admit one thing: If that worked, it would have been one heck of a great trick."

"It's my fault, really. I washed my hands this morning and now I can't do a thing with them."

"Gee! And only a few minutes ago, that used to be my favorite card trick."

I'm sure you can think of dozens of other silly excuses. The point is: Say something somewhat amusing and then get on with it; show another trick—preferably one that you're sure will work. Most will forget that you ever goofed up. And many will think it's all part of the show.

Above all, don't let it bother you. Remain composed as you proceed with your tricks. The old show-biz saying applies here: "Don't let them see you sweat."

TRICKS

Mental Tricks

Strictly speaking, the following four tricks are forces—that is, you know the name of the "freely" chosen card in advance. They are, however, perfect for performing mental tricks. Apparently, a card is selected in the fairest possible way; yet you are able to read the spectator's mind and divine the name.

So with these four selections, you can either force the card for use in some other trick, or you may perform a feat of mind reading. If you decide to read a person's mind, you should reveal the name of the chosen card gradually—first revealing the color of the card, then the suit, and finally the value. In revealing the value, you apparently run into some confusion. For example, you know that the card is the ace of clubs. You have already divined the color and the suit. Concentrating fiercely, you say, "I can't seem to get the value. It looks like a four. No, no! Not a four. It looks *like* a four. Let me see. It's an ace!" Pause. "The ace of clubs."

Similarly, you might at first confuse a three with an eight, or a two with a five—any two cards that are moderately similar will do. Such nonsense is designed to convince spectators that mind reading is extremely difficult and is seldom precise. Deep down, everyone *knows* that this is baloney. But just maybe . . .

The last three tricks in this category are not forces; they are quite clever and certainly worthy of your consideration.

The Way Back

Since the dirty work for this one is done behind your back, you'd better make sure no one is behind you.

One way or another, you must know the name of the top card. You can sneak a peek in advance, but I recommend this: Say, "I wonder if the joker is in here." Fan through the cards, apparently seeking the joker. The joker isn't there, but you do get a look at the top card of the deck.

Announce, "I'm going to attempt a feat of telepathy, so I don't guarantee any degree of success."

Place the deck face up onto the table. Gary knows his way around a deck of cards, so get him to assist you. Say, "Gary, please cut off a huge pile of cards and turn them over on the rest of the deck."

Gary lifts off a large number of face-up cards, turns them over, and sets them, face down, onto the remaining face-up cards.

Continue, "Please cut off a smaller pile, turn it face up, and set it on top of the remaining cards."

He does it. You may tell him to cut off another small pile, turn it over, and set it back onto the remaining cards. In fact, this can be done several times.

"They should be pretty well mixed." Pick up the cards with your right hand and place them in the dealing position in your left hand. The lowermost card is the one you sneaked a peek at.

Move your left hand behind your back. At the same time, turn away from the group. Your back is now to the group, the deck behind your back in your left hand.

"Gary, I'd like you to cut off a pile of cards. But please cut into the *face-down* cards so that no one else can see the card that you choose."

Gary cuts off a pile.

Turn back toward the spectators, keeping your left hand behind your back. The right hand remains in front of you where the group can see it.

Ask, "Did you cut into the face-down cards?"

At the same time, stick your left thumb underneath the pile and flip the cards over (Illustration 108).

Gary says yes.

Instantly turn around. Once again the spectators are looking at your back and the cards in your left hand.

"Gary, please look at the card you cut to. And show it to only one other person. I don't want anyone to think that one of the spectators is helping me." Pause. "When you're done, put the card back on top and put the rest of the cards on top of it. Then take the deck into your hands and concentrate on your card."

Naturally, the card Gary looks at is the original top card of the deck. Since you know the card, gradually read his mind.

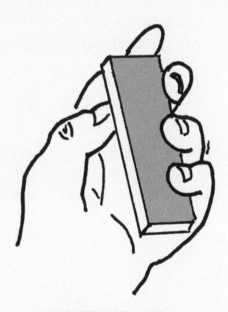

ILLUSTRATION 108

Out of My Hands

You need to know the bottom card. This is relatively easy. You can sneak a peek as you pass the deck from hand to hand. Or you can tilt the deck forward and get a glimpse as you hand it to a spectator (Illustration 109).

Let's assume that Linda has agreed to help out. Hand her the deck, saying, "Please cut off a pile of cards and put it on the table."

She does.

"Turn over the top card of those you're holding. Put it, face up, on top of the cards on the table."

She does.

"Put the rest of the cards you're holding on top of those on the table."

She follows your instructions perfectly.

"Now, Linda, please pick up the deck and fan through the cards so that only you can see the faces. Fan to the card you turned over. The card right after that is your card. Remember the

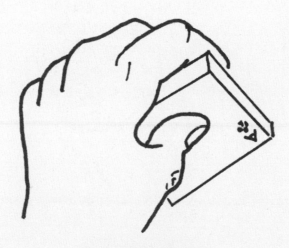

ILLUSTRATION 109

269

name of that card." Wait until she's ready. "Turn the face-down card over and give the deck a good shuffle."

Linda has looked at the original bottom card of the deck. With your usual dramatic presentation, read her mind.

My Variation

I recently read a book in which a simplified version of this really old principle was presented as a wonderful force. It would not fool a soul, of course. Who would be fooled? To paraphrase S.J. Perelman, "It's hard to imagine where you would find such a collection of addlepates and feebs."

Here is a variation that seems to fool people, however. You must know the name of the eighth card from the top of the deck.

Start by having Henry shuffle the deck. Take it back and turn it face up so that all can see the cards. Start fanning through the deck, saying, "The cards look pretty mixed up to me."

After fanning out ten cards or more, place these cards on top (the back of the deck). Fan through further. After you fan through several, take note of an inconspicuous card. Consider it as the first card, as you go on fanning. Continue counting to yourself as you fan through the cards. (Count in threes; it's less obvious.) When you reach eight, place all the cards you've fanned on top (the back of the deck).

That inconspicuous card you noted is now eighth from the top of the deck.

Fan through another large group of cards, but don't place them on top; simply close these up.

Say these exact words to Henry: "Name a number between one and ten." Chances are very strong that he'll name either seven or eight. If he names seven, deal seven cards into a pile, counting aloud. Without saying anything, hold the deck out to Henry. Point to the top card. He takes it and looks at it.

If Henry says eight, hand him the deck and ask him to count down to the eighth card and look at it.

If he names a number from two to six, you simply subtract that number from eight. For instance, if he chooses five, you subtract five from eight, getting three.

"Here's what I'd like you to do, Henry. Just count out your number, like this." As you utter the last sentence, deal three cards into a pile one by one. Drop the deck on top of the dealt cards. Pick up the entire deck and hand it to Henry. "Then look at the card that lies at your number."

He deals out five cards and then looks at the original eighth card from the top.

Similarly, if he chose the number two, you'd subtract two from eight, getting six. This time you demonstrate by dealing six cards into a pile. Drop the deck on top of the six. Pick up the entire pile and hand it to Henry. Again he gets to choose the eighth card from the top.

Understand that you're not going to have to do this very often; most of the time Henry will choose either seven or eight.

But what if that sneaky guy chooses nine. Nothing to it. You'll resort to an old ruse. Spread out three cards from the top of the deck. Deal them onto the table into a loose pile, saying, "Three." Take two more and place them on top of those on the table, saying, "And two is five." Add two more, saying, "And two is seven." And toss on a final two, saying, "And two is nine."

Promptly even up the pile and place it on top of the deck. Extend the deck toward Henry, indicating that he should take the top card. That top card, of course, is actually the original eighth from the top.

Unless Henry is hearing impaired, he will not choose one or ten. After all, you *did* say "*between* one and ten."

Henry can put the deck together and shuffle the cards as you gradually read his mind.

Five-and-Ten

Following a similar principle to that mentioned in the previous force, get a known card to the *seventh* position from the top.

Ask Mary Lee to help out. Say to her, "Mary Lee, give a number between five and ten." The phrasing restricts her choices to six, seven, eight, and nine.

If the choice is six, deal off six cards one at a time and place the next card aside. If the choice is seven, hand her the deck, saying, "Please count down to the seventh card."

If the choice is eight, deal the cards by twos onto the table, one pair on top of the other. "Two, four, six, eight." Place the packet on top of the deck, and then stall for a moment. You might say something like, "You had complete freedom of choice of any number you wished." Extend the deck toward Mary Lee for the removal of the top card.

If the choice is nine, deal the cards in groups of three, saying, "Three, six, nine." Place the packet on top of the deck and follow the procedure indicated when the choice is eight.

In each instance, Mary Lee has chosen the original seventh card from the top. And, of course, you're delighted to read her mind.

Let's Prognosticate

This spectacular Michael Jeffreys invention is perfect, if you don't mind ruining a deck of cards. Let's assume that you're looking forward to a special occasion and that the guest of honor will be John Jones. Prepare a deck of cards like this: Count off 26 cards. With a marking pen, print *John Jones* on the back of all 26.

On the backs of the other 26, print a variety of names—making sure you include both first and last names. Place these face up onto the table. On top of them, place the *John Jones* cards face up. You're ready.

At the celebration, approach Mr. Jones. Remove the cards from your pocket so that they are face up.

"Mr. Jones, I wonder if you'd be kind enough to touch one of these cards."

Slowly fan the cards from the uppermost down. Jones should have no trouble touching one of the 26 *John Jones* cards.

If you feel daring, you might name the card selected, and then close up the cards. Say, "If you like, you might touch a different card. It's strictly up to you, sir."

Again fan through slowly, making sure he touches one of the *John Jones* cards.

But let's assume that you don't feel daring. Have Jones remove the card from the deck.

Turn the deck so that it's face down. Slowly fan through at least 20 cards from the top. "Notice, sir, that on the backs of the cards are different names."

Since you're showing the various names, progress through the deck will be quite slow. Jones should be happy when you stop after 20 cards.

Close up the deck and stick it into your pocket.

"Out of all those different names, I wonder which one you chose, sir."

Jones turns the card over. On the other side, of course, is his name.

Take the card from him. Remove the deck from your pocket and replace the card somewhere in the middle.

But won't Jones want to examine the deck? Maybe. Give it to him. On the backs of all the cards are different names. Really?

Yes, you rapscallion. You took another deck and wrote on the backs of 26 cards all the names you had put down originally and added different names to the other 26. The trick deck was in your right-hand pocket originally. This deck was in your left-hand pocket. When you placed the trick deck in your left pocket, you simply released it and gripped the other deck. You then left your hand in your pocket as you said to Jones, "Out of all those different names, I wonder which you chose, sir."

Pause for a bit, giving Jones a chance to restore his senses. Then hold out your hand for the card as you remove the deck from your pocket.

It's a bit of trouble, but miracles aren't always easy.

Note: Suppose Jones examines the deck and notices that there is another card of the same value as the one he chose. Simple. Explain, "That's right. The one you chose is an extra card that I added to the deck. Amazing, eh?"

Two for One

Here we have two tricks that form a perfect routine. The first is the invention of Bob Hummer. Both tricks have appeared in other books of mine, but in this form they become twice as effective.

Part One:

To start, you have the deck shuffled. Take the cards back and begin dealing them into a face-down pile, counting to yourself. After you've dealt ten cards, say to Angela, "Please tell me when to stop."

Continue counting as you deal. When Angela says "stop," cease dealing. *But* make sure you have an even number of cards on the table. If, for instance, she says "stop" as you deal down the 15th card, deal one more to make sure you have an even number.

Let's suppose that Angela stops you after you've dealt 22 cards. Set the deck aside and pick up the 22 cards. Rapidly fan off exactly half the number of cards—in this instance, 11. Turn these face up. Shuffle the entire packet.

Hand the packet to Angela. "While I turn my back, shuffle these cards, Angela. When you're done, place the cards in my hand."

Turn away. Place your left hand behind your back for the placement of the cards. When she's done shuffling, Angela places the cards on your hand. Turn around so that you once more face the group.

Quickly count off 11 cards from the top of the packet. Turn your left hand over so that it's palm down; your right hand remains palm up (Illustration 110). Bring both piles forward and set them down.

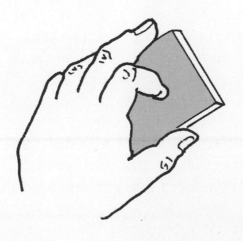

ILLUSTRATION 110

Update: You have counted off half the cards. These are brought forward in the right hand. The bottom half is turned over, and this half is brought forward reversed in the left hand.

"In that short time, I have managed to put the same number of face-up cards in each pile."

The piles are examined. Sure enough, each contains the same number of face-up cards.

The trick is strengthened by a repetition.

Part Two:

"It's very strange, but somehow or other I seem to have control over face-up cards. Let's try another experiment, this time in precognition. To start, I'll make a prediction, using two cards."

Fan through the deck, making sure no one else can see the faces. Remove two cards and place them face down onto the table. The total should be somewhere between 15 and 20. Let's assume that you remove a 9 and an 8, the total being 17. "My prediction is the total of these two cards."

Hand the deck to Augie, turn away, and say, "Augie, please make two piles of cards, about a dozen in each pile. But you don't need to have the same number in each pile." Pause. "Pick up one of the piles and turn some cards face up. You may turn over a group of cards or turn over cards at different places." Pause. "Fan through that pile and see how many cards you've turned over." Pause. "Set that pile down and pick up the other pile. Turn over that same number of cards in that pile. You can turn them over wherever you wish in that pile also."

When he is done, continue, "Please put one of the piles on top of the deck and hide the other pile."

Put your hands behind your back and ask him to give you the deck.

With the cards behind your back, face the spectators and say, "Let's see if I can make my prediction come true." Count off from the top the number of cards in your prediction and turn them face up on top. In this instance, you would count off 17 cards and turn them face up on top. The quickest way to count off the cards is to take them one under the other.

Bring the cards forward and tell the spectator to place his other pile on top. "The question is," you say, "how many face-up cards do we now have?"

Fan through the deck, tossing out and counting aloud the face-up cards as you come to them. When your helper turns over your two prediction cards, he finds that the total precisely matches the number of face-up cards.

Something Old, Something New

In Pensacola, Florida, I was fortunate enough to be able to associate with a wonderful group of magicians. Among them was John Braun, president of the local Society of American Magicians. At the meeting, John performed a clever variation of an old, old trick. Here it is, for your edification.

First, let me explain the original trick. Sneakily get a peek at the bottom card of the deck. Set the cards down on the table and ask Diane to cut off a pile. Point to the original bottom portion and say, "Please set these crosswise on top of the other pile." (See Illustration 111.)

ILLUSTRATION 111

Provide a bit of time misdirection by making this sort of comment: "You cut the cards exactly where you wanted, right?" It doesn't much matter what you say, as long as it makes some kind of sense and eats up a little time.

Say, "Lift off the packet, please, and look at the card you cut."

Diane lifts off the top packet and looks at the card you previously peeked at. She concentrates on the card as you divine the suit and value bit by bit.

What did John add to the trick? He has someone shuffle the cards. If they are giving the deck an overhand shuffle, he says, "Go ahead, give them a good riffle-shuffle."

There's a good chance the spectator will riffle-shuffle the ends together, giving you a peek at the bottom card. If this happens, say, "Fine. Just set the cards onto the table, please."

If the person *doesn't* give you a peek, have someone else come up and give the cards a shuffle. You may have to try yet a third person. In fact, John had to wait till the third person shuffled the cards before he caught his glimpse.

As soon as you get your peek, step back and provide the appropriate directions. Step away even farther as the spectator looks at the card and begins to concentrate.

A small variation, to be sure, but it makes the trick much more effective.

Coincidence Tricks

Very Little Turnover

How about a lively trick requiring no skill and with a wonderful surprise climax?

A little preparation is needed. Let's assume that you're going to use the two black queens. Put one face down on top. Turn the second card from the top face up. The third card is the other black queen, also face up.

Position from the top down: face-down black queen, any card face up, face-up black queen. (See Illustration 112.)

This should be your first trick. Remove the cards from the card case. Turn the deck face up. Fan through the face-up cards, saying, "Here we have an ordinary deck of marked cards." Stop before you get too close to the top.

Close up the cards, keeping them face up.

This is the Queen of Spades on Top of the Deck.

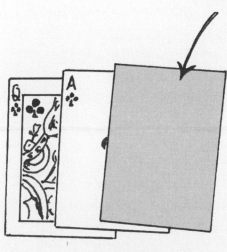

ILLUSTRATION 112

Marie is very agreeable, so she will undoubtedly agree to help out. "Marie, would you please cut off a pile of cards and place it *face down* onto the table."

She does.

"You may cut off more if you like, or put some back—whatever you choose."

Turn the remaining cards *face up* and place them right on top of the cards Marie cut off. "We'll just mark the spot."

So you have a face-down pile on the table, with a face-up pile on top of it.

Presumably you're marking the face-down pile with a face-up packet.

Why are you marking the spot? You have something very important to say: "Marie, was there any way at all that I could have influenced the spot at which you cut the cards?"

Of course not.

"Very well." Pick up the entire deck. Fan through the face-up cards until you come to the first face-down card. This is the queen that was originally third from the top of the deck. Below it is another face-down card. And below that is the other queen, face up.

Make sure you fan through the cards slowly enough so that you don't reveal the face-up queen.

Set the face-up cards onto the table. Hand Marie the face-down queen, again making sure you don't spread out the cards.

"Here's your chosen card, Marie."

Pick up the face-up cards on the table and place them *face down* on top of the deck. Presumably, the deck is now all face down.

"What card did you choose, Marie?"

She names it. Let's say that she got the QC.

"The queen of clubs? That's a very magical card. Please tap the top of the deck with it. Something wonderful might happen."

She taps the deck with the QC. You fan through the cards, showing that the QS is face up.

"Good for you, Marie. You caused the exact sister of the queen of clubs to turn face up."

Who Has a Match?

You may prefer this trick, based on the principle used in the trick just described.

As before, a bit of preparation is necessary. Remove from the deck two cards of the same value and color, plus an indifferent card. Let's suppose that you remove from the deck the black sixes. Place one six face up on top of the deck. On top of this, place the indifferent card face up. On top of all goes the other black six face down.

The position: a black six face down on top, below it a face-up card, below that a face-up black six.

Take the deck from the card case. Turn it face up.

Ask Tim to assist you. Fan through several cards from the bottom, letting Tim see the cards. Explain, "I have reversed one card in the deck. I wonder if you can, somehow, figure out which one it is. Let's start by having you cut off a packet of cards. To keep everything aboveboard, we'll have you cut from the face-up cards."

After he has cut off a group, say, "Is this how many you want? You can replace those and try again if you wish."

When he is done, have him place his cut-off pile *face down* onto the table. You're still holding a packet of face-up cards. Place this packet face up on top of the face-down pile on the table, saying, "So that's exactly the number of cards you want."

Your cards should be set on top so that they're offset a bit, as in Illustration 113.

"Remember now, we're looking for you to somehow identify the one face-up card in the deck."

Pick up both piles together, closing them up as you do so. Fan down through the face-up cards to the first face-down card. (Go slowly near the end, so that you don't fan out too many cards and reveal the true position.)

Set the face-up cards aside for the moment. Carefully remove the top card of those you're holding and place it face down before Tim.

Pick up the pile you just placed on the table and put it on top of the cards you're holding. Put the combined pile face down onto the table.

"Let's review. I put one card face up into the deck. You cut the cards exactly where you wished." Tap the card before Tim. "And here's the card you chose. Let's find the face-up card."

Fan through the deck to the face-up six—let's say the six of clubs. Take it out and place it next to Tim's card.

"And which card did you choose, Tim? Turn it over, please."

He turns over the six of spades.

"Unbelievable! You selected the perfect match."

ILLUSTRATION 113

It's All Up to You

Helen always displays an extraordinary interest in how you perform your tricks. It's time that she tried a little magic herself.

Hand Helen the deck, saying, "I'd like you to do a card trick for me, Helen. First, so no one will be suspicious, you should give the cards a good shuffle."

When she's done, continue, "Now fan out the cards in front of me so that I can see the faces. When I see one I like, I'll take it out."

Note the top two cards. If Helen fans right by them, spread the top several cards yourself so that you can get a look at the top two. Let's suppose that the top two are the 3C and the 4H. You are going to find a card that combines the two. In other words, you will choose either the 3H or the 4C. It doesn't matter which. Let's say that you pick out the 3H.

Take your selected card from the deck and set it face down onto the table.

"Close up the cards, please, Helen."

She does.

"Now you should do something mysterious, like deal the cards into a pile."

She deals about ten cards into a pile.

"And you should stop dealing whenever you feel like it."

Eventually, she stops dealing.

"Excellent. You'd better set the rest of the deck aside."

She does.

"Let's make it really complicated. Take your pile and deal it into *two* piles. First, deal a card here . . . " Indicate a spot on the table. " . . . and then a card here." Point to a spot next to the first spot. "Then continue dealing alternately, making two piles."

She does.

"Well, I can't think of anything else, Helen. Can you?"

No, she says. But if she does make a suggestion, negate it, saying, "No, I think that's a little too complicated."

Continue: "Let's see . . . why don't you turn over the top card of each pile."

She does.

"I'll be darned," you declare, "a heart and a three. In other words, a three of hearts."

Turn over the card you chose.

Note: If the top two cards are of the same value or suit, tell Helen, "I think the cards should be shuffled some more, Helen." She shuffles, and everything is fine. But suppose the two top cards are again of the same value or suit. Tell her the same thing. This could be very humorous, since everyone assumes that you're just being amusing.

Another Way

Let's follow that up with a trick with a similar climax, but a much different method.

This time, let's work our magic on Raymond. Hand the deck to Raymond, asking him to shuffle. When he's done, take the deck, saying, "I'll have to find the perfect card for you to stick into the deck."

With the cards face up, quickly fan through to the end, noting the top card. Also, take a look at the bottom card. Let's suppose that the top card is the 8C, and the bottom card is the AH. You need to combine the value of one of these with the suit of the other. Look through the deck and remove either the 8H or the AC. Let's assume that you take out the AC. Hand the card, face down, to Raymond.

"This should be an absolutely suitable card for you to stick into the deck. Please push it into the deck partway."

Hold the deck out face down. Raymond sticks the card partially into the deck. Naturally, since you handed him the card face down, he sticks it into the deck face down.

"I'm sorry, Raymond, it's supposed to be face up."

Fan down to the protruding card with both hands palm up. Separate the right hand from the left (Illustration 114). On top of the cards in the left hand is the card that Raymond just pushed into the deck. Turn the left hand palm down. This brings these cards face up (Illustration 115). Put the protruding card face up on top of the face-down cards in the right hand. The right thumb assists in taking the card (Illustration 116).

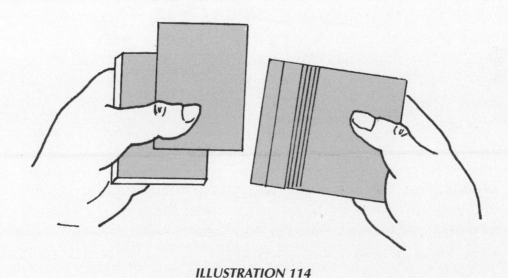

ILLUSTRATION 114

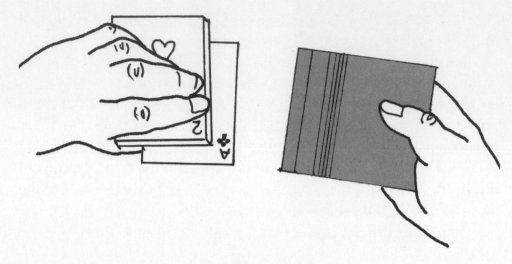

ILLUSTRATION 115

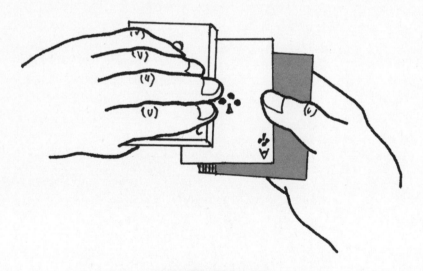

ILLUSTRATION 116

Turn the left hand palm up. The cards in the left hand are now face down and the AC is face up on top of the face-down cards in the right hand. Place the cards that are in your left hand face down on top of the face-up selection.

It all seems very natural. But the face-up card is now between the original top and bottom cards.

Set the deck down. It's time to help the group forget about what just happened and to build to a climax.

"Raymond, you could have stuck your card in anywhere. But you chose that particular spot. Let's see if you managed to accomplish anything really mysterious."

Pick up the deck. Fan through and remove, in a group of three, the face-up card and the card on either side of it. Set the three cards onto the table (Illustration 117).

"You shoved the ace of clubs into the deck. Let's see the other two cards."

Turn over the other two cards. Tap the club. "Here we have the eight of clubs, and your card is a club."

Tap the AH. "Here we have the ace of hearts, and your card is an ace."

Tap the AH. "Ace of . . . " Tap the 8C. " . . . clubs."

ILLUSTRATION 117

287

Pause. "I can't believe it, Raymond. You found the two cards that match your card. Good going!"

Just a Little More

I worked out a variation on the preceding trick that is very effective. Perhaps you'll like it also.

Tracy plays bridge quite often, so she would be the perfect assistant. Hand her the deck and ask her to give it a good shuffle.

Take the cards back, saying, "Tracy, I'd like you to name any card at all."

After some thought, she names a card. Let's say that she names the KS.

"I'll find it for you."

Start fanning through the deck, faces toward yourself. After fanning out 20 cards or so, cut the cards you've fanned off to the top. This is to throw off suspicion when you cut the cards later.

Continue fanning. You're looking for a king (other than the KS), with a spade on one side of it. Your chances are excellent. When you find the match you're looking for, cut between the cards. This puts a K on the top and a spade on the bottom, or vice versa.

Start all over, fanning through the deck, this time really looking for the KS. When you find it, take it out of the deck. Hold it up so that all can see the face. Hand the card to Tracy *face down*.

"Here's your card, Tracy. Please push it into the deck partway."

She puts the card in face down. As in the previous trick, you turn the card face up, and eventually show that she has located two cards that match her selection.

This is quite a powerful effect, so I recommend that you don't fool with it. If, for example, you can't find a spade and a king together, *don't* fiddle with the cards, trying to arrange them properly. Instead, perform the previous trick. Hand the deck to Tracy, saying, "I have a better idea, Tracy. Shuffle the deck, and then *I'll* pick out a card for you to use."

Continue performing "Another Way."

Dynamic Duo

This clever trick was developed by Bill Martin and mathematical wizard Martin Gardner.

A bit of preparation is necessary. Remove from the deck one card of each value—the suits are irrelevant. Set these up so the highest card (king) is on top and the lowest (ace) is on the bottom. Place the rest of the deck on top of these. The result is that the bottom 13 cards are set up like this:

K Q J 10 9 8 7 6 5 4 3 2 A

The ace is the bottom card.

You're ready to roll.

You'll need someone to assist who will do a good job of riffle-shuffling the cards, so you'd better select Edith, who plays bridge nearly every afternoon.

Set the deck onto the table. Say to Edith, "Please cut off about half the cards, Edith."

She does.

"Now give those a good shuffle."

She shuffles.

"Turn your packet face up, Edith. Hold that in one hand. Take the other packet *face down* in the other hand. Now riffle-shuffle the two packets together."

When she finishes, there should be a fairly even mix of face-up and face-down cards. Take the deck from Edith and fan the cards out so that she can see the cards that were originally face down, including your setup.

"I think the cards are well mixed."

She will not notice the setup.

Spread the deck out on the table so that your setup is face down. Make sure that all the cards near the bottom are spread out so that you can tell all the cards in your face-down setup. As you will see, this is quite important.

"Edith, please look over the face-up cards and pick out any one you wish."

She picks a card. Have her place it aside on the table. Let's suppose that she chooses a three.

"Let's see if I can pick a good card."

Count *up* to the third face-down card from the bottom. It, too, is a three. Remove it and place it face down next to Edith's choice.

"Pick another one, Edith."

She does. Have her place it a little distance from her first choice. If she takes a card of the same value as her first choice, tell her, "No, you've already taken one of those, Edith. Try something different."

But she's very cooperative today, so say, "That's an excellent card. Maybe *I* can find a good one also."

Again count from the bottom to a card that will match Edith's. (If the second card is higher than the first, you will have to count to one card less than the value of Edith's selection.) Place this card next to Edith's second choice.

Gather up the cards on the table, placing the face-up cards face down. You don't want to leave any evidence of your setup. As you do this, chat about the present situation. You might say, "So, you've chosen two cards, Edith, and I've chosen two cards. I have no idea of what I've chosen except that I had a strong feeling that they were good cards. Did you have that same feeling about the ones that you picked?" She responds. "Well, let's see what we accomplished."

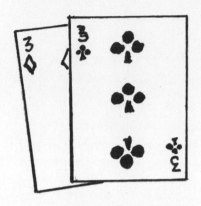

ILLUSTRATION 118

Turn over your first choice, placing it partially on Edith's card (Illustration 118). "My goodness, they match. Let's check the other one."

Turn over your second choice and, as before, place it on Edith's second choice.

"Two matches! You did an incredible job, Edith."

Location Tricks

Don't Take That Tone with Me

There's nothing wrong with an old-time trick—especially a good one. And more especially, if you can patch it up a bit and give it a new lease on life. Here's one that's a real fooler.

You'll need to prepare a little. Remove all the clubs from the deck. Place six on top of the deck and seven on the bottom. Take any three cards from the middle of the deck and put them on the bottom.

Since Paul is quite the wheeler-dealer, start by handing him the deck and saying, "Paul, please deal out six cards in a face-down row."

He does (Illustration 119).

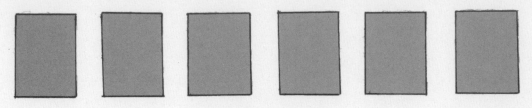

ILLUSTRATION 119

"In the same way, deal another six on top of them. Then just continue on, all the way through the deck."

When Paul gets to the last four cards, tell him, "Just set those aside, Paul. We won't need them."

If he has already dealt one or two of the four on top of the piles, just pick them off the piles and add them to those Paul has already set aside.

On the table are six eight-card piles. A club is at the top and bottom of each pile.

"I'm going to turn away, Paul. While I'm not watching, please take a card from the middle of any of the piles. Look at it and show it around."

Turn your back while Paul does his duty.

"Now place that card on top of any one of the piles. Then gather up the piles one on top of the other . . . in any order you wish."

Paul is done at last. Turn back to the group. Have Paul give the deck a complete cut. Others may cut the deck as well.

"Believe it or not, Paul, through years of experience I can tell when a person names his chosen card. Now that's no great trick if I ask you to name your card and then say, 'Yep, that's your card.' Nor would it be wonderful if I told you to name three cards with one of them being your chosen card. After all, one out of three isn't so great. But I'm going to ask you to name all the cards in the deck one by one, and—from the tone of your voice—I'll be able to tell your chosen card. Come to think of it, you may not have to go all the way through the deck. Would you start naming the cards, please, Paul. You can go fairly fast."

Of course he can. You're listening to hear clubs named. Chances are, he'll mention two clubs in a row at least once before he gets to the chosen card. How can you tell when he gets there? Easy. He'll mention a club, another card, and then another club. That card between the two clubs is the one chosen.

Paul might say, "Seven of hearts, eight of spades, two of clubs, three of diamonds, six of clubs, nine of hearts, queen of . . . "

"Did you say three of diamonds?"

"Yes, I did."

"Just as I thought. That's your card."

Double Discovery

Charles Jordan, I think, came up with the original idea. It has been expanded on by many writers, but the original idea is still very strong. I have added a few notions which lead the spectators to believe that two chosen cards are hopelessly lost.

Start by handing the deck to Estelle and asking her to shuffle the cards. When she finishes, ask Claude to take the deck. "Please deal quite a few cards into a pile, Claude. Stop whenever you wish."

As he deals, pretend to pay no attention. Actually, count the cards mentally. For, in a moment, Estelle will turn a card face up and place it into this group. The number of face-down cards *must* be even.

So if you mentally count 21, for instance, you say to Estelle, "Please pick up the pile that Claude just dealt out. Turn one of the cards face up—any card you wish." Now an even number of cards is face down and one card is face up.

Suppose Claude deals out 20 cards—an even number. Say to Estelle, "Please take the rest of the deck from Claude. Take any card from this group. Turn the card face up and add it to the group that Claude just dealt out." Again, an even number of cards is face down and one card is face up.

One way or the other, you must remember the number of face-down cards. The remainder of the deck is set aside.

"That face-up card is going to help each of you choose a card."

Have each spectator shuffle the packet. Take the cards and fan down to the face-up card. Tilt the cards up so that Estelle can see the faces (Illustration 120). "Estelle, I'd like you to remember the card that's on my side of the card you stuck into the deck. In other words, look at the card that's face to face with that card." Make sure she remembers the right card.

Let Claude see the faces of the cards. "Claude, I'd like you to remember the card that's on your side of the card that Estelle stuck into the deck. In other words, look at the card that's back to back with that card." Make sure that he gets a good look at the right card.

"Please don't forget your cards; that would ruin everything." Set the packet onto the table. "Now I'd like each of you to give the packet a complete cut."

They do so.

You pick up the packet, saying, "I think I'd better mix them up even more."

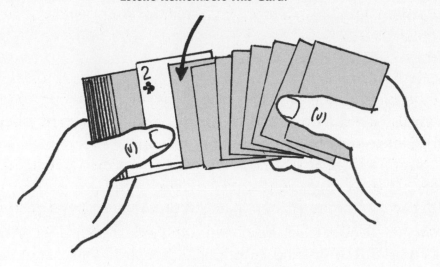

Estelle Remembers This Card.

ILLUSTRATION 120

You're about to perform the "Up-and-Down Shuffle," described on page 19. In this instance, pass the cards from your left hand to your right, one at a time. Push the top card upward, the second one down, the third card upward, the fourth down, and so on through the packet. When you're done, strip out the lower section of cards (second, fourth, sixth, and so on). Place this section on top of the other section. Even up the cards. Set the pile onto the table. Alternatively, you push the first card *downward*, the next card *upward*, and so on. And, after you strip out the lower section of cards, you may place this section on top.

Now that you know how to do the shuffle, continue: "I'm going to give the cards an up-and-down shuffle. Estelle, should I push the top card up or down?"

Do whatever she indicates. The next card goes in the opposite direction, and so on. You strip out the lower section.

Turn to Claude. Indicate the pile you stripped out, saying, "Should I place these on top or on the bottom of the others?" Do whatever he says.

"It might be a good idea to have the cards mixed a little more. How about each one of you giving the cards one more cut."

They do.

"We'd better try another up-and-down shuffle."

Again, let Estelle choose whether the first card should go up or down, and let Claude pick whether the stripped-out cards should go above or below the others.

Set the packet onto the table and invite Estelle and Claude to cut the cards yet again.

After they finish, pick up the packet and fan through it, passing the face-down cards from your left hand to your right. When you come to the face-up card, place the cards that are in your right hand onto the table. The face-up card is on top of the cards remaining in your left hand (Illustration 121).

"We won't need this any more," you say.

ILLUSTRATION 121

Take the card with your right hand and place it with the discarded remainder of the deck. With your right hand, take the cards remaining in your left hand and place them onto the packet on the table.

In effect, you've removed the face-up card and have cut the cards at that point.

One of the selected cards is at the same number from the top of the packet as the other is from the bottom of the packet. And you know what the number is.

You know the total number of cards in the packet—in our example, 20. Divide this number by four. If the number won't divide evenly by four, add two to it and then divide by four. Suppose the number is 18. You divide 18 by 4, but it will not divide evenly. You add 2 to 18, giving you 20; 20 divided by 4 is 5. So the selected cards are 5 from the top and 5 from the bottom.

Suppose the packet contains 28 cards. You divide by 4, getting 7. The selected cards are 7 from the top and 7 from the bottom.

There are many ways in which you can reveal the cards. My favorite method is to milk the cards—that is, taking the top and bottom cards together and placing them into a pile. (See "Milking the Cards," page 18.) Repeat the procedure. Continue fairly rapidly until you're three deals from the chosen two. Suppose that the chosen cards are at the seventh position. Milk cards four times rapidly. Stop and say to *both* assistants, "Tell me when to stop, please."

Fairly slowly, deal one and then another. If someone says "stop" at this point, you milk the next two but continue to hold them. Set the rest of the packet down. The top card of the two is Claude's; the other is Estelle's.

Ask Claude to name his card. He names it and you show it. Ask Estelle to name hers; sure enough, you also have her card.

If neither says "stop" when you've dealt off the next two, look at the couple inquiringly. If neither responds, say, "How about these two cards?" If one or both utter an affirmative, proceed as described above. If not, say, "I think they might do." Set the cards in your hand aside. Pick up the two chosen cards and proceed as described.

With two persons involved, you have an excellent chance of one of them stopping you appropriately. But if not, it's still quite an astonishing trick.

Note: As you have undoubtedly figured out, it doesn't matter what decisions are made on the up-and-down shuffles. If you perform two shuffles, everything will turn out properly.

Another way to finish is to turn the packet face up and begin milking the cards. Say, "If one of you sees your card, please stop me." When you are stopped, show that the lower card is also a chosen one.

The Long Count

I am convinced that there's nothing wrong with trying to revive a wonderful device that has been terribly neglected for the past several decades. I'm referring to the "faced deck." That is, unbeknownst to the spectators, the upper half of the deck is face down and the lower half is face up.

But before you "face" the deck, there's quite a bit more to do. Start off by having someone shuffle the deck. Sam is always helpful, so ask him to give a hand.

He shuffles the cards thoroughly and gives the deck back.

"Now, Sam, I'd like you to think of a number from one to five. Got one?"

He does.

"I'll show you the cards one by one. Please note the card that lies at your number. And—here comes the tough part—please remember both your card and the number."

Avert your head. Hold up the top card so that Sam can see it. Announce, "One."

Take the next card from the deck. Hold it *in front of* the first card as you show it to Sam. Say, "Two."

The third card goes in front of the other two. Show it to Sam and say, "Three."

Continue until you've shown the top five cards, announcing each number as you show it.

Because of the way you've shown the cards, the top five go back on top in the same order as they were before.

It's time to ask Angie to also help out.

"Angie, please think of a number from ten to twenty. Do you have one?" She does. "Good. I'm now going to put the deck behind my back and make a certain clever arrangement."

Place the cards behind your back. Turn the top half face up and place it on the bottom. The half in which Sam's card lies is now face up below the face-down half. Bring the deck forward. Be careful not to tilt it upward so that spectators can see the bottom card.

"First of all, Sam, let me show you that your card is no longer at its original number. What number did you pick?"

Suppose he says four.

You deal off four cards into a face-down pile. Turn over the last card dealt, showing that it is not Sam's card.

"Angie, what number did you choose?"

She names her number. Let's suppose that it's 13. Mentally subtract Sam's number from Angie's number. In this instance, you'd subtract 4 from 13, getting 9.

You have already dealt four cards from the top and turned over the fourth card, proving that it's not the chosen one. Say, "All right, this is number four." Turn the card face down. Continue dealing, saying aloud, "Five, six, seven, eight, nine."

You have stopped as the result of subtracting Sam's number from Angie's number. Drop your left hand to your side. At the same time, tap the ninth card, saying, "That's my lucky number." Turn over the ninth card. Look at Sam and say, "I hope it didn't turn out to be your selected card."

As you almost complete the sentence, bring the hand back up, only with the palm down (Illustration 122). You have reversed the deck. The half containing Sam's card is now in the top face-down group. As you converse with the group, take the deck into your palm-up right hand. Then casually place it into your left hand, in the dealer's position.

Turn the ninth card face down, saying, "So that's nine." Continue dealing, saying aloud, "Ten, eleven, twelve, thirteen. Thirteen was your number, right, Angie?"

Right.

"And what was your card, Sam?"

He names it. You turn over card number 13, the last one you dealt out. Somehow you have managed to bring Sam's card to the number chosen by Angie.

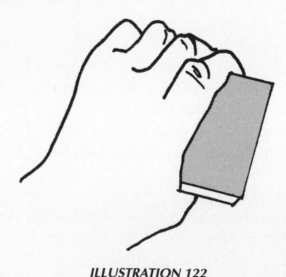

ILLUSTRATION 122

Review: (1) Sam thinks of a number from 1 to 5. You show him the first five cards, numbering them aloud. Sam is to remember his number and the card that lies at that number. The five cards are returned to the deck in their original order.

(2) Angie thinks of a number from 10 to 20.

(3) You put the deck behind your back. The top half is placed face-up on the bottom.

(4) Bring the deck back to the front. Ask Sam his number. Deal that many cards into a pile. Show that his card is no longer at that number.

(5) Ask Angie for her number. Subtract Sam's number from Angie's number. Suppose Sam chose 3 and Angie chose 17. Subtract 3 from 17, getting 14. You have already dealt out 3 cards. Continue dealing to 14, which happens to be your lucky number. As this card is revealed, you drop your hand and bring it back up, reversing the deck.

(6) Continue the deal to 17. Show that the 17th card is Sam's.

Note: The deck is still faced; how do you fix it?

Do a trick requiring that a card be chosen. Fan out the top several cards, asking a spectator to choose one. If the spectator is unreceptive and seems intent on taking a card farther down in the deck, choose someone else.

Once the card is chosen, turn away, saying, "Please show the card to the rest of the group."

Your back is to the group; you might as well straighten out the deck. Turn back and complete your trick.

Impromptu Liar's Trick

A card is chosen and returned to the deck. The magician asks the spectator to name a color—either red or black. The spectator may give the same color as the chosen card or a different color. The magician spells out the answer, dealing out one card from the deck for each letter in the spelling. The card on the last letter of the spelling is turned over; it is the same color as that of the chosen card—regardless of whether the spectator has lied or told the truth.

The same procedure is followed for the suit and value of the chosen card. At last the final card is turned over. It is the chosen card.

A wonderful trick, and, in most instances, it requires a modest setup of the deck. But here we have my invention, a sort of satirical version of the same trick.

Don's reputation is that he's very good at exaggeration, so he'd be the ideal helper for this trick. Hand him the deck and ask him to give the cards a good shuffle.

Have Don choose a card and return it, using the method described in "Simplicity Itself," on page 11. This means that you know the card above the one chosen.

Turn the deck so that the faces are toward you. Fan through till you come to the "key" card, the one just beyond the chosen card. *Starting with the key card*, count eleven cards as you continue fanning through the face-up deck. Your best bet is to count the cards in threes and, after you have counted nine, add two more cards to those in your right hand.

Separate the cards after counting eleven. Tilt the deck down so that all can see the faces of the cards. Place the cards that are in your right hand below those in the left hand, so that when the deck is face down, the cards that were in your right hand would be on top. Even up the cards.

The result of this is that the chosen card is now 12th from the top of the deck. But, after the cut, keep the cards face up, for you are about to offer the goofiest excuse ever for fanning through the cards.

"See this card?" you say, calling attention to the card at the face of the deck. All can see the card. "I can tell you right now that *this* is not your card." Pause, as though waiting for approval. "Now if I could do that fifty more times, we'd have a *real* trick. But let's try something else."

Turn the deck face down. "Let's play the liar's game. The liar's game is to lie sometimes and to tell the truth at other times so that no one else can tell the difference. Sound exciting? You bet. I'm going to ask you some questions, Don, and when you answer, you can either lie or tell the truth—whatever you want. Ready?"

He is.

"Is your card red or black—lie or tell the truth."

It doesn't matter what he says. If he says red, you spell it out, dealing one card face down for each letter in the spelling, forming a pile on the table. If he says black, you say, "Maybe yes, maybe no. I'm going to spell red." And you proceed to spell out red, as described.

"Let's see what we got." Turn over the next card. Whatever the color is, name it and say, "Just as I thought." Place the card face down onto the pile.

Pause. "Name a suit, Don. You can name the actual suit of your card, or some other suit. Clubs, hearts, spades, or diamonds—what do you pick?"

He names a suit. If he names clubs, you say, "Excellent!" Spell it out, adding the cards to the top of the pile. If he names another suit, say, "Oh, sure! Well, I'll just spell out clubs." Proceed to spell it out.

You turn over the next card and comment on it. Here is where your ability to ad-lib will sparkle. It doesn't really matter what you say, but it should have some relevancy to the card turned over. If it turns out to be a club, fine. Say, "Just as I expected."

If it's a spade and Don named something different, you might say, "See? I knew it would be a black card."

If it's a red card, you might comment, "Notice, Don, that we got the *opposite* color. Now we're getting somewhere."

Turn the card face down on top of the pile. "Was your card high or low, Don—lie or tell the truth?"

Whatever Don says, you say, "It definitely is a low card, so we'll spell out 'low.'"

Turn over the next card. To some extent, your remarks will be based on what you've said previously. For example, if you previously mentioned that you got the opposite color, you might either say, "Ah, naturally, we once more have the opposite—a low card, rather than a high card," or, "Ah, naturally—just as I predicted—we get a low card this time." If the card is what Don mentioned, you could say, "Congratulations, Don—exactly as you said."

In each instance, you have something to say. The idea is to pretend that each card that you turn up is exactly what you expected. Sometimes there is a certain logic to it all. For instance, on occasion, every single card you turn over will be inaccurate—which seems to be your exact intention. Sometimes, every card you turn over will match the spectator's choice—which is *real* magic.

Now comes some real sneakiness. If you ask Don to choose the value of a card, chances are strong that the choice will be seven, eight, or—occasionally—three. All three of these are spelled with five letters.

And you have two additional chances: (1) Don may name queen, which is also spelled with five letters. (2) He may name five, which can simply be counted out, rather than spelled.

"We should start getting a little more truthful, don't you think, Don? At least I should get more truthful. Name the value of a card, Don. Again, it could be the same as your card, or it could be a lie."

Quite often, Don will name seven, eight, or three. And perhaps he'll choose queen or five. If he happens to choose one of these, continue, "As I say, let's deal out your exact choice." Spell out the value, and turn over the next card.

But suppose Don is not quite normal and chooses a different value, such as four. Say, "Oh, what a silly choice, Don. Let's try lucky seven." Spell out seven, and turn over the next card.

If the card turns out to be of the same value as Don named, you obviously have a miracle feat. If it turns out to be the same value as the one *you* chose, you also have a miracle feat. Remember when you fanned through the deck to bring Don's selected card 12th from the top? Well, the card *before* the key card is the selected card. If your memory is pretty good, you could make a mental note of the value of the chosen card. Once in a great while, this will come in handy. For instance, you count down five cards and turn over the next and it turns out to be the same value as the one selected. If this happens, say something like this: "My goodness, it *is* time for the truth. Here we have a card that's exactly the same value as the one you chose."

Suppose that the card is the same suit as the selected card. "A heart. Oh, sure! *Now* we get a card of the same suit as the one you chose."

This might make the trick even stronger, but you don't really have to note the selected card. Nevertheless, you absolutely must make some sort of comment, just as you've done the other three times. You might comment on the card's relationship to the spectator's choice or your choice. For instance, if the card is a four and the spectator chose six, you could say, "You chose six and this card is a four. Amazing! They're both even numbers." Or you could be amazed that you chose an odd number and that the card is also odd. Or you could be absolutely flabbergasted that you both chose an odd number, yet the card is even; what a coincidence!

As you can see, what you say doesn't have to be clever; it just has to be prompt.

Turn the card face down on top of the pile. *Pick up the pile and place it on top of the deck.* As you're doing this, say, "It's time for the truth, Don. Both you and I have to be truthful, all right?"

Of course it is.

"So we'll spell out . . . *the truth.*"

Spell out *the truth* exactly as you did the other words. Take the next card from the deck and hold it out face down. "The truth now, Don. What was the name of your card?"

He names it. You turn it over. It's the chosen card.

"I knew this would work. Remember, I told you that this is the liar's game? Well, nobody's a better liar than I am."

The truth is . . . you're terrific.

Notes: (1) Here are the words you spell out, in order:
(color): RED
(suit): CLUBS
(low or high): LOW
(value): SEVEN (also possible: EIGHT, THREE, QUEEN)
THE TRUTH

(2) Hard to believe, but with all the counting, a couple of cards could get stuck together or something else could go wrong. In the unlikely event that this occurs and you end up with the wrong card, you might say, "As I said, we need the truth. And to tell you the truth, I don't know why I even tried that trick." Immediately swing into a trick that will work.

(3) When you read this long description, you might get the impression that this trick is difficult. It's not. Yes, you'll need to run through it several times before trying it out on friends and

then strangers. But once you master it, you'll find that it's quite easy and moves along rapidly.

What Else?

Dave Altman seems to specialize in tricks with unusual endings. Here is one I think you'll like.

The only requirement is that you get a peek at the top card. You might try the method recommended at the beginning of "The Way Back," on page 23. Be sure to remember that top card, for it's your key card.

To begin, pick out someone who plays enough cards to be able to give the deck a good riffle-shuffle. Andy would be perfect.

Set the deck onto the table. Tell Andy, "Please cut off about half the cards. Look at the card you cut off and show it around."

Andy shows his friends the bottom card of the packet he cut off.

You turn your back and continue: "Please turn the cards on the table face up. Now do one riffle-shuffle, shuffling the *face-down* cards into the *face-up* cards. When you're done, set the deck onto the table." Pause. "Is the deck on the table? Good. Give the deck a complete cut."

You can have it cut again if you wish.

Turn back to the group. Pick up the deck and turn it over. Spread the cards out so that all can be seen. Both your key card and the chosen card will be among the face-up cards.

As you spread the cards, note your key card. Following it will be a face-down card, or perhaps several face-down cards. But the first face-up card beyond it is the chosen card. Don't pause at it, of course, but be sure to remember it.

Let me quote Dave:

"Now comes the fun. To reveal the spectator's card, have the spectator pull out from the tabled fan four face-down cards that he *feels* have some connection with the noted card. The magician turns them face up and, whatever their value/suit/pictures, uses them to pinpoint the noted card.

"For example, assume that the noted card is the 7S, and the four cards selected are 10S, JH, KD, 3S. Discard the two picture cards, explaining that they have no numerical value. Point out that the two remaining cards are spades, and that 10 − 3 = 7, so that the noted card must be the 7S! Congratulate the spectator on picking out the four appropriate cards."

Dave gives another example: The noted card is the QC, and the four pulled-out cards are 4D, QH, 9S, AD.

Say, "You'll notice that only one of these cards is a picture card, the queen. Also, every suit is represented except clubs. Therefore, the chosen card must be the queen of clubs."

Dave tells us, "The more ridiculous or far-fetched the pinpointing, the more the fun. Enjoy, and don't forget to congratulate the spectator."

Notes: (1) Obviously, if you wish, you can eliminate Dave Altman's clever ending and simply locate the selected card and name it, or produce it in some other way.

(2) I really like Dave's method of locating the chosen card. But, if you prefer, you can simply force a card and use Dave's method of revealing the name. (See the first four tricks under the heading "Mental Tricks," on pages 23 to 33.)

Piles of Magic

To perform this trick, you must be able to get a sneaky peek at the bottom card of the deck. I find it fairly easy to do as I riffle-shuffle the deck while standing up. Others may prefer to simply tilt the deck a bit while chatting with spectators. Yet others might find it convenient to turn the deck face up and quickly spread the cards, saying, "Note that it's an ordinary deck." In the process, they take note of the bottom card.

Now that you know the bottom card, you're ready for Evelyn to assist you. "Think of a number from two to ten, Evelyn." She does. "Please remember that number."

Turn away from the group.

"Evelyn, please look at the card that lies at your number from the top. Let everyone else see that card. Be sure to keep that card at your number from the top."

When Evelyn is ready, continue, "Evelyn, please give the deck a complete cut."

She does.

"You're about to deal out some cards, Evelyn. When you do, deal them slowly and quietly so that I'll have no idea as to the number. Now start by dealing into a row the same number of cards as your number from the top. For example, if your number were three, you'd deal three cards into a row, from left to right. Be sure to take a little extra time so that I won't get the number."

She finishes.

"Now please wait till I complete all these directions. In the same way as you dealt before, deal out one more card on top of each one you dealt out. Continue dealing like this until all the deck is dealt out. You can start now. Let me know when you're done."

When she's done, continue: "Gather up the piles one on top of the other in any order you wish."

Finally Evelyn announces that she's finished. You turn back to the group and take the deck. Fan through with the faces toward yourself. The card to the left of the one you peeked at is the chosen card. In other words, as you fan through the face-up deck, the chosen card is the one immediately after the one you peeked at. Remove the selected card from the deck and place it face down onto the table. Ask Evelyn to name her card. When she does, you turn over the selection.

It hardly seems possible, but the method of dealing always ensures that the card you peeked at will be on top of the chosen card.

Meet Madam Flaboda

You go through a bit of business at the beginning of this trick; after this, the spectator handles the cards throughout. Apparently, the trick can't possibly work. But it certainly does, and quite amusingly.

My friend Wally Wilson has a mysterious invisible acquaintance named Madam Flaboda. She frequently helps him with his magic tricks. Here we have an excellent example. I have changed the working slightly.

Incidentally, I present two possible ways to present the beginning portion of the trick. The one I present first is simple and deceptive. The other method, which is also quite effective, appears in the note at the end of the trick.

To start, you must have a full deck. Have Gloria shuffle the cards. Take the deck back and turn it face up.

"The cards are well mixed, as you can see."

Fan through the face-up cards, mentally counting them in threes. When you reach 18, separate the two face-up groups, holding one section in each hand. Turn to Gloria, saying, "You did an excellent job, Gloria."

Set the pile of 18 cards onto the table face down. Set the remainder of the deck face down next to it. Point to this pile, saying, "Please cut off a pile, Gloria, and put it on the table."

She does.

"Nice job, Gloria. Now let's select a pile together. First, I'll take a pile."

Pick up one of the piles that does *not* contain the 18 cards. "Now you take one."

If Gloria picks up the 18-card pile, say, "Excellent," and proceed with the trick. If she picks the other pile, hold out your empty hand. She gives you the pile. Indicate the 18-card pile. "Please pick it up."

Set the piles you're holding back onto the table.

Gloria is now holding the 18-card pile. You tell her to take it and shuffle it. Add, "Please take a look at the top card of the pile. Then set the pile onto the table."

She is then told to pick up one of the other piles, pick it up, shuffle it, and place it on top of the one she just placed on the table. She is also to shuffle the third pile and place it on top of all.

The chosen card is now 35th from the top.

"I'm sorry, Gloria, but I have to ask you to do a bit of work. Would you please deal the deck into four piles, going alternately."

She deals out the cards as requested (Illustration 123). Each pile contains 13 cards.

You apparently fall into a trance—your eyes are almost shut and your voice is fainter and almost a monotone. "I think I hear the voice of Madam Flaboda. She has volunteered to help me with this effect. "What do you want, Madam Flaboda?" Pause. "Madam Flaboda tells me that you should pick up this pile . . . "

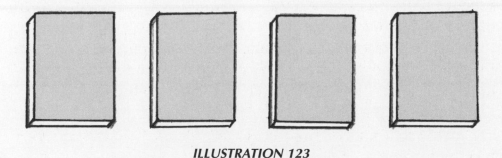

ILLUSTRATION 123

Indicate the third pile that was dealt out. " . . . and deal it into three piles, just as you dealt before."

You pick up the other three piles and set them aside.

Gloria does as requested. There are now three piles; the first pile contains five cards, the other two contain four cards each (Illustration 124).

"What next, Madam Flaboda?" Apparently the Madam speaks to you for a few moments. Indicate the middle pile of the three. "Madam Flaboda tells me that you should pick up this pile and deal it into two piles."

Pick up the other two piles and set them aside with the other discards.

Again Gloria follows Madam Flaboda's directions. There are now two piles, each containing two cards.

Listen to Madam Flaboda again. "Gloria, the Madam wants you to pick up this pile and deal it into two piles." Indicate the *first* pile she dealt to.

Pick up the other pile and place it with the other discards.

Gloria deals out the two cards separately. Listen again to Madam Flaboda.

Point to the first card Gloria dealt. "The Madam says that this is your chosen card."

Set the other card with the discards.

ILLUSTRATION 124

"Please turn the card over."

Unbelievable! Madam Flaboda is right.

Review: (1) Gloria looks at the top card of the 18-card pile and places the other two piles on top of it.

(2) She deals the entire deck into four piles.

(3) She deals the *third* pile into three piles. (The other cards are set aside.)

(4) She deals the middle pile into two piles. (The other cards are set aside.)

(5) She deals the first pile into two piles. (The other cards are set aside.)

(6)- Two cards are on the table. Point to the first card, saying, "The Madam says that *this* is your chosen card."

Note: As I promised, here is another way to begin the trick. After Gloria shuffles the cards, say, "Gloria, I'd like you to just pile up some cards, like this."

The cards are face up, so you fan out three face-up cards and drop them face up onto the table. Fan out four face-up cards, and toss them face up on top of the first group. Make sure the cards are not in a neat pile but form a rather sloppy group. Do the same with five more cards, and then with six. So into a face-up group you've tossed three cards, four cards, five cards, and six cards—18 in all. Straighten your pile a bit.

Hand the face-up deck to Gloria. Indicate a space in front of her on the table. She deals out a pile of cards, several at a time, just as you did. She should have some face-up cards left.

Take them from her and place them face down onto the table. Straighten up your pile and put it face down next to the ones you just set down. Finally, take her pile, straighten it, and place it face down next to the other two.

You now complete the trick exactly as described above. First, you force Gloria to choose the 18-card pile. Then you have her perform the various deals.

These Are Gold

Professor Hoffmann (Angelo John Lewis), a 19th-century magician, wrote three exhaustive books on magic. In one of them, *Modern Magic*, he explained this trick. It's hard to believe that a trick that's more than 100 years old can still fool people, but I have performed it successfully many times. I have modernized it slightly, tossed in a touch of my own, and thrown in few patter points.

Explain to the group: "I believe many of you are familiar with a trick in which three columns of seven cards are dealt out. The spectator thinks of his card and tells the magician which column his card is in. The magician gathers up the cards and then deals them out again in three columns. Again the spectator tells him which column, and again the magician deals the cards into three columns. In fact, the magician does this three times in all. Finally, the magician tells the spectator the name of his card.

"I intend to do better than that. Jennifer, will you help me?" She will. "I'm going to deal out as many columns of cards as you want, Jennifer—five columns of five cards each, six columns of six cards each, or seven columns of seven cards each. Which would you like?"

She makes her choice.

Let's suppose that she chooses six columns of six cards each. You deal out six cards face up in a row. Starting at the left you next deal a face-up card on top of each of the original six, all cards overlapping so that spectators can see the indices of the first six. In Illustration 125, you can see the first card covered appropriately. Continue in this way until all remaining 36 cards have been dealt out face up.

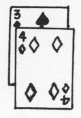

ILLUSTRATION 125

Ask Gary to also assist you. "Jennifer, I'd like you and Gary to each mentally choose a card. It would be better if you don't both choose the same card, so I'll turn my back while you point out your choices to one another."

Turn your back. When you face the group once more, say, "The trick I just explained to you deals with threes—three columns, three choices. My attempt at mind reading deals with twos. Two persons choose a card, and two times I'm told in which columns the cards lie.

"Jennifer, in which column is your card?"

She points it out. You note the top card of that column and commit it to memory. Do I mean that you have to actually remember the name of this card? Yes, I do. And another one besides. Hold it! I'll explain how easy it is. Let's suppose that the top card in that row is the QS. Say to yourself, "Queen of spades, queen of spades, queen of spades, queen of spades." And every time you have a few seconds, repeat, "Queen of spades, queen of spades."

Turn to Gary. "Which column is your card in, Gary?" He tells you. Note the top card of that column. Suppose that the top card in that column is the 7C. Say to yourself, "Queen of spades, seven of clubs. Queen of spades, seven of clubs. Queen of spades, seven of clubs." And when you pause in your delivery, repeat the names again.

You, yourself, must close up each row of cards, because you can't explain in a short time precisely how this should be done. All you do, really, is push each column up from the bottom (Illustration 126). The cards remain precisely in the same order.

You make this generous offer: "Jennifer, please gather up the piles, one on top of the other. You can gather them up in any order you wish."

Big deal! If it mattered, you'd have never made the offer.

Guess what you're doing mentally as she's gathering up the piles. That's right. You're saying, over and over, "Queen of spades, seven of clubs." Or the names of whatever cards you're supposed to be remembering.

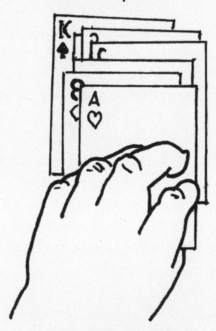

*Your hand slides
the cards upward.*

ILLUSTRATION 126

Take the collected piles from Jennifer and turn the combined pile face down. Deal the cards face up precisely as you did at the beginning, ending up with six columns of cards. (And while you're dealing, what are you saying mentally? That's right. You're repeating the names of your key cards.)

Ask Jennifer, "Which column is your card in?" She tells you. Your job now is to find the card which you remembered as the top card of the pile Jennifer originally selected. So you look around until you find the QS. Note the position that it is from the top of its column. Let's suppose that it is third from the top. Note the card that is third from the top of the pile Jennifer just pointed out. That's her card. (You can count this out either from the top or the bottom, but—and I hate to insult your intelligence, but I have a lot of time on my hands—you must count from the same place with both piles.) Pick out her card and hand it to her.

Do exactly the same thing with Gary. He tells you which column his card is in. You find your original key card for Gary—in our example, the 7C. Note its position from the top. His card is in the same position in the column he pointed out. Pick it out and hand it to him.

The trick has a powerful effect. Someday you may just be able to do it with three spectators.

Note: Occasionally, the two spectators will initially choose a card from the same pile. Nothing changes except that you must remember only one card—the one at the top of the pile which contains both cards.

You Need All 52

That's right. The trick will probably work if you have fewer than 52 cards, but to be on the safe side, use a complete deck.

Once more I'm indebted to my good friend Wally Wilson for this fascinating trick. As always, I've made a few adjustments, and have made it nearly 100% perfect by offering a few "outs" in case you have a stubborn spectator.

Maria seems to think she's psychic, so let's give her an opportunity to display her technique.

"Please shuffle the cards, Maria. And then cut the deck into three piles, approximately even. You can move cards around to make sure the piles are fairly even."

Turn your back and add, "Please pick up one of the piles. Turn them so the faces are toward yourself. Fan the cards out so that you can see the faces. Now think of a card somewhere near the center of the group."

Pause.

"Now close up the cards. Place that pile on top of one of the piles on the table. Place the other pile on top of all."

Pick up the deck and begin an overhand shuffle, running off several cards. Stop suddenly, saying, "Wait! I'll mix them up in a much better way."

Place the cards in your right hand below the cards you shuffled off. Thus, all you've done really is mix up the top dozen cards or so.

(If you find this part is too difficult, just eliminate it.)

You now mix the cards like this:

(1) Deal off, singly, three cards, placing them in a row on the table.

(2) Fan off two cards and place them on top of the first card. Do the same for the other two.

(3) Fan off three cards and place them on top of the first group. Do the same for the other two.

(4) Fan off two cards and place them on top of the first group. Do the same for the other two.

(5) Deal off, singly, three cards, placing them on top of each pile.

Say, "Let's start all over again."

(6) Deal off, singly, three cards, placing one on top of each pile.

(7) Fan off two cards and place them on top of the first group. Do the same for the other two.

(8) Fan off three cards and place them on top of the first group. Do the same for the other two.

(9) Fan off two cards and place them on top of the first group. Do the same for the other two.

You have one card remaining. Place it on the bottom of the middle pile.

It's easy enough to remember:

1 2 3 2 1 (Let's start all over again) 1 2 3 2 (1 card left)

Even up the packets. "Now let's see how psychic you are, Maria. Which packet do you think your card is in?"

She chooses one. "See if your card is there, Maria." Turn your head away and fan though the cards face up.

If it's there, congratulate her on her magnificent powers. If not, ask her to choose one of the two remaining piles. Again, turn your head away and fan through the cards face up. If it is, tell her, "Not bad, Maria. Not perfect, but not bad."

If it's not there, tell her, "Maria, congratulations. You have 100-percent-perfect negative psychic power."

In any event, collect the cards, placing the pile that contains the chosen card on top.

"Maria, I believe that we can find your card. What's the name of the card?"

She tells you. Let's suppose that it's the KS. "Good. Now what we must do is test your faith. We'll find out if you believe me. Let's spell it."

The selected card can be in any of four positions in the pile and you will spell to it. The card can be in the 6th, 7th, 8th, or 9th position from the top. Here's how you do it:

Deal the cards into a face-up pile, placing down one card for each letter in the spelling of the word BELIEVE. If the KS comes up as you deal the last E, stop, saying, "You do believe, Maria." If it does not, turn over the next card. If it's the KS, make the remark to Maria. If it's not, immediately continue by spelling the word ME. Say the letter M for the card you just turned up.

Turn over the next card, saying E. If that's the KS, say, "Believe me, Maria, you have faith in me."

If not, the next card should be the KS. Turn it over, making the comment to Maria.

Suppose the spectator is a real chowderhead and that the chosen card is not one of the four cards. Look through the pile until you find the card and cut it to the top, all the while declaring how disappointed you are.

You now have the card on top. Say, "Let's try something different." Proceed to force the card on Maria, using one of the four forces at the beginning of "Mental Tricks," on pages 23 to 33.

When Maria chooses the card, say, "What did you select?" She names the card. "Oh, sure," you say, still miffed. "Now it shows up."

Note: You have just finished reading my so-called surefire version of Wally's trick. Wally, however, assures me that his version hardly ever fails. He suggests that you take the pile in which the spectator's card lies and say, "To locate your card, we must use the mystic expression, 'I believe.'"

You then spell out I BELIEVE and the selection should appear on either the last card of the spelling or the next card.

Wally assures us that we don't have to worry too much about saving the trick: "I have found by experimenting over and over that the thought-of card will end up in the 8th or 9th position after the shuffle. Rarely will it be the 7th or 10th. The odds are so great in your favor, it is a worthy effect, I have found. Try it and see for yourself. What makes it work is the subtle suggestion, 'Think of a card, somewhere near the middle of the fan.'"

If the card is not in the eighth or ninth position, you can always resort to the forcing method I described earlier.

Take Your Q

Ed Marlo, master card-trick performer and inventor, occasionally would develop a trick that was far more complicated than it needed to be. Case in point is this variation of an old favorite, familiarly known as "The Q Trick." Marlo, for some unfathomable reason, felt there had to be a memorized setup. Actually, an easy variation can be performed with a bit of subtlety, as I will explain.

The original basic trick is this: A number of objects—coins, for instance—are placed in a circle. A tail is added, consisting of, let's say, three coins (Illustration 127). A spectator—Melissa, for instance—is told to think of a number from five to ten. She is told, "Starting at the bottom of the tail, please count your number up the tail and around the circle to the left. Then, starting with the coin you landed on, count the same number back around the circle to the right. But don't go down the tail—just stay on the circle."

You turn away while Melissa does this. Regardless, when you turn back, you know exactly which coin she landed on. How? There are three coins in the tail. In Illustration 128, X marks the coin in the circle to which the tail is attached. Start with the coin

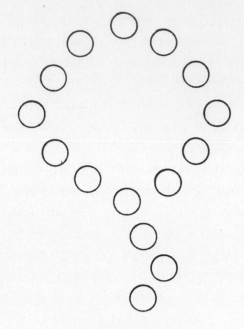

ILLUSTRATION 127

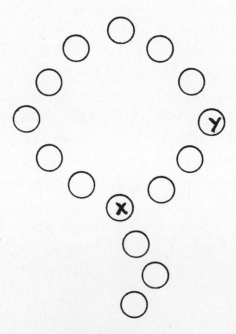

ILLUSTRATION 128

to the right of this coin and continue counting counterclockwise to the exact number of coins in the tail—in this instance, three. The last coin you count is the one chosen. In the illustration, this is marked with a Y.

The trick may be repeated, but you must slyly change the number of coins in the tail; otherwise, Melissa will end up on the same number.

Marlo's version is done with playing cards. He decided to form a Q of face-up cards and then have two cards chosen as described: the one the spectator lands on first, and the one the spectator lands on after counting back. Both cards are revealed.

This can be done by using an elimination process, but here is a much easier trick that seems to accomplish the same thing.

We might as well have Melissa help out. Ask her to shuffle the deck. When she finishes, say to her, "Please deal out 12 cards face up in the form of a clock." She does. The result should resemble Illustration 129, except that the cards would be face up.

Take the remainder of the deck from her, saying, "Now we'll add a little tail."

The cards are actually face up.

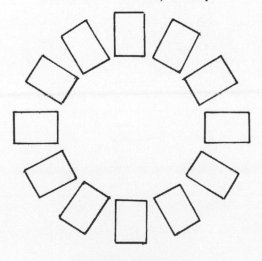

ILLUSTRATION 129

Place a two-card tail on the circle, connecting them at the card that would represent 6 if the layout were a clock (Illustration 130).

"Here's what we'll do, Melissa. We'll have you choose a card. You'll think of a number from five to ten. Let's say you think of six. You count up the tail like this."

You demonstrate by counting up the tail and then to the left, stopping at the card at the count of six. "Then you start on the card you land on and count back the same number, going to your right. But don't go down the tail; just keep going around the circle. The card you land on will be your choice."

Show the direction of the count back, but don't actually perform it.

Turn away while Melissa performs her duties. Turn back and, after concentrating, divine the name of her choice. As with the

ILLUSTRATION 130

coins, you simply start counting with the card to the right of the card to which the tail is attached. And you count counterclockwise to the same number of cards as are in the tail—in this instance, two. The last card you count is the one chosen.

"Now let's try for two cards," you say. "To make it even more difficult, let's make the tail a bit longer."

Add two cards to the tail.

Carefully explain: "Again I'd like you to think of a number from five to ten. You can even choose the same number if you wish—anything to fool me. Follow the same procedure as before—counting up this side . . . " Indicate counting up and going to the left. " . . . and, starting on the card you land on, counting the same number back this way." Indicate the counterclockwise direction.

"The card you land on will be your choice, just as before. But then I'd like you to choose a second card. And I want you to use a lucky number for that. What would be a good lucky number?"

If Melissa should say any number other than 7, say, "That is a good lucky number, but I think a better one would be seven. So start on your first choice and count off seven cards, going either way. The card you land on will be your second choice."

Make sure she understands the directions; then turn away. When you turn back, you again concentrate fiercely and eventually name both cards. You count to the first card by counting four cards counterclockwise, starting with the card to the right of the one to which the tail is attached. The second card? Oh, you've already figured that out. It's seven cards away from the first choice, no matter which direction you count.

Note: You do not immediately do a two-card revelation, because you want Melissa to become familiar with the basic procedure first. It's possible that she might become confused if she must choose two cards to begin with.

Let's Lose Your Card

An extremely observant spectator would be able to perform this trick after watching it once, but fortunately there is sufficient folderol to cause confusion. The spectator would have to recall how the cards are cut, the exact sentence you use, and the precise procedure at the end.

Charles is seldom surprised by anything, so it's time you caused his eyes to widen somewhat. Hand him the deck and ask him to give it a good shuffle. Continue with appropriate pauses:

"Set the deck down, Charles, and then divide it in half. It doesn't have to be exact—just about in half."

"Push one half the deck aside and cut the remaining cards in half—again, just about half."

"Push one of those piles aside."

"Charles, please pick up the remaining pile and give it a shuffle."

"I'll turn my head while you take a look at the bottom card of the pile. And show it to the rest of the group, please."

"Now let's lose your card. Spell out, 'Let's lose your card,' transferring one card to the bottom for each letter in the spelling."

Make sure he understands what to do and that he does it properly.

"Let's mix them further. Please deal the top card onto the table, and move the next card to the bottom. Deal the next card on top of the first card, and move the next card to the bottom. Please continue until all the cards are in a pile on the table."

Then say, "For the first time, I'll touch the cards."

Show that both your hands are empty. Pick up the pile and straighten it out. Hold it in your left hand in the dealer's grip.

"What's the name of your card, Charles."

He names it.

"Watch."

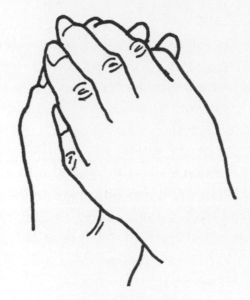

ILLUSTRATION 131

Place your right hand over the deck, completely concealing it (Illustration 131). Give your hands a little up-and-down shake. "And here it is." Turn over the top card of the packet.

Notes: (1) It's hard to believe that this trick actually works. But, as you'll discover, it does, and most entertainingly. Why all the cutting? For one thing, the trick would be much too cumbersome with a full deck. For another thing, the trick only works if there are eight to sixteen cards. The cutting makes sure that the number of cards is right.

(2) Why do wc always have the spectator show the card to others? Hard to believe, but once in a while a spectator will actually lie about his chosen card just to goof you up. So it doesn't hurt to take out a little insurance that this won't happen.

(3) If you are skilled at performing an overhand shuffle, you might try this when you take the packet from the spectator: Shuffle the top card to the bottom of the packet, and then shuffle it back to the top. Now reveal the chosen card.

Easy Speller

To perform this excellent spelling trick, you must be familiar with "Simplicity Itself," a method of locating a chosen card. As described, you have arranged to have your key card just above the chosen card.

Let's suppose that Nancy has chosen a card and that you know the card above it in the deck. Say to her, "I want you to be sure that your card has not been removed from the deck. Watch for it, please, but don't say anything when we come to it."

Fan through the deck until you come to the chosen card (on the near side of the key card, of course). Notice the value and suit of the chosen card. Let's suppose that it is the nine of clubs. Starting with the chosen card, proceed to spell it out; pass one card to the right-hand pile for each letter in the spelling.

Note the suit and value of the next card.

You can now forget about the chosen card. Let's suppose that the next card is the queen of spades. Spell this out mentally as you fan through the cards, in the same way as you did with the chosen card.

Cut the cards so that the last card in the spelling goes to the top.

Everyone is now observing the new bottom card. Proudly announce, "I think I can say with authority that this is not your chosen card, right?"

Of course you're right.

"Let's see if we can locate your card by spelling it out. Suppose your card were the queen of spades." Name the second card you spelled out. Make it casual, as though you're naming a card at random. Spell out the queen of spades, dealing one card into a pile onto the table for each letter. Turn over the last letter of the spelling.

"There it is—the queen of spades."

Hand Nancy the deck. "What was the name of your card, Nancy?" She names it. Have her spell it out. When she turns over the last card of the spelling, she, along with everyone else, will be quite surprised.

General Tricks

I could discover no other category for these tricks—which means they are unique. Perhaps these are the most interesting tricks in the book.

Point with Pride

Required here is a modest amount of nimbleness. I recommend that you at least give this a try; it has a powerful effect on viewers.

It's essential that the deck be shuffled, so you might as well call on Sal, who fancies himself an expert with the pasteboards.

Take the deck back, saying, "I've acquired a certain amount of skill with this finger." Hold up the first finger of your left hand. "Sometimes I can rub this finger on the back of a card and tell what it is." Pause. "And, of course, sometimes I can't. Let's try it out."

Hold the deck in the dealing position in your left hand. With your right hand, cut off a small packet of cards and set it onto the table. Still holding the deck, extend the first finger of your left hand. Rub the tip of the finger against the top card of the packet on the table, preferably in the upper right corner (Illustration 132).

As you rub the card, the left fingers have pushed over the top card of those in your left hand so that you can see the value and suit (Illustration 133). After you have seen the card, push it even with the others. Do this while stopping the rubbing movement and turning the hand back to its normal position.

Shake your head. "I can't seem to get that one. Let's try another."

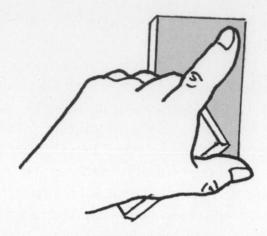

ILLUSTRATION 132

With your right hand, cut off a small pile from the cards you're holding and place it on top of the pile on the table. Naturally, you know the top card of those on the table.

Perform the rubbing procedure again. As you do, name the card. At the same time, you push the next card over for a peek. Return the left hand to its normal position.

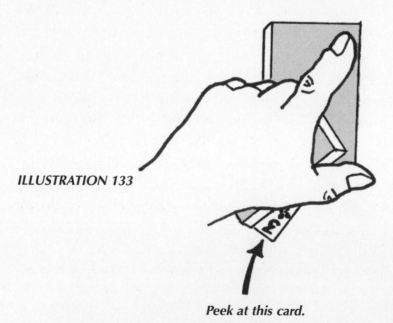

ILLUSTRATION 133

Peek at this card.

"Let's see how I did." With your right hand, turn over the top card of the packet on the table. "I can't believe it; I got it absolutely right. Let's try again." Turn the card face down.

Cut off another small packet and place it on top of the pile on the table. Rub the top card of the packet. This time, however, do not peek at the top card of those in your left hand. Move your left hand away from the tabled cards. "I can't seem to get it."

Transfer the remainder of the deck to your right hand. Presumably, these cards are interfering with your rubbing ability. Rub the top card of the tabled cards again. Gradually name the card. For instance, you might say, "I think I'm getting the suit. It's a six. No, I'm confused because the cards are reversed; it's a nine." You could equally well confuse a five and a two, a three and an eight, an ace and a four, any two face cards.

Give the cards another rub and reveal the suit. The idea is to stress that it's not easy, and that you're not perfect.

Turn over the top card of the packet, showing that once more you are correct. It's quite enough to detect two cards; no need to go further. If the group insists, you might say, "No, I was pretty lucky to get two out of three. I'd better not try again."

If, however, you feel confident in your ability to peek, you might proceed. Fail on the next card while taking another peek. Then, with great difficulty, detect the card after that.

As with the revelation of the second card, first rub with the deck in your left hand. Run into difficulty. Transfer the deck to the right hand to make the rubbing easier. After considerable tribulation, you name the card.

Under no circumstances do the trick more than three times.

Crime Does Not Pay

This idea is another Wally Wilson invention. The principle is used in a number of tricks, but the actual working here is unique.

Spread the cards from left hand to right, counting off 15. Hand the packet to Janet, asking her to shuffle them. Count off another 15, handing the packet to Ron, also requesting a shuffle. (Incidentally, as you count off the 15, don't make it clear that you're counting. You might do well to pass the cards three at a time to help conceal the process.)

Have Janet and Ron set their packets face down onto the table.

"Now I'd like you both to cut off a pile from your packet and set the pile down right next to your packet."

Make sure that the two sets of packets are fairly widely separated (Illustration 134). This is so that future directions will not be misunderstood.

Have both Janet and Ron choose a card from the rest of the deck. The cards are turned face up so that all can see them. (The rest of the deck is set aside and will not be used for the rest of the trick.)

"One of those cards will be a detective, and one will be a criminal. I don't like to hurt your feelings, Ron, but I think you'll make a better criminal. Janet, you'll be the detective."

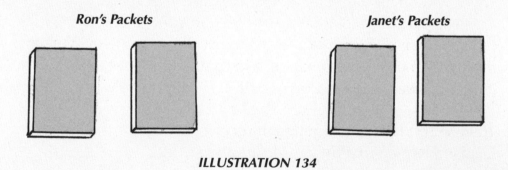

ILLUSTRATION 134

"Janet, please place your card face up onto either one of your packets."

She does.

"Ron, pick up either one of your packets and put it right on top of Janet's card."

He does.

"Now, Ron, put your card—the criminal—face down onto your packet. We need him face down so that he'll be harder to find."

He does.

Point to the packet that does not contain Janet's selected card. "Janet, please put this pile on top of Ron's pile."

She does. Instruct Janet to place either pile on top of the other one.

Both Ron and Janet give the entire packet a complete cut. If they desire, the packet may be cut again.

"Which of you wants to be the big dealer?"

Let's suppose that Ron volunteers. Have him deal the cards alternately into two piles.

"Obviously, we have to keep the packet with the detective."

Set the other packet aside.

The remaining cards are dealt into two piles. The pile containing the detective is retained; the other is set aside.

This is continued until only two cards are left.

"We have tried our best to confuse the detective. Let's see if she was able to overcome the odds and capture the criminal."

Turn over the face-down card. It's the criminal.

Review: (1) Ron and Janet each receive 15 cards.
(2) Both divide their cards into two piles.
(3) Each chooses a card from the remaining deck.

(4) Janet's card is the detective and is placed face up on top of one of her packets.

(5) Ron places one of his packets on top of Janet's card.

(6) Ron's card is the criminal. It's placed face down on top of his remaining packet.

(7) You point to the packet that does not contain Janet's card and tell her to place this packet on top of Ron's packet.

(8) Janet is told to combine the packets, placing either one on top.

(9) The combined packet is given several complete cuts.

(10) One of your assistants deals the combined packet alternately into two piles. The pile containing the face-up card is kept, while the others are set aside. The deal is repeated until only two cards remain. Turning over Ron's selected card, you declare that the great detective has found the criminal.

B'Gosh

A good magician learns early on that the most important part of a trick is the effect. Yes, the presentation should be entertaining, and the magician should have a pleasing personality, but if the result is mediocre, everything else is a waste of time. Good magicians will tell you that if you need a special card to make a trick work, that's just fine. Or, if the deck must be secretly set up in advance to perform a super-miracle, that's delightful. And, if a spectator is a confederate (or plant) and the result is remarkable, that's absolutely perfect.

Such is the case with this trick, which Martin Gardner credits to Chris Schoke.

Let's suppose that your secret helper is Grace. Tell the group that you'll need two volunteers. Naturally, Grace raises her hand and is chosen. Of the half-dozen other eager helpers, you pick Arnold.

Hand the deck to Arnold and ask him to shuffle the cards. He does.

"Arnold, please give the deck to Grace, who will also give the deck a good shuffle."

Grace shuffles the deck thoroughly. But, at the end, she casually glances at the bottom card and then sets the deck face down onto the table. Let's say that the bottom card is the six of clubs. Grace will remember this card. Later on, she will pretend that this is the card that she has chosen.

"Arnold, please cut off about half the cards and set them in front of you."

He does.

"Now, Arnold, you can take the top card of either pile and look at it. Don't let anyone else see it, please."

He does what you ask.

"Grace, I'd like you to choose a card from the top of either pile. Look at it, but don't let anyone else see it."

Grace takes a card, all right, but the card she remembers is the six of clubs that was on the bottom of the deck.

"Arnold, please put your card back on top of either pile. And Grace, put your card back on top of the other pile." Pause. "Now on top of either pile is a chosen card. Grace, I'd like you to put the two piles together and then give them a cut, or give each pile a cut and then put them together—your choice."

On the bottom of one pile is the six of clubs that Grace sneaked a peek at. If Arnold's card is on top of this pile, Grace gives the pile a complete cut—that is, she takes off a portion from the top, sets it onto the table, and then puts the balance of that pile on top of the pile she just placed on the table.

She gives the other pile a complete cut. Then she puts one of the piles on top of the other. The upshot is that the six of clubs is now on top of the card that Arnold selected.

Suppose that on the bottom of the first pile is the six of clubs and that Arnold's chosen card is on top of the second pile. Grace places the first pile on top of the second pile. This puts the six of clubs on top of Arnold's chosen card. Then she gives the entire deck a complete cut. Little known to the general public is that a complete cut does not change the basic order of the cards; regardless of the number of complete cuts, the cards remain in the same relative order. Therefore, Grace may cut the cards again. And Arnold should give the deck a few complete cuts as well.

Pick up the deck. Give the cards a snap, or riffle the ends. You can do the latter by putting your fingers at the outer end and your thumb at the inner end. Bend the cards upward (Illustration 135); let them fall quickly. The whole idea is to do something that could pass for a clever move. You don't want the group to think that the trick is automatic, or—heaven forbid—that one of the participants assisted you.

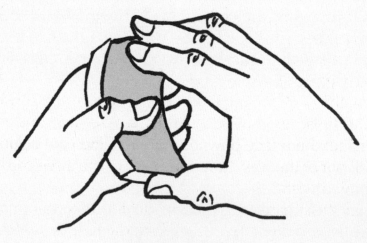

ILLUSTRATION 135

Address Grace and Arnold: "I'm going to deal the cards out face up. If either of you sees your card, tell me immediately."

From the face-down deck, slowly deal the cards into a face-up pile. Eventually, Grace will see the card she glimpsed on the bottom of the deck, the six of clubs. The minute she does, she says, "Stop! That's my card."

"Fair enough. Grace, your card and Arnold's card were separated in the deck. And the deck was given several cuts. The only thing I did was give the deck a magical snap. Let's see what happened." Deal the next card face down in front of Arnold.

"What was your chosen card, Arnold?"

He names it.

Turn it over, showing that the two chosen cards have somehow joined together in the deck.

Thank the two for their assistance and move on to your next trick.

The Ten Trick

Once more I'm indebted to my good friend Wally Wilson, who showed me this extraordinary stunt many years ago. I have no idea who invented it; I do know that I have added a few wrinkles that I think enhance it.

You really should try this out on your friends; it may well be the most impressive trick in this book.

Hand the deck to Sally and ask her to give it a good shuffle. When she finishes, continue, "Now please pick out any three cards and set them face down over here." Indicate a spot on the table well out of the way. "You may look at the three cards or not, whatever you wish."

When she's ready, say, "Please deal four rows of cards face up. Each row should consist of five cards. Put the rows one below the other."

The rows should look like Illustration 136, except that the cards would be face up.

Take the deck back from Sally.

"I'm going to go through all the cards in the deck, trying to check out all thirteen values. I'll go through the cards only once, and then I'll try to tell you the value of each one of your chosen cards."

All of that is baloney, of course. You'll go through the deck, all right, but you'll do it in such a way that you'll know absolutely what the three cards are.

The cards are actually face up.

ILLUSTRATION 136

Look over the 20 face-up cards. You're seeking a pair that adds up to ten—5 and 5, 6 and 4, 7 and 3, 8 and 2, 9 and 1 (1 is an ace).

Take off the top card of the deck and turn it face up; place this card face up on one card of the pair you've discovered—a 6, for instance. Take off the next card, turn it face up, and place it onto a 4. Since 6 and 4 add up to 10, you've correctly covered your first pair. Naturally, you've now added two new face-up cards. Look for another pair that adds to 10 and cover each of the cards with a face-up card from the deck.

There is only one other combination that you cover. See if a combination of these three values is showing: king, queen, jack. If so, cover each one with a face-up card.

How about 10s? You don't cover 10s; you just let them be.

Continue covering pairs that add to 10 and K-Q-J combinations until you hold no more cards. Look over all the face-up cards. How many 10s are showing? Let's suppose that four 10s are showing; obviously, 10 is not one of the chosen cards. If, however, there are three 10s showing, then one of the chosen cards is a 10. If two 10s are showing, Sally has chosen two 10s. And in the extremely unlikely event that one 10 is showing, goofy old Sally has selected three 10s. If Sally has chosen any 10s, you tell her about it at the end of the trick, not now.

You now pick up all the cards on the table, based on the top face-up card of each pile. You pick up each pair that adds up to 10, each K-Q-J combination, and each pile topped by a 10. Each pile is picked up by your right hand and placed face up into your left hand.

(Sometimes, before picking up the cards, you'll be holding one card which could not be dealt out. What do you do? For your first pick-up from the table, select a stack on which the top face-up card will add up to 10 with the card you're holding. If you're holding a face card, pick up the two piles that complete the K-Q-J combination.)

At the end, there will be some cards left on the table—these cards do not get picked up, because they do not fulfill the requirements. Let's say that the cards are a 3, a 6, and an 8. You subtract each from 10. This gives you the values of the three selected cards. Three subtracted from 10 gives you 7. Six subtracted from 10 give you 4. Eight subtracted from 10 gives you 2.

As you gather up the last cards, remember the values 7, 4, and 2. Tell Sally, "I can't tell you the suits of your cards, but I know the values. You selected a 7, a 4, and a 2." Repeat to make sure it's clear. Sally turns over her cards to reveal that you're correct.

Suppose that the cards remaining include two face cards—a K and a Q, for instance. The card missing from the K-Q-J combination is the J. So one of Sally's selections was a J. Clearly, whatever value is missing from the combination is held by Sally. If at the end you have a spot card and one face card, you subtract the value of the spot card from 10 to determine one of the chosen cards. The other two are cards that complete the K-Q-J combination. If the card is a Q, for instance, Sally holds both the K and the J.

Oh-oh! Big trouble. After the pickup, only one card remains on the table. This means that Sally holds two cards that add up to 10. After all this work, are you defeated? Of course not.

Let's suppose that the only card left on the table is an ace. You know that one of the cards held by Sally is a 9 (10–1 = 9). You say, "Sally, I'm having big trouble today. I know absolutely that one of your cards is an ace, right?"

She looks at her cards. You're right.

"I just can't get the other two. I have sort of an idea. Maybe I can work it out if you tell me one of the other two cards."

Oh, you sly little rapscallion. When she tells you the value of one of the cards, you subtract that value from 10, which gives you the value of the other card.

Let's say that Sally tells you that one of the cards is a 6. "Six?" you say, looking quite puzzled. Murmur, "What can the other one be?" Ponder a moment. "Oh, of course. The other card is a four."

Right you are.

There's no reason why you can't perform the trick again. Believe me, no one will catch on to how you determine what cards to cover.

Four of a Kind

Piles of Aces

Years ago, William Simon came up with this excellent four-ace trick. As with most tricks, a great deal of its effectiveness depends on the proper presentation.

A bit of preparation is necessary. You need two aces on top of the deck, and two aces together somewhere in the middle.

To start, get the aid of two assistants. Humphrey and Adele are always hanging around together, so they would be perfect.

Fan through the face-up deck so that all can see, saying, "As you'll notice, it's a regular deck of cards."

Raise the cards toward you as you near the middle. Watch for the two aces in the middle. Make them the last two cards that you pass into the right hand. Separate the cards at this point (Illustration 137). You should be holding a face-up pile in each hand. On the bottom of each face-up pile are two face-up aces. Illustration 138 shows the position of both sets of aces. The aces are not actually fanned out. Even the cards up and lower your hands.

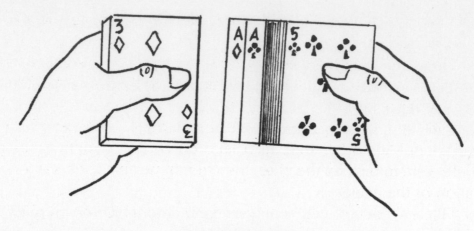

ILLUSTRATION 137

Set the two piles face up onto the table.

Point to the pile nearest Adele. Say to her, "Adele, I'd like you to cut some cards off this pile and hand them to me."

She does.

"Humphrey, please cut some cards off the other pile and hand them to me."

ILLUSTRATION 138

After you receive the cards, form them into a single pile and set them aside.

"It would seem that each of you started with a different number of cards. And then each of you undoubtedly cut off a different number of cards."

Pick up Humphrey's pile, turn it face down, and hand it to him. Hand Adele her pile, also face down. (If Humphrey and Adele were to pick up the piles, there might be an accidental revelation of the aces.)

"Please, each of you deal your cards into a face-down pile."

After each has dealt out several cards, say, "Each of you can stop whenever you want. But please don't stop at exactly the same time."

They stop dealing. Take the cards they're still holding and set them aside with the other discards.

"Now, Humphrey, I'd like you to pick up your pile and then deal your cards into two piles, alternating—first one card on the left, then one on the right. Continue until all your cards are dealt out."

When he's done, direct Adele to do the same thing. Finally Adele finishes. Line up the piles as in Illustration 139.

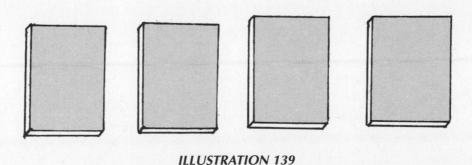

ILLUSTRATION 139

343

"I hope everyone noticed that Humphrey and Adele each cut off a different number of cards. Then they dealt out as many cards as they wanted. And again, each chose a different number. So, of course, we have considerable variation between the two sets of piles. Despite all these differences, I'm sure that Humphrey and Adele have a certain compatibility, a mysterious mutuality. Let's see if I'm right."

Turn over the top cards of the four piles, revealing the four aces. Let everyone have a look for several seconds.

Aces by the Number

Frank Garcia applied an old principle to a four-ace trick. I've spruced it up a bit to simplify the trick and eliminate a sleight.

Before starting, you must have the four aces on top. Later, you will secretly move fifteen cards on top of them. If you want to make this your first trick, put the four aces on top; then count fifteen cards from the bottom of the deck and place them on top of the aces. You're ready to go.

Or you can try it this way: Start your performance with the four aces on top of the deck. Perform a few tricks that will keep them there. Or perform a few tricks that will keep them together somewhere in the deck. When you're ready, without explanation casually fan through the deck and cut the aces to the top. Chat with the group for a minute or two. Now you're ready to add 15 cards to the top.

Turn the deck face up so that all can see the bottom card (Illustration 140). Start fanning through the deck, saying, "The cards seem to be well mixed."

Count off eight cards as you fan through the deck. Place these eight cards to the back (top) of the deck. Count off seven more cards and also place these on top of the deck. Spread out

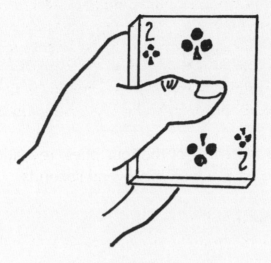

ILLUSTRATION 140

several more cards, saying, "I think you'll agree." Close up the cards and turn the deck face down.

You now have fifteen cards on top, followed by the four aces.

I don't see where Donna has any right to sit there like a lump, while you're working your head off; she should be willing to assist you.

"Donna, please name a number between 15 and 20." The word "between" confines her choice to four numbers: 16, 17, 18, and 19. This is important, as you'll see.

Let's say that Donna names 18. Fan out the cards at the top of the deck. Let everyone see that you're taking five cards. Take the five cards into your right hand and set them face down onto the table, saying, "Five."

Do it again, taking another five cards and setting them to the right of the first group. Say, "Ten."

Repeat, saying, "Fifteen." This pile goes to the right of the others.

Fan off three more cards, saying, "And three is eighteen." Place these to the right of the other three piles. (If Donna had chosen 16, you would place one card here. If she had chosen 17, you would place two cards here. And, of course, if she had chosen 19, you would place four cards here.)

Point to the pile on the left, saying, "Five."

Place the cards you're holding on top of this pile.

Touch the next pile to the right, saying, "Ten." Touch the next pile to the right, saying, "Fifteen." Touch the three-card pile, saying, "And three is eighteen."

Take the top card of this pile and place it, face down, forward of the other piles (Illustration 141). This card is an ace.

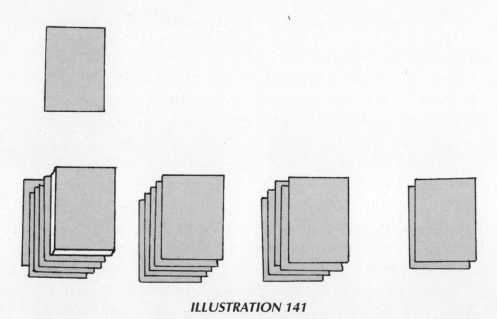

ILLUSTRATION 141

Pick up the remaining cards in this pile and place them on top of the deck, which is resting on top of the first pile you placed down. (Where the chosen number is 16, there will be no cards left, which works out fine.)

Place the other two piles onto the deck in any order. Pick up the deck.

"More work, Donna. Please name a number between 10 and 15."

Let's say that she names 12.

As before, you place down five cards, saying, "Five." Then place down five more to the right of this pile, saying, "Ten." Place two cards to the right of all, saying, "And two is twelve."

Point to the pile on the left, repeating, "Five." Place the rest of the deck on top of this pile. Point to the next pile to the right, saying, "Ten." Point to the two-card pile, saying, "And two is twelve."

Remove the top card of this last pile and place it, face down, to the right of the first ace you've set down (Illustration 142).

Place the remaining card (or cards) in this pile onto the deck, which rests on top of the first pile you set down. (If Donna chose 11, no cards will remain in this last pile—which is all right.)

Place the five-card pile on top of the deck.

"Once more, Donna. This time, please name a number between five and ten."

Suppose she says nine. Fan out five cards and place them onto the table, saying, "Five." Fan out four cards and, placing them to the right of the first pile, say, "And four is nine."

Touch the first pile, saying, "Five."

This time do not place the deck onto the five-card pile. Simply point to the four-card pile, saying, "And four is nine."

Take the top card of this pile and place it to the right of the other two aces (Illustration 143).

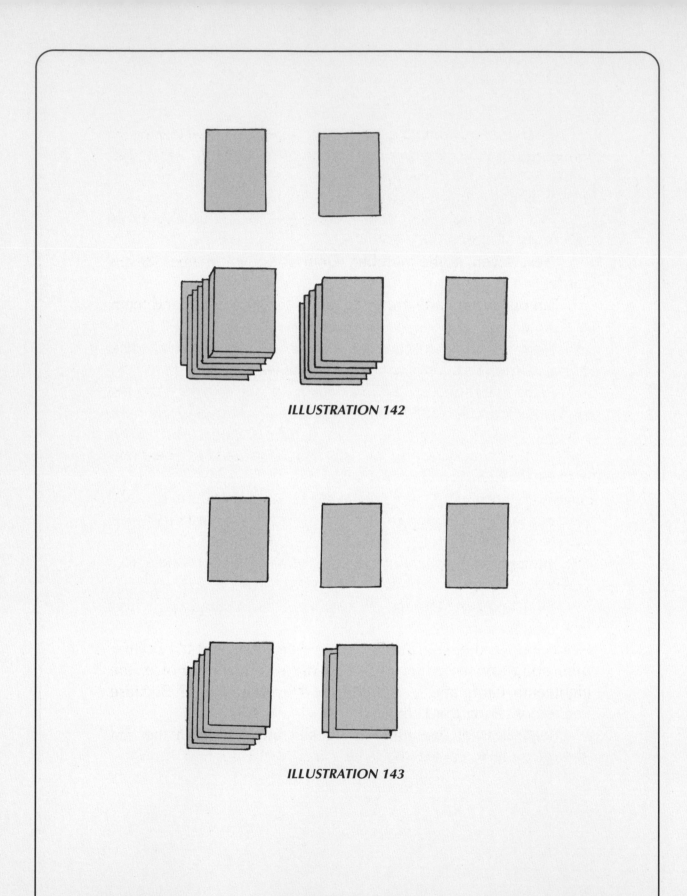

ILLUSTRATION 142

ILLUSTRATION 143

Place the remaining cards in this pile on top of the deck, which you are still holding. Set the five-card pile on top of the deck.

Pick up the deck. "What's the lucky number?"

You must hope that she's knowledgeable enough to guess seven. If not, you'll have to tell her.

"Yes, seven is the number, Donna. So you'll need seven cards."

Fan out seven cards from the top of the deck and hand them to Donna.

"And who are the luckiest people in the world? The Australians. So I'd like you to give the cards the down-under shuffle. So put the top card down on the table, and then put the next one under—on the bottom of the deck."

She does this.

"The next one goes on top of the first card, and the next one goes on the bottom. Continue on."

When she's done, the cards are in a pile on the table. Take the top card and place it to the right of the other three cards on the table (Illustration 144).

"Remember, Donna, you chose the numbers. Let's see how you did."

Turn the aces over one by one.

Note: After you have laid out the five-card piles and the smaller pile, don't say something like, "So we'll take your choice, the eighteenth card, and . . . " Why don't you say that? Because you're not taking the 18th card.

Regardless of the numbers chosen by Donna, in the first instance, you're taking the 16th card. In the second instance,

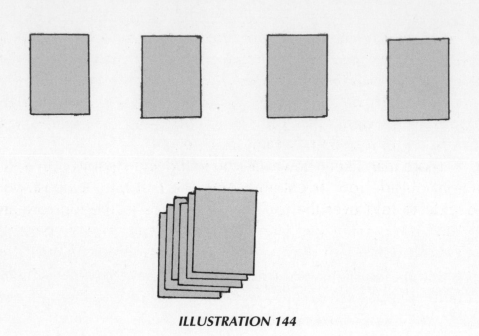

ILLUSTRATION 144

you're taking the 11th card. And in the third instance, you're taking the 6th card. It's best that the spectators not be made aware of this.

Kings in a Blanket

A complex version of this trick appears in my book *Easy Card Tricks*. This variation is quite startling and considerably easier.

First, you must learn how to "fold the blanket." Start by dealing 16 cards face down, so that they form four rows and four columns (Illustration 145).

You can fold over any row or column and continue folding until you have just one pile of cards. How do you "fold over"? Simply turn over all the cards on one outside row or column and place them, reversed, on top of the cards next to them. Let's suppose that you turn over all the cards in the far right column and place each card on top of the card to its immediate left. The column on the right will now consist of four piles of two cards each; the bottom card of each pile is face down and the top card face up.

You may continue by folding over the column on the right again, which would give you two columns—the one on the right consisting of four piles of three cards each.

More than likely, however, you will decide to fold over a different outside row or column. After the first fold, suppose you decide to fold over the top row. The cards in the top row are turned over and placed face up onto the card directly beneath them. Now you would have three rows and three columns. The top row would now consist of three piles. The pile on the left and

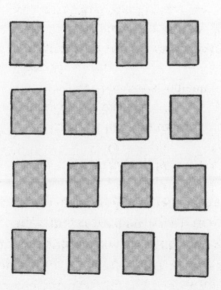

ILLUSTRATION 145

the one next to it would contain two cards each. The pile on the right would consist of four cards—the top card and the third card from the top being face up.

You would continue folding like this until only one pile remains. On with the trick.

Fan through the deck with the faces toward yourself. Place a few random cards on top. Explain, "I have to find certain cards or this will never work."

Continue fanning through. Place the four kings on top, one by one.

"All set," you declare. Turn the deck face down. The kings are now on the bottom of the 16-card pile.

Deal out the kings face down from the top of the deck so that they are roughly in the positions indicated by K's below. Deal out 12 more cards face down so that they fill the positions indicated by the O's below. Make sure that the kings are in the proper position.

```
O    O    K    K
O    O    O    O
K    O    O    K
O    O    O    O
```

"Hazel, I'd like you to watch carefully as I make a magic symbol on the blanket."

Turn over the cards indicated by X's in Illustration 146.

"Hazel, do you see the letter that the face-down cards make?" If she puzzles over it too long, add, "It makes the letter K, Hazel." Run over the face-down cards with your finger so that she can really see the K. "That K stands for King, Hazel. I'd like you to remember that as you fold the blanket. Oh, that's right, I have to explain to you how to fold the blanket."

The "K" is facing away from you.

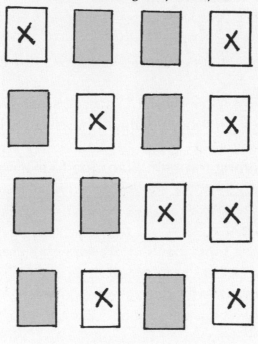

ILLUSTRATION 146

Explain how to Hazel. Believe me, it's much easier when you have the cards laid out. Explain to her the various options. Make sure she understands that she can fold it in any order she wishes. She can start at the bottom, then repeat with another bottom fold, or go anywhere else—whatever she wishes.

As she folds, you might well have to help her, making sure she doesn't goof up. When she's done, straighten out the single pile.

"Do you remember the magic sign I made on the blanket, Hazel?"

She does.

"And what did that letter K stand for?"

"King" she says.

"That's right." Pick up the pile. "Watch." Spread the pile out so that the four face-up kings show. As you spread the pile, you may see that a number of cards are face up. This means that you must turn the pile over to show the face-up kings.

Better Than Four of a Kind

Ken Beale had the original idea, and a mighty fine notion it is. I tossed in the ending, which I believe adds a stronger climax.

You must make a minor setup in advance. Remove from the deck the four aces and five spades: 6, 7, 8, 9, 10. Place the five spades face down on top of the deck in any order. On top of them, place the four aces face down.

Start by saying, "I'll teach you all to play Australian poker. We'll need the jacks for this."

Fan through the cards with the faces toward yourself and toss out the jacks, face up, one by one. Put them into a row.

"The jacks, of course, are the critical cards. But we also need twelve additional cards."

Fan off three cards, even them up, and place them face down into a pile on the table, saying, "Three cards." Fan off two more cards, even them up, and place them on top of those on the table, saying, "And two is five." Deal one card on top of the others, saying, "And one is six."

Add, "And we'll need six more." Address Shirley, who has been very attentive: "We need six more, Shirley. How should we do it? Should I deal the way I did—three, two, one? Or should I deal one, two, three? Or should I just deal out six cards one at a time? It's up to you."

Deal the remaining six cards on top of the other six, in the manner directed. Set the rest of the deck aside.

Turn the jacks face down in place.

"To start with Australian poker, you must first deal the cards out in the regular way."

From left to right, deal a card on top of each of the jacks. Repeat three times, exhausting the cards you're holding. Pick up the pile on the far right. Place it onto the pile to the left of it. Place the combined pile onto the pile to its left. Place the combined pile onto the last pile on the left.

"Now we deal the cards in the Australian way, which is like this." Deal a card face down onto the table and put the next one under the packet. "Do you catch on, Shirley?" Pause. "One down and one under." She will probably tell you that the deal is, like Australia, "down-under." If not, you tell her.

Continue by dealing a card face down onto the one on the table, and the next one under the packet. Continue until you hold only four cards. Turn them face up.

"There you are—the four jacks."

Set them aside, face up and spread out.

"So what do you do when an Australian is lucky enough to deal himself four jacks? I'll show you what I do. We'll do the down-under deal again."

Deal a card down, and put the next one under the packet. Continue until you hold only four cards. Turn them face up.

"There you are—the four aces. Now that's a real winner."

Place the aces aside near the jacks. Make sure they're face up and spread out.

"But if you really want to win, you should milk the cards—the American way."

Proceed to milk the cards as described in "Milking the Cards," on page 18. First, draw off the top and bottom cards together, placing the two face down onto the table. Again, draw off the top and bottom cards together, placing them on top of the two on the table.

"But in America, we need five cards."

Place the top card on top of the four cards on the table.

Set the remaining three cards on top of the deck that you set aside earlier. Pick up the five cards on the table. Hold them so that the faces are toward you. One by one, place the cards face up onto the table in this order: six, seven, eight, nine, ten.

"There you are—a straight flush. I think that'll beat any four of a kind."

Notes: (1) How is it that you can allow Shirley to direct the placement of the second six-card group? Simple. I figured out that whichever way you do it, the straight flush will be properly set up.

(2) It takes quite a while to do the down-under shuffle, no matter how fast you go. So while you're dealing, converse about something. The best bet is to provide some amusing comments. You might discuss, among other things, the koala, the kangaroo, and anything else that begins with K. Or you might point out that you happen to know that the Outback is where they keep the barbie. Whatever.

I Win, You Lose

Here are four amusing propositions. In the first two, the odds are heavily in your favor; in the third, you almost can't lose; in the fourth, you absolutely can't lose.

For me, the best part of these propositions is that you provide instruction. To paraphrase Damon Runyon, the old guy tells his son, "Someday you're going to come across a guy with a sealed deck of cards. He'll bet you that the jack of spades will jump out of the deck and squirt cider in your ear. Don't bet him, son. 'Cause sure as you do, you're gonna get an ear full of cider."

In other words, don't play the other person's game; you'll lose.

Suits Me

Ask Joe to shuffle the deck. When he's ready, tell him, "I'd like you to deal out any three cards face down."

He does.

Say, "I'll bet my house, my car, and my children that two of those cards are of the same suit."

Joe turns the cards over. Sure enough, you're right—about two out of three times. So the third time, you'll be awfully lonesome out on the street.

Do it a number of times with Joe so that he can see that, in the long run, he couldn't possibly win.

Big Odds

Ask Frank to give the deck a good shuffle and then cut it into three piles.

"If I owned a mint, Frank, I'd be willing to wager half of it that I can name three values, and that at least one of them will be on top of one of those piles. Obviously, the odds are against me. When I name three values, there are only 12 of those cards in the deck, and I have only three chances to get one."

Sounds good, right?

"I'll name five, six, and seven." You can name any three values.

Frank turns over each of the top cards. Chances are very good that one of them will be a 5, 6, or 7. How good? Well, you actually told a little fib to Frank. When he turned over the top card of the first pile, you had 12 chances in 52 to get one of your values. When he turned over the next top card, you had another

12 chances in 52. And the same for the last top card. In other words, you had 36 chances in 52.

Want a better deal? Have Frank cut the deck into four piles. Again you name three values. You poor guy! There are only 12 possible cards for you out of 52 cards. Actually, of course, the odds are even more in your favor.

Very Close

Perhaps Louise could use some instruction.

Ask her to shuffle the deck. She does.

"Name two values, Louise—two, five . . . king, jack . . . whatever you wish."

Let's say that she names six and eight.

"I can't believe you named those two, Louise. They love to be together in the deck. In fact, I'm willing to bet anything that a six and an eight are together in the deck."

Take the deck and turn it down so that all can see the cards as you fan through. If you find that a six and an eight are together, great.

"I'm not surprised. I just knew they'd be together."

Otherwise, fan back to where a six and an eight are separated by one card. Suppose that a jack divides the two.

"Just as I thought, a jack. That's the guy who's always trying to come between them."

And if a six and an eight aren't even close together, say, "Just my luck, they happen to be on the outs on this one particular occasion. Well, let's try something else."

Don't worry about it; very seldom will you totally fail.

When you do succeed, explain to Louise that the odds were heavily in your favor. Have her name several more combinations and show her that the vast majority work out.

Lower Is Higher

Time to provide suitable instruction to Ralph.

"Let's cut for higher card, Ralph. You first."

He cuts; you cut. Your card is higher.

Of course it is! Beforehand, you separated all the values in the deck. Then you put the 2s on top, followed by the 3s, the 4s, and so on, all the way down to the aces.

To beat Ralph, all you have to do is have him cut off a pile first. Your card is bound to be higher than his.

Put your cards back and have Ralph put his cards back. Do the stunt again.

If, after you've done it a few times, Ralph insists that you cut first, simply cut off a huge pile, show the bottom card of it, and return the pile to the deck. If Ralph hasn't caught on yet, he'll probably cut a smaller pile and lose again.

Eventually, of course, you should reveal all to Ralph. This should provide some amusement, but also a degree of wisdom.

Solitaire

If you don't play regular or Canfield solitaire, you might as well skip this section.

In the next two items, the idea is to set the deck up so that it is virtually impossible to lose at solitaire. How can this be useful?

You could say to someone, "Are you good at solitaire?" Whatever the reply, hand the person the setup deck and say, "I'll bet you have a really good chance to win with this lucky deck."

Or, you could say to someone, "See this deck? I believe that a great card player like yourself can win at solitaire right now." Immediately commence your game.

Or say to a friend, as though joking, "Here's a deck of cards. Why don't you try some solitaire. I've already set them up, so don't change anything." Hand over the deck. "Go ahead. If you do it right, you can't lose."

When your friend wins, say, "I was just kidding. I can't believe you won."

Then, if you wish, burst the balloon by admitting that you actually did set up the deck. Perhaps even reveal the system.

The assumption in all the items is that your friend can play solitaire well. It might not hurt if you watch the deal and point out plays that are missed.

Can't Lose 1

Here we have what I call regular solitaire. You deal out one card face up, followed by six face-down cards in a row. Deal a face-up card onto the second card, followed by a face-down card on each of the other cards. Continue until, from left to right, you have one card, followed by two cards, followed by three cards—all the way up to seven cards. The first card is face up, and the top card of all the other piles is face up.

Then there are two possible variations:

(1) You go through the cards, three at a time. You can go through as many times as you wish. I'll not explain further; it would take up too much space. I just wanted to make clear which solitaire game you're playing.

(2) This is called Canfield Solitaire. The assumption is that you pay 52 dollars for the deck and that you get five dollars back for every card that you get on top, including the aces themselves. You go through the deck that is not laid out one card at a time. You're allowed to go through the cards only once.

Fortunately, this layout will work for either variation.

To win, here's the way you set up the deck. Separate the suits. Put every suit in order, from the A to the K. The order, from the top down:

A 2 3 4 5 6 7 8 9 10 J Q K

Put the club suit face up onto the table. On top of it put the hearts suit face up. On top of that put the spade suit. And on top of all put the diamond suit.

Pick up the pile. Deal out three cards face down in a row. Go back to the first card and deal a card on top of it. Deal a card on top of the second. Deal a card on top of the third card. Continue with this until all the cards are dealt out.

Place the first pile on top of the second pile. Place the third pile on top of all. The deck is now stacked to win at solitaire. Make sure you stay alert so that you can spot every possible play. Otherwise, you might just lose. In fact, with this setup it will look as though you're going to lose and then—aha! another play.

I think you'll particularly like the ending in the Canfield version.

Can't Lose 2

Let's try another setup, this one quite similar to the first one.

Again separate all the suits and then arrange them in the same order as described above.

This time, take the cards face down and deal out six piles as described above. The last card will be dealt on the fourth pile from the left. Gather the piles up by placing the first pile on top of the second, the combined pile on top of the third, the combined pile on top of the fourth, and so on.

Deal the cards out in the regular way. In this setup, there are two things to keep in mind.

(1) If taking three cards at a time, remember this: When more than one king is available to go into an empty space, choose the one on the left.

(2) If taking one card at a time (Canfield), choose the king on the right.

Again, either type of solitaire should be a sure winner. I think you'll particularly enjoy the Canfield version. Give it a shot.

The Time Is Now

I love clock tricks. That is, I love tricks in which 12 cards are dealt out to match the numbers on a clock. For one thing, such tricks usually offer a colorful display. For another, they are quite different from the usual card trick and, therefore, create considerable interest.

Here are two very good ones.

Mistakes Are Fun

A friend of mine tried three times to perform a clock trick for a small group. It finally occurred to me what trick he was trying to do. I pointed out to him that he had forgotten an important part of the trick, that his method made success impossible.

The following day, I figured out a variation of the original method. Here it is.

Some preparation is necessary. Remove from the deck all of the clubs and hearts. Arrange the clubs so that they run in this order, from the top down:

Q J 10 9 8 7 6 5 4 3 2 A

The king of clubs gets stuck into the remainder of the deck.

Place the club stack on top of the deck. On top of the clubs, set the hearts, in any order.

Start by getting Janice to assist you. Fan off the top 13 cards and hand them to her. These, of course, are 13 hearts.

"Give these a good shuffle please, Janice."

As she does, take the deck and deal out a clock face down, starting at 1 and ending at 12. Push the card at 12 upward, saying, "We'll put the 12 o'clock card here so we'll be sure which one it is." (See Illustration 147.)

Then carefully explain, "Janice, I'm going to turn away. When I do, please cut off a portion of the cards you're holding and hide them. Put the rest of your cards on top of the deck."

Make sure she understands. Turn away while she does her job.

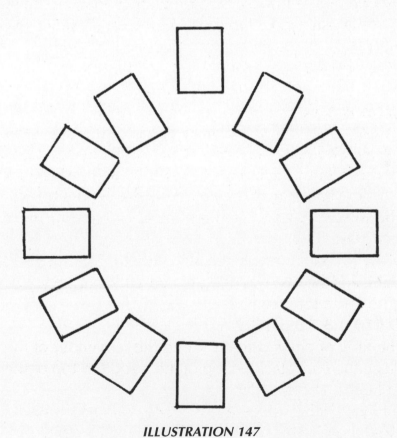

ILLUSTRATION 147

Turn back and continue explaining: "In a moment, I'm going to turn my back again, Janice. When I do, I'd like you to take the cards you cut off . . . "

As you talk, casually pick up the deck. " . . . and count them. But don't tell me the number. Then look at the card that lies at that time. For example, if you count four cards, you'd look at the card that lies at four o'clock. Show the card around and then replace it face down. Hide your packet again. Tell me when you're done."

Turn away. Let your arms hang low as you turn the deck face up and count the number of hearts on top. Close up the deck and let your hands drop to your side. You now know the chosen card. It is the same value as the number of hearts on the deck. And it is, of course, a club. For example, if you count eight hearts, the chosen card is the 8C.

When Janice says she's done, turn back. Don't look at the clock formation. Instead, say, "Janice, please gather up the cards in the clock and give them one shuffle."

Casually set the deck down. Avert your head. "Please add your secret packet to the cards you just shuffled. Give those cards one shuffle. Now put the packet on top of the deck and give the deck one shuffle."

Look back at the group. Take the deck from Janice. Give the cards a riffle shuffle. Everyone expects that you'll glance through the deck to find the card. Instead, hold the deck silently for a moment. Then stare into Janet's eyes. "Janet, it's perfectly obvious that your card is the nine of clubs (whatever)."

The shocked response is very strong.

Note: I especially like the fact that you're absolutely "clean" at the end of this effect. There is no evidence whatever of what you've done. In fact, you can proceed with other tricks immediately.

It's That Time

Again, my pal Wally Wilson has come up with a superb clock trick. I have added a bit.

Preparation: Let's say that you're using a deck with a red back. Look at any card that's near the top of the deck. From a blue-backed deck, remove a card of the same value and suit. Place this card 13th from the bottom of the red-backed deck. Remember the name of this card. Let's assume that it's the 6D.

You're ready to perform. We'll assume that this is the first trick you'll do for this group. Remove the deck from the card case and turn it face up. Genevieve is good with numbers, so ask her to think of any number from 1 to 12. Hand her the faceup deck.

"Genevieve, I'm going to turn away. While my back is turned, please deal into a face-up pile the same number of cards as the number you just thought of." Pause. "Deal right from the face-up cards, please."

Turn away.

When Genevieve announces that she's finished, say, "Please hide the cards that you counted off."

When she's done, turn back to the group. Take the cards from Genevieve. "Let's make a clock." Still holding the deck face up, count off 12 cards from the face-up deck. Either deal them into a face-up pile, or count them from the deck, taking one on top of the other. Set the rest of the deck aside. Pick up the 12 cards and deal them into a face-up clock, starting at 1 o'clock and ending at 12.

"Genevieve, I'd like you to look at the card that lies at the number you thought of. I'll turn my head away so I won't get any clue as to your card."

You avert your eyes while Genevieve notes the card at the number she chose.

Say, "Now, everyone, don't stare at the card, but please concentrate on it."

Naturally, you know the card. It's the one that you placed 13th from the bottom of the deck—in our example, the 6D.

"I'll try to eliminate some of the ones I'm sure you didn't choose." Slowly, one by one, turn over all the cards except the one chosen.

"I believe that this is your card, Genevieve—the six of diamonds. Am I right?'

Of course you are.

Casually turn the card over. "Look at this!"

Everyone looks and observes that the card has a different-colored back.

Notes: (1) To continue with your performance, simply remove the "stranger" card and proceed.

(2) If you wish to do the trick without the climax provided by the "stranger" card, just note the 13th card from the bottom of the deck. At the end, arrive at the chosen card exactly as described.

Number Tricks

Usually, tricks involved with numbers are fairly easy to perform. Unfortunately, spectators have a tendency to put down such tricks, believing that they are mere mathematical stunts. The idea, then, is to persuade onlookers that mathematics is not involved with your tricks; you are only using numbers to demonstrate a magical principle. You don't exactly say that, but your presentation should push this notion.

In the next two tricks, the mathematical aspect is minimized by the nature of the tricks and by subtle patter.

Twenty-Card Trick

This trick was originally done with matches. Actually, any objects could be used. I prefer doing it with cards.

Dan is noted for his ability to count, so ask him to assist you.

Count 20 cards from the deck and hand them to Dan. It's best to count the cards in groups of three to create a feeling that the number is irrelevant. Set the rest of the deck aside.

"Dan, in a moment I'll turn away. While my back is turned, please give the cards a shuffle. Then think of a number from one to ten. Take that many cards from your packet and put them into your pocket."

When he's done, say, "Now count the cards that you have left."

He does.

"Do you have two figures in your number?"

Yes, he does.

"Well, add those two digits together, and put that many more cards into your pocket. For instance, if you have thirteen cards, you'd add the one and the three together, getting four. So you'd add four more cards to the ones in your pocket."

Make sure he understands, and then have him proceed.

"One more thing, Dan. Take some cards from those you have left and hide them under your hand. Make sure you hide them well, so that when I turn around, I won't be able to tell how many you have."

Wait a bit, and then turn and face the group again.

Pick up the remaining small packet of cards.

"I don't think there's any doubt, Dan, that I couldn't possibly know the number of cards in your pocket. And I certainly don't know how many cards you're hiding under your hand. But even though you're hiding them, I'm going to try to make an accurate guess."

While blabbing away, you casually fan out the cards you're holding to see how many there are. Once you have the number, fiddle with the cards briefly and then drop them onto the deck that you set aside earlier.

Concentrate for a bit and then tell Dan the number of cards he's hiding under his hand. Have him lift his hand and count the cards out. Your powers are unbelievable.

Actually, the only power you needed was the ability to subtract. When you counted that small packet of cards, you subtracted the total from 9. This gave you the number that Dan was hiding under his hand.

There's no reason why you shouldn't repeat the trick.

Note: Obviously, you could tell Dan how many cards he has in his pocket. You simply add the number of cards you put back onto the deck to the number of cards he's holding under his hand, and then subtract from 20. But I don't do that. It's quite enough of a trick as it is. If you use the recommended patter, however, a spectator will sometimes ask, "How many cards does he have in his pocket?"

This is perfect! Feign befuddlement. Then concentrate. Let's say that Dan has six cards in his pocket. You slowly say, "I believe that Dan has . . . let's see . . . oh, I'd say, six cards in his pocket. Please take the cards from your pocket and count them, Dan."

This is a very strong finish. When this occurs, don't repeat the trick.

A Prime Trick

In my *Magical Math Book* is a trick derived, I think, from Martin Gardner. You hand a spectator seven cards. He chooses one and gives back the other six. He shows the card around and then gives it to you. You hold the chosen card in one hand and the six-card packet in your other hand. You say that you'll stick it in among the other six and put your hands behind your back. Actually, you place the card on top of the packet.

Bring the cards forward. It's time for the spectator to locate his card. The spectator names a number from 2 to 7. Counting aloud, you place one card short of that number on the bottom and turn the next card face up. In other words, if the spectator names four, you place three cards on the bottom and turn up the next one. You then count out that same number again. The first card you place on the bottom is the face-up card. You continue counting out the original number, placing cards on the bottom. When you reach the original number, you turn the card face up and leave it on top for the moment. Repeat this procedure until only one card remains face down. It is, of course, the spectator's. The trick can be repeated.

I have worked out a variation of the original trick.

First, a brief explanation. The trick will work with any prime number. A prime number is one that cannot be divided by any number but itself. For instance, it would be reasonable to perform the above trick with a fairly low number of cards that make up a prime number: 7, 11, 13, 17, 19. Although it would be tedious, you could continue on into higher numbers: 23, 29, 31, 37, 39, and so on. Note that none of these numbers is divisible by any other number. (Clearly, prime numbers lower than 7 would not be suitable for this trick.)

Let's begin. Solicit Marty's help; after all, he's always eager to help out.

Hand Marty the deck, saying, "Please deal the cards into a face-down pile, Marty."

As he deals, count the cards to yourself. After he has dealt five cards, say, "Stop whenever you wish."

You hope that he'll stop at seven and that you can do the above trick. But it doesn't matter as long as he deals no more than 20 cards. If he happens to deal beyond this, say, "Very good, Marty. You've proved yourself an excellent dealer, but I don't think we should wait for you to go all the way through the deck."

Take the cards from Marty and add the dealt cards to them. "Let's see how well Nellie does."

Have Nellie deal the cards into a pile. After she has dealt out five, tell her to stop whenever she wishes. Nellie will probably stop before hitting 20; you're not likely to run into two ninnies in a row.

Let's assume that Marty behaves himself and deals out fewer than 20 cards. You have been keeping track of the number. If he has dealt out a prime number, take the deck from him and set it aside. Proceed as with the original trick.

But what if he deals out 6, 8, 9, 10, 12, 14, 15, 16, 18? Let's say that he has dealt out one less than a prime number—notably 6, 10, 12, 16, or 18. Take the balance of the deck from Marty. Fan out the cards so that he can choose one. Set the deck aside. Take the chosen card in one hand and the dealt cards in the other and place your hands behind your back. Proceed as with the original trick.

The remaining possibilities: 8, 9, 14, 15.

The numbers 8 and 14 are one more than the prime numbers 7 and 13. Take the deck from Marty and set it aside. Pick up the dealt cards. Fan them out so that both Marty and Nellie can choose a card.

Address the group: "Which one should we use—Marty's or Nellie's?"

You take the one selected by the group. The number now is right, so you can proceed as with the original version.

How about 9 and 15? Both are two above a prime number, so you must ditch two cards. Easy. Have three persons select cards from those counted out, and let the audience choose one of the three.

Note: When two persons have chosen cards, you can perform an additional trick. After you have shown that Marty's card is the last remaining face-down card, you can remove his card and add it to the discarded deck. Then take Nellie's card in one hand and the packet in the other hand, place both hands behind your back, and put Nellie's card on top. Proceed with the trick.

When you have three cards chosen, you can work the trick with one of the three and then discard it. Then have the crowd choose one of the two other cards. Behind your back, you place this card on top and go ahead with the trick.

You might assume that you could then perform the trick yet a third time. I wouldn't recommend it. That would make for an awful lot of counting, and even the friendliest audience can get bored.

A Fun Trick

Clearly, any magic you perform should provide fun for the audience. But the next item is specifically designed to cheer a group up.

Nothing Up My Sleeve

John Murray developed the basic idea; I provided the revelation of a chosen card.

Some preparation is necessary. You'll need a slip of paper about 11 inches long and two inches wide. This need not be exact. You can take a regular sheet of paper and carefully tear off a piece that will do the job (Illustration 148).

ILLUSTRATION 148

On one side of the sheet print in bold letters the word NOTHING (Illustration 149). On the other side, print the name of a card—six of clubs, for instance (Illustration 150).

NOTHING

ILLUSTRATION 149

SIX OF CLUBS

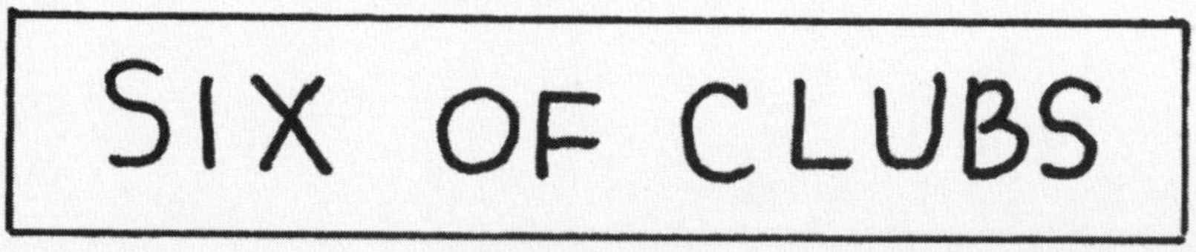

ILLUSTRATION 150

Slide the paper up your sleeve so that when you pull it out spectators will see only the side that says NOTHING.

Go through the deck and find the card you named on the slip—the six of clubs, in our example. Place it in the deck so that it can be forced on a spectator, using one of the four forces at the beginning of the "Mental Tricks" section, page 23.

Ready?

Ask Ginny to select a card from the deck and show it to all the spectators. Naturally, the card is not exactly chosen; you force the six of clubs on her. Let her hang on to the card.

"I can assure you, Ginny, that I use no sleight of hand in performing my wondrous tricks. The cards aren't marked, and—believe me—there's nothing up my sleeve." Pause. "Ah, some of you seem to doubt me. I told you I have nothing up my sleeve. Look."

Pull the slip from your sleeve so that all can see the word "Nothing."

This should get a laugh, or at least a mild chuckle.

"Now that I've proved to you how fair everything is, it's time for magic. Ginny, what's the name of your card?"

She might be reluctant to tell you, but someone in the group will be cooperative. The minute the card is named, turn the paper around so that all can see the name of the chosen card printed on the other side.

Don't neglect this one; it's well worth the modest preparation.

PARTING THOUGHTS

Write It Down

Go through the tricks again and jot down the page numbers of the ones you particularly like. When you finish, try out your selections—first on yourself, and then on others. It is easy to get into the habit of performing certain favorites, and letting other excellent tricks fade from memory. You can prevent this by keeping a record right from the beginning.

When you find a good card trick, perhaps you should make a memorandum of it—jot some notes down on a file card or in a notebook. From time to time, you can consult your notes and freshen up your routines.

Simplify

Some say that the perfect trick is one that has been simplified to the point that it requires no sleight of hand. I don't know about that, but I believe that you *should* try to simplify every trick as much as possible. Do you really need all those sleights? Can you substitute subtlety for a sleight, or simply drop one altogether? Think it through. At least in some respect, every trick you do should be uniquely yours.

Stay Within Yourself

You have heard the expression, usually in sports, that a certain person should "stay within himself." For instance, if a player tries to do too much, he will probably mess up altogether. Similarly, when you do card tricks, you should stay within yourself. Don't try tricks you haven't mastered. Don't experiment with sleights in public. Practice in private until the sleight is perfected. Why risk exposure when there are so many tricks that you do perfectly?

Be Prepared

Should you carry a deck of cards with you wherever you go? Although this may not be a bad idea, what you should *definitely* know is what you're going to do when someone hands you a deck.

It's quite simple, really. It doesn't matter whether you're at a party, in a small group, or with an individual—your response is the same. Have in mind three or four tricks that are particularly effective and that you perform especially well. The tricks need not be related or sequential—just *good*.

Suppose these tricks are well received and you are encouraged to do more. *Now* you're ready to perform a routine. The makeup of this program is your choice, of course. It can consist of all gambling tricks or all mental tricks, for example. Personally, I prefer variety. Whatever you decide, perform no more than five or six tricks, closing with one of your best, a guaranteed eyepopper.

AFTERWORD

You're interested in card magic. Let's suppose you do all the right things. You learn a dozen really good card tricks. You practice them till you have them down perfectly. You toss in some superb, imaginative patter. Then you try them out on susceptible, trusting friends and relatives—with great success! Now what? Where do you go from here?

It depends on how interested you are. Do you aspire to become one of the all-time greats, or would you prefer to dabble in magic? Do you want to become a professional, or remain an amateur? Nothing wrong with any of these.

Obviously, if you plan to make money performing magic, you'd better be prepared to practice a great deal. Furthermore, you'd better be creative, because very few spectators are interested in stale patter or ordinary tricks. Are there jobs? Yes. Probably more jobs than ever before. But there are more magicians than ever before, too. So you'd better be good. And dedicated. Furthermore, you'd better realize that very few magicians make their living solely doing magic. Most have a full-time job and perform magic as a sideline.

On the other hand, being an amateur magician has its rewards. There is certainly less pressure. No one expects you to be as good as a professional, so when you do a trick especially well, you hear things like, "You're a regular professional." It's much more gratifying than being a professional and hearing the reverse. Also, as an amateur, you view magic as a hobby. You can devote as much time to it as you choose, attaining perfection in your own good time.

Whatever your aspirations, you should get together with fellow magicians. They are a surprisingly helpful and friendly lot.

Check your phone book to see if there's a magic shop in your area. If so, you can drop in and get all the information you need about local organizations. Furthermore, you might just meet other magicians who can help you out with advice.

What if there is no magic shop in your area? Again, check the phone book. If any professional magicians are operating in your area, they will probably be listed. Feel free to give a call. Explain your situation and ask about any local group, formal or informal. Chances are, you'll get all the information you need about local magicians and organizations.

INDEX

A

Ace Collection, 201–203
Ace Surprise, 125–126
Aces by the Number, 344–350
And Another, 256
Another Way, 284–288
Astounding Appearance, 140–142

B

B'Gosh, 334–337
Behind My Back, 89
Better Than Four of a Kind, 354–356
Big Deal, 154–155
Big Odds, 357–358
Big Turnover, 223–225
Blackstone's Stunt, 36
Blind Chance, 190–192

C

Can't Lose 1, 360–361
Can't Lose 2, 361–362
Cards, control of, 17–24
Casual Cut, 25
Color Confusion, 170–172
Colorful Prediction, 54–56
Control. *See* Cards, control of

Countdown, 127
Crime Does Not Pay, 331–334
Crisscross Force, 40
Crisscross, 152–153

D

Delayed Shuffle, 18
Digital Estimation, 82–83
Discovery, 173–189
Do-It-Yourself Discovery, 87–88
Don't Pass It Up, 19–20
Don't Take That Tone with Me, 291–293
Double Cut, 17
Double Discovery, 293–298
Double Discovery, 178–180
Double or Nothing, 204–205
Double-Lift, 42–47
Double-Match Trick, 138–139
Double-Turnover Force, 39
Drop Sleight, 41
Dunbury Delusion, 243–245
Dynamic Duo, 289–291

E

Easy Aces, 62–63
Easy Estimation, 80–81
Easy Match, 226–228

Easy Speller, 328–329
Easy/easier control, 21–23
Efficient Double-Lift, 44–46
Either/Or Force, 161
Estimation, 80–86

F
Face-Up Force, 39
Face-Up Miracle, 197–198
Face-Up, Face-Down,
    87–95
False Cuts, 25–28, 255
Five-and-Ten, 272
Flush of Success, 120–122
Forces, 34–40
Four Aces Again, 128–129
Four Aces, 199–214
Four Times Four, 181–184
Freedom of Choice,
    108–111
From the Land Down
    Under, 112–114

G
Gall Cut, 26
Gambler's Bonus, 117–126
Gambling Aces, 123–124
Gambling, 105–116
Get Out of This World,
    130–135
Glide, 15–16

Good Choice, 236–237
Gotcha!, 240–245
Grab Bag, 127–147
Grand Illusion, 213–214
Groups of cards, control of,
    32–33

H
Hindu Shuffle, 29–30
Hot Spell, 103–104

I
I Guess So, 215–217
Ideal Card Trick, 193
Impossible Poker Deal,
    105–107
Impromptu Liar's Trick,
    301–307
Impromptu Speller, 96–97
In the Palm of Your Hand,
    149–151
It's All Up to You, 283–284
It's Out of My Hands,
    199–200
It's That Time, 365–366

J
Join the Knavery, 73–76
Joker Helps, 71–72
Just a Casual Cut, 255–256
Just a Little More, 288–289

K

Key cards, control of, 23–24
Kings in a Blanket, 350–354

L

Let's Lose Your Card,
   326–327
Let's Prognosticate,
   272–274
List to One Side, 229–230
Long Count, The, 298–301
Lower Is Higher, 359
Lucky 7, 168–169

M

Meet Madam Flaboda,
   310–314
Milking the Cards, 261
Mind Control Poker,
   118–119
Mind Reading, 148–161
Miscellaneous, 215–239
Mistakes Are Fun, 362–364
More Oily Water, 220–221
Most Oily Water, 222
Moves and Maneuvers,
   250–265
Multiple-Pile Cut, 26
Murder, 143–145
My Favorite Card, 92–93
My Variation, 270–272

N

No Touch, No Feel,
   173–175
No Wonder, 242
Nothing Up My Sleeve,
   371–373

O

Oily Water, 218–219
One in Four, 66–68
One-Cut Force, 38
One-Finger Cut, 26–28
Original Double-Lift, 47
Out of My Hands, 269–270
Out, An, 246–247
Overhand Shuffle, 18,
   30–33

P

Patter, 250–251
Peek, 14
Perfect Pile, 84–86
Piles of Aces, 341–344
Piles of Magic, 308–310
Point with Pride, 329–331
Poker, 118–119
Pop-Up Card, 231
Practice, 10
Prediction, 50–59
Preparation, 10, 162–172
Presentation, 11

Presto Prediction, 50–53
Prime Trick, A, 368–371
Process of Elimination,
    136–137

Q
Quaint Coincidence,
    146–147
Quick Speller, 98–102
Quick Trick, 36
Quite Quaint Queens,
    77–79

R
Rare Reverse, 90–91
Recovery, 246–247
Riffle Force, 36–37
Roll-Up Cut, 257

S
Second Deal, 240–241
Setup, 190–198
Seven for Luck, 194
Sheer Luck, 176–177
Shuffles, 29–33
Simon Says, 37
Simple Overhand Shuffle,
    18
Simplicity Itself, 252–254
Simplify, 374
Sixes and Nines, 185–189
Snap Double-Lift, 42–44

Sneaky Aces, 212
Something Old, Something
    New, 277–278
Spelling, 96–104
Spin-Out!, 238–239
Standard Force, 34–35
Stay Within Yourself, 374
Suits Me, 357

T
Take Your Q, 321–325
Ten Trick, The, 337
These Are Gold, 314–317
Those Mysterious Ladies,
    232–235
Three Location, 158–160
Three Piles, 156–157
Three-Card Surprise,
    57–59
Tick Tock Trick, 60–61
Tips, 12–13
Transposition, 60–79
Travelling Hearts, 69–70
Tricky Transpo, 64–65
Twenty-Card Trick, 367–368
Two for One, 274–277
Two-Faced Card Trick I,
    162–163
Two-Faced Card Trick II,
    164–167
Two-Handed Poker,
    115–116

U

Up-and-Down Shuffle, The, 262–264

Ups and Downs, 94–95

Very Close, 358

Very Little Turnover, 279–281

W

Wally's Wily Ace Trick, 206–211

Way Back, The, 266–268

What Do You Think?, 195–196

What Else?, 307–308

Who Has a Match?, 281–282

Write It down, 374

Y

You Need All 52, 317–321